RELIGION AND WOMEN IN BRITAIN, c. 1660–1760

Religion and Women in Britain, c. 1660–1760

Edited by

SARAH APETREI
University of Oxford, UK

and

HANNAH SMITH
University of Oxford, UK

ASHGATE

Published by
Ashgate Publishing Limited
Wey Court East
Union Road
Farnham
Surrey, GU9 7PT
England

Ashgate Publishing Company
110 Cherry Street
Suite 3-1
Burlington, VT 05401-3818
USA

www.ashgate.com

British Library Cataloguing in Publication Data
A catalogue record for this book is available from the British Library

The Library of Congress has cataloged the printed edition as follows:
Religion and Women in Britain, c. 1660–1760 / edited by Sarah Apetrei and Hannah Smith.
    pages cm
    Includes bibliographical references and index.
    ISBN 978-1-4094-2919-7 (hardcover: alk. paper)—ISBN 978-1-4094-2920-3 (ebook)—ISBN 978-1-4724-0558-6 (epub)
    1. Women in Christianity—Great Britain—History—17th century. 2. Great Britain—Church history—17th century. 3. Women in Christianity—Great Britain—History—18th century. 4. Great Britain—Church history—18th century. I. Apetrei, S. L. T. (Sarah Louise Trethewey), 1979– editor. II. Smith, Hannah, editor.
    BR757.R46 2014
    274.1'07082—dc23

                                                                        2014008227

ISBN 9781409429197 (hbk)
ISBN 9781409429203 (ebk – PDF)
ISBN 9781472405586 (ebk – ePUB)

MIX
Paper from
responsible sources
FSC
www.fsc.org FSC® C013985

Printed in the United Kingdom by Henry Ling Limited,
at the Dorset Press, Dorchester, DT1 1HD

Contents

Notes on Contributors

Sarah Apetrei is Departmental Lecturer in Ecclesiastical History at the University of Oxford. Her book, *Women, Feminism and Religion in Early Enlightenment England* was published by Cambridge University Press in 2010, and she is currently working on a second monograph on mystical theology in seventeenth-century Britain.

Sarah Hutton currently holds a chair at Aberystwyth University. Her main area of research is seventeenth-century intellectual history, with a special interest in the Cambridge Platonists and women philosophers. Recent publications include *Anne Conway: A Woman Philosopher* (Cambridge University Press, 2004) and *Benjamin Furly (1646–1714), a Quaker Merchant and his Milieu* (Olschki, 2007). She is director of the series, International Archives of the History of Ideas.

William Kolbrener is Chair of English Literature at Bar-Ilan University. His publications include *Milton's Warring Angels* (Cambridge University Press, 1997), *Mary Astell: Reason, Gender, Faith* (Ashgate, 2007), co-edited with Michal Michelson, and *Open Minded Torah: Of Irony, Fundamentalism and Love* (Continuum, 2011).

Emma Major is Lecturer in English at the Department of English and Centre for Eighteenth-Century Studies at the University of York. She has published on eighteenth-century national identity, religion and politeness, including *Madam Britannia: Women, Church, and Nation 1712–1812* (Oxford University Press, 2011), and was a contributor to the *Oxford Dictionary of National Biography* (2004). She is now working on two projects: a study of Anna Laetitia Barbauld, and a book on religion and national identity in the 1840s.

Alasdair Raffe is a Chancellor's Fellow in History at the University of Edinburgh. He is the author of *The Culture of Controversy: Religious Arguments in Scotland, 1660–1714* (Boydell and Brewer, 2012) and several articles on seventeenth- and eighteenth-century religion and politics.

Alison Searle is an ARC DECRA postdoctoral research fellow at the University of Sydney. Her current research project analyses the relationship between religion nonconformity and performance in seventeenth-century Britain. She is also working on an edition of James Shirley's play, *The Sisters*, for Oxford University Press and, with Johanna Harris, on a complete edition of the letters of Richard Baxter.

Hannah Smith is a Tutorial Fellow and University Lecturer in History at St Hilda's College, University of Oxford. She has published *Georgian Monarchy: Politics and Culture, 1714–1760* (Cambridge University Press, 2006) and co-edited with Erica Charters and Eve Rosenhaft, *Civilians and War in Europe, 1618–1815* (Liverpool University Press, 2012).

Claire Walker is a Senior Lecturer in History at the University of Adelaide. She has written extensively about post-Reformation English nuns in exile on the Continent, and is the author of *Gender and Politics in Early Modern Europe: English Convents in France and the Low Countries* (Palgrave Macmillan, 2003). She recently co-edited *Moral Panics, the Press and the Law in Early Modern England* (Palgrave Macmillan, 2009), and is currently co-writing *Governing Emotion: The Affective Family, the Press and the Law in Early Modern Britain* with Katie Barclay and David Lemmings, and co-editing *Fama and Her Sisters: Gossip and Rumour in Early Modern Europe* with Heather Kerr.

Melinda Zook is Professor of History at Purdue University. She is the author of *Radical Whigs and Conspiratorial Politics in Late Stuart England* (Penn State Press, 1999; paperback, 2009) and *Protestantism, Politics and Women in Britain, 1660–1714* (Palgrave, 2013); she also co-edited *Revolutionary Currents: Nation-Building in the Transatlantic World* (Rowman & Littlefield, 2004), and *Challenging Orthodoxies: The Social and Cultural Worlds of Early Modern Women* (Ashgate, 2014).

Acknowledgements

This volume has its origins in a conference on women and religion in late seventeenth- and early to mid-eighteenth century Britain held at St Hilda's College, Oxford, in June 2009. The editors thank all who gave papers, chaired sessions, contributed to discussion and participated in the conference. They also wish to thank the Centre for Early Modern British and Irish History, University of Oxford; the Faculty of Theology, University of Oxford; the John Fell OUP Fund; and the Royal Historical Society for sponsoring the conference. Thanks are also due to Felicity Heal, Stephanie Jenkins and St Hilda's College, Oxford, for support with the conference organization.

The editors wish to thank Erika Gaffney at Ashgate for her assistance with this volume, and the anonymous Ashgate readers for their constructive comments and suggestions. Hannah Smith also wishes to thank the Leverhulme Trust for funding a period of research leave which helped to facilitate the preparation of the volume for publication.

The cover image from Jeremy Taylor and William Cave, *Antiquitates Christianæ*, 10th edn (London, 1742) (Vet. A4 c.386, plate between pages 2 and 3) is reproduced by kind permission of The Bodleian Libraries, The University of Oxford.

Chapter 1
Introduction

Sarah Apetrei and Hannah Smith

Seeing that the chiefest commendation, if not the onely, both in men and women, is to bee piously devoted unto God, it is worth our enquiring, whether women herein may not bee compared with men. Yes surelie and for ought I can finde, in zealous devotion, and piety towards God they doe farre excell even the best men of notable example of constant and couragious piety.

> —'Womans Worth. Or a Treatise Shewing and Proveing by Sundry Reasons that Women doe Excell Men'[1]

If indeed your Sex should enter into the irreligious Notions which now prevail too much amongst the Men, the next Generation would be irrecoverably lost.... But, God be thanked, Religion keeps up its Authority in a great measure with your Sex still, and God grant it may ever do so!

> —William Wotton[2]

Who do we find attend his Ordinances so frequently as the Women? May I not venture to say, there are at least five Women to a Man, every Lord's Day in the House of God; and does there want Demonstrations of five more at the holy Sacrament? Men, and especially Gentlemen, will follow the Ladies any where but where they should.

> —James Bland[3]

The Learned understand *Religion*, the Vulgar believe it, and *Women* spoil it: For the first seek it, the second follow it, and the last counterfeit it.

> —Thomas Brown[4]

The years between 1660 and 1760 represent a remarkably vibrant and formative era in British religious history. Characterized by resurgent Anglicanism, a royally sponsored Catholic renaissance in the mid-1680s, the consolidation of Dissent, vocal Deist and Arian heresy and, at the end of the era, the Evangelical

---

[1]   Bodleian Library, Oxford, MS Rawl. D.1,125 (c. 1660), p. 45.

[2]   William Wotton, *A Letter to Eusebia: Occasioned by Mr Toland's Letters to Serena* (London, 1704), pp. 73–4.

[3]   James Bland, *An Essay in Praise of Women: Or, A Looking-Glass for Ladies* (London, 1733), pp. 237–8.

[4]   Thomas Brown, *A Legacy for the Ladies: Or, Characters of the Women of the Age* (London, 1705), p. 17.

Revival, the period also saw the emergence of important secular features that distinctively shaped the lived experience of religion. This was an era of increasing urbanization and enhanced communication networks, in which a dynamic public sphere developed, fostering an expansive and evolving print culture that boomed after the demise of the Licensing Act in 1695. The idiom of politeness, with its fundamental implications for religion and gender, became a dominant social paradigm. The horizons of British men – and women – were expanding with greater opportunities for interaction with other religious cultures in continental Europe, the colonies and the distant lands of other trading partners. In an age intensely concerned with preserving the established Protestant confession, and Christian faith more generally, female piety took on a particularly serious social and political significance. As the remarks by William Wotton and James Bland that preface this introduction suggest, the religion of women was viewed as a key to the survival of godliness into the next generation and, to some observers, in its innocence and fervour seemed to stand as a reproach to the faithless masculine establishment: rather like the devotion of the women in the Gospels, who preached the resurrection to the defeated (male) apostles. However, feminine spirituality was also delicate and volatile, susceptible to popery, enthusiasm and – as Thomas Brown insinuated – hypocrisy; it needed to be patrolled and safeguarded.

Religion and Women in Britain takes as its focus the religious worlds of women in Britain, at a time when the Church seemed to be increasingly under siege and the culture of British Christians was being transformed by Enlightenment discourses about 'Reason', 'sensibility' and 'politeness'; by encounters with other world religions; by political responses to two Protestant revolutions; by urbanization and the vibrant public sphere. It seeks to examine the particular religious experiences of women within these contexts, to assess their contributions to renewal and change and to consider the ways in which women negotiated institutional and intellectual boundaries. The essays contained in this volume examine not only contemporary perceptions of female piety and attempts to circumscribe it, but also the reality of women's experiences and women's concrete roles in shaping religious identities. This volume will argue that a focus on women's various religious roles and responses will help us to understand better the structures of lay religious commitment which were not separate from, but also not exclusively shaped by, the political, intellectual and ecclesiastical disputes of a clerical elite and will help to deepen our understanding of both popular and elite religious cultures in this period and the links between them. It aims to offer a reassessment of the religious history of the period 1660 to 1760 as one in which female participation was central to the formation of new practices and discourses, and, in some contexts, pious femininity became a totem of religious responses to the Enlightenment.

The precise bookends of 1660 and 1760, whilst they indicate changes of regime, are, of course, somewhat arbitrary in terms of marking thresholds in major processes of cultural, political and social change. However, they do helpfully parenthesize a period in British history which has come to claim its own coherence on a number of levels. In social and economic terms, this was the age of 'financial revolution', of an expansion of global trade and consumerism, of emerging iron and pottery industries, and the renaissance of the provincial town.[5] In high culture, the years between 1660 and 1760 correspond closely to the Augustan era of literary neoclassicism and aesthetic refinement.[6] It was also a seminal moment for British political and religious ideologies, as party competition became institutionalized in Parliament and Church, and ecclesiastical politics oscillated between the poles of toleration and Anglican hegemony.

I

The backdrop to any consideration of gender, society and culture in the post-Restoration period has to be, of course, the profound political and even spiritual trauma of the civil wars in the three British kingdoms, and the experience of the Interregnum. In 1993, reflecting on the impact of the dramatic events of the 1640s and 1650s on sexual politics, Patricia Crawford asked (echoing Joan Kelly), 'did women have a revolution?' Crawford noted that this question had prompted a pessimistic response from historians like Keith Thomas: namely, that yes, the radical sects opened up a temporary window of opportunity, but that from a longer-term perspective this period of enthusiasm 'was not of great significance for the history of women's emancipation'.[7] Despite the force of Crawford's argument that the unprecedented involvement of women in printing, petitioning and prophesying during the revolution was in fact decisive in transforming women's self-understanding as participants in public religious debate and reform, the narrative of immediate patriarchal reassertion after an euphoric and egalitarian moment continues to influence characterizations of women's roles in the Interregnum sects.[8] Institutionalization and separation of spheres of authority in, for instance, the Quaker movement has been seen as indicative of this decline

---

[5]   See Angus McInnes, *The English Town, 1660–1760* (London, 1980); Peter Borsay, *The English Urban Renaissance: Culture and Society in the Provincial Town, 1660–1770* (Oxford, 1991); Lorna Weatherill, *Consumer Behaviour and Material Culture in Britain, 1660–1760* (London, 1988); Henry Roseveare, *The Financial Revolution, 1660–1760* (London, 1991).

[6]   See, for instance, Ian A. Bell, *Literature and Crime in Augustan England* (London, 1991), p. 2: 'The terminology of a new Augustan Age is most conventionally associated with some of (or all of) the period from 1660 to 1760, from the restoration of Charles II to the accession of George III'. See also Clare Haynes, *Pictures and Popery: Art and Religion in England, 1660–1760* (Aldershot, 2006).

[7]   Patricia Crawford, *Women and Religion in England, 1500–1720* (London, 1993), p. 5.

[8]   The classic version of this account is Keith Thomas, 'Women and the Civil War Sects', *Past and Present*, 13 (1958): pp. 42–62. For more recent treatments, see Catie Gill, *Women in the Seventeenth-Century Quaker Community: A Literary Study of Political Identities, 1650–1700* (Aldershot, 2005), p. 186; B.J. Gibbons, *Gender in Mystical and Occult Thought: Behmenism and its Development in England* (Cambridge, 1996), pp. 48–9.

from utopian beginnings.[9] Outside the sects, among the High Church satirists and commentators, the memory of disorder and heterodoxy shaped the association between women and fanaticism, which clearly helped to discredit public displays of female piety. It seemed apparent to such commentators that the inverted world of female prophets, tub-preachers and military tyranny illustrated perfectly the evil consequences of rebellion against the paternal monarch and an emasculating toleration.[10]

However, the possibility of a paradox, that the legacy of the Interregnum was both the continuing expansion (in certain contexts) of female involvement in religion and public life and a patriarchal reaction which sought to limit that contribution, has not adequately been accounted for. Indeed, we might surely expect to see these two mutually reinforcing outcomes developing in parallel, just as the Tory and Whig parties represent two antagonistic but correlated political legacies of the civil wars. The essays in this volume do not conceive of two discrete cultural trajectories ensuing from the mid-century revolution – one pro-feminist and one anti-feminist – which can easily be mapped on to the political landscape. It has long intrigued and perplexed feminist historians that some of the most vociferous apologists for female authorship and autonomy after the civil wars were High Churchwomen; recent scholarship on Whig women writers and supporters indicates that this was not universally the case. It is equally clear that the rise of the published female author from the 1650s was not an exclusively sectarian phenomenon. Demure poetic works by Katherine Philips and philosophical discourses by Margaret Cavendish supplied rather different models. Yet most women publishing after 1660 had, explicitly or implicitly, to negotiate the uneasy memory of the revolution.

The 'Wars of Religion' in the British Isles, as they were so memorably described by John Morrill, created an environment in which some women felt authorized to speak publicly about things that mattered.[11] Of course, this sense of permission had much to do with the changed climate of press censorship, as well as the apocalyptic fervour of the sects. These conditions were temporary (though Warren Johnston has recently reminded us that 'apocalyptic thought did not disappear in 1660', even in Anglican circles).[12] But the interventions of women, in print, in theological and religio-political controversies proved to be an enduring feature of the British public sphere after 1660. Elizabeth Bathurst, for instance, became

---

[9]   See H. Larry Ingle, *First Among Friends: George Fox and the Creation of Quakerism* (Oxford, 1994), pp. 250–65; Su Fang Ng, 'Marriage and Discipline: The Place of Women in Early Quaker Controversies', *The Seventeenth Century*, 18/1 (2003): pp. 113–40.

[10]   On the gendered imagery of inversion see Sharon Achinstein, 'Women on Top in the Pamphlet Literature of the English Revolution', *Women's Studies*, 24/1–2 (1994): pp. 131–63.

[11]   John Morrill, 'The Religious Context of the English Civil War', *Transactions of the Royal Historical Society*, 5th ser., 34 (1984), p. 178.

[12]   Warren Johnston, *Revelation Restored: The Apocalypse in Later Seventeenth-Century England* (Woodbridge, 2011), p. 1.

one of the earliest 'systematizers' of Quaker theology in the 1670s. The works of the London visionary Jane Lead, claiming prophetic inspiration for bold new theological claims, inspired Pietist readers across Europe in the 1680s and 1690s. The Tory pamphleteer Elinor James was a prolific apologist for the Church of England throughout the Exclusion Crisis and 1688–89 Revolution, and her fellow Anglican apologist Mary Astell also entered into learned debates about patristic ecclesiology and scriptural exegesis. Might it be that the failure of the churches in the British Isles to establish consensus, to deal with dissent and to impose an authoritative settlement had something to do with the space created for female voices in this period? Many of the women mentioned above and represented in the chapters which follow are critically engaged with religious politics: either seeing themselves as substituting for absent or corrupt masculine authority or as censors of clerical power.

The transformations in the relations between church, dissent and state which informed their identity as pious critics have become increasingly central to our understanding of the post-Restoration period.[13] As one historian of the eighteenth century puts it, religion 'conditioned attitudes to the State; it determined or excluded political participation; it defined emerging ideas of national identity; it framed moral expectations and contributed to ideas of continuity and change and of urbanity and ruralism'.[14] Endeavours to put back religion into the history of this period have taken various directions. Firstly, scholars have been particularly active in demonstrating the continuing impact of religion in shaping the political life of the post-1660 era. Indeed, the concept of the 'politics of religion' has become the predominant analytical framework for the later Stuart period, an approach immensely strengthened by an emphasis on the popular as well as the elite concerns, and the significance of the localities as well as the metropolitan centre. Such work has underscored the role played by Dissent in forming the intellectual character and personnel of early Whiggism and emphasized the force of defensive and alarmed Anglicanism in personifying and propelling Toryism.[15] While the driving forces behind the Revolution of 1688–89 have been subject to much – and continuing – debate, contemporary fears over James VII and II's Catholicizing, popish policies

---

[13] See, for example, Stephen Taylor, 'Church and Society after the Glorious Revolution', *The Historical Journal*, 31/4 (1988): pp. 973–87; G.M. Ditchfield, 'Religion, "Enlightenment" and Progress in Eighteenth-Century England', *The Historical Journal*, 35/3 (1992): pp. 681–7; Susan Rosa, 'Religion in the English Enlightenment: Review Essay', *Eighteenth-Century Studies*, 28/1 (1994): pp. 145–9; Jonathan Sheehan, 'Enlightenment, Religion and the Enigma of Secularization: A Review Essay', *American Historical Review*, 108/4 (2003): pp. 1061–80.

[14] William Gibson (ed.), *Religion and Society in England and Wales, 1689–1800: Documents in Early Modern Social History* (London, 1998), p. 14.

[15] Tim Harris, Paul Seaward and Mark Goldie (eds), *The Politics of Religion in Restoration England* (Oxford, 1990); Jason McElligott (ed.), *Fear, Exclusion and Revolution: Roger Morrice and Britain in the 1680s* (Aldershot, 2006).

must always form a major part of any explanation of the Revolution's causes.[16] Religion's importance to the Revolution is further suggested by the language used by William III's and Mary II's supporters to justify their accession. Williamites depicted the joint monarchs as having a godly, Protestant mission and tellingly took recourse to the enduring language of Providentialism rather than Lockean contractualism.[17]

Religious concerns and fears continued to have a major impact upon early to mid-eighteenth-century politics.[18] This was most dramatically manifested in 1709–10 when the High Church clergyman, Dr Henry Sacheverell, was impeached for a sermon preached before the lord mayor of London on 5 November 1709 that denounced Dissenters and claimed that the doctrine of non-resistance had not been challenged by the Revolution. Sacheverell quickly became a celebrity. His sermon sold around an estimated 100,000 copies and the trial sparked rioting that brought about the destruction of a number of London Dissenting meeting houses, in a fury of sectarian violence.[19] If fears over Protestant Dissent remained vivid, much more widespread was the era's savage anti-Catholicism. Anxieties over the future of Protestant Britain ensured a majority of support for the succession of the house of Hanover, commonly termed 'the Protestant Succession', after the death of Queen Anne in 1714 in preference to her Catholic half-brother, and it was as doughty Protestant champions that the early Georgian monarchs were depicted by their supporters.[20]

After 1714–15, religion no longer had quite the same potent political force that it had throughout the seventeenth century. This can be seen, however, as a result of the legislation passed in 1689 and 1701 which ensured that the throne could only be inherited by a Protestant (thus removing one of the main and long-running sources of political-religious tension between the Crown and its subjects), and the care which George I's and George II's ministers, most notably Sir Robert Walpole and the duke of Newcastle, took to assuage Anglican anxieties over Dissent.[21] Having felt the brunt of pro-Sacheverell feeling in 1710 and opposed

---

[16]   W.A. Speck, *Reluctant Revolutionaries: Englishmen and the Revolution of 1688* (Oxford, 1988); Lois G. Schwoerer (ed.), *The Revolution of 1688–1689: Changing Perspectives* (Cambridge, 1992); Tim Harris, *Revolution: The Great Crisis of the British Monarchy, 1685–1720* (London, 2007); Steve Pincus, *1688: The First Modern Revolution* (New Haven, 2009).

[17]   Tony Claydon, *William III and the Godly Revolution* (Cambridge, 1996).

[18]   See, for example, Robert D. Cornwall and William Gibson (eds), *Religion, Politics and Dissent, 1660–1832: Essays in Honour of James E. Bradley* (Farnham, 2010).

[19]   Geoffrey Holmes, 'The Sacheverell Riots: The Crowd and the Church in Early Eighteenth-Century London', *Past and Present*, 72 (1976): pp. 55–85.

[20]   Colin Haydon, *Anti-Catholicism in Eighteenth-Century England, c. 1714–80: A Political and Social Study* (Manchester, 1993); Hannah Smith, 'The Idea of a Protestant Monarchy in Britain, 1714–1760', *Past and Present*, 185 (2004): pp. 91–118.

[21]   Stephen Taylor, '"The Fac Totum in Ecclesiastic Affairs"? The Duke of Newcastle and the Crown's Ecclesiastical Patronage', *Albion*, 24/3 (1992): pp. 409–33; Stephen

the Stanhope-Sunderland ministry's attempts in 1719 to assist Dissenters through repealing the Occasional Conformity and Schism Acts, Walpole was sensitized to the grievous impact that religious partisanship could have on political stability. Indeed it was only in the early to mid-1730s when Walpole was under attack from Opposition Whigs, that he was forced to court Whig anti-clericalism in particular by supporting the Quakers Tithe Bill of 1736. The resulting political furore suggests Walpole's basic political instincts were correct. Anglican fears over any challenge to the Church of England's hegemony remained acute.[22] The Jewish Naturalisation Bill in 1753 was contested by an outcry sardonically described by Horace Walpole as 'a Christian zeal, which was thought happily extinguished with the ashes of Queen Anne and Sacheverell'.[23] The Gordon Riots of 1780 can be viewed as part of a continuing and popular expression of anti-Catholicism.[24]

If British domestic politics were still shaped by religious concerns, so too were British responses to the lands beyond Britain's shores. Protestant confessionalism continued to be important both to forming foreign policy and moulding and complicating senses of national and transnational identity.[25] Tony Claydon has recently argued for the century after the Restoration that it saw the birth of English national self-consciousness, emerging from its developing sense of situation as a Protestant power in Europe.[26] This was a strongly confessional self-perception, formed in England's continuing preoccupation with Protestant ecumenical ambitions and the 'evil empire' of Popish tyranny, embodied in the aggressive

---

Taylor, 'Queen Caroline and the Church of England', in Stephen Taylor, Richard Connors, and Clyve Jones (eds), *Hanoverian Britain and Empire: Essays in Memory of Philip Lawson* (Woodbridge, 1998), pp. 83–101; Jeremy Gregory, *Restoration, Reformation and Reform, 1660–1828: Archbishops of Canterbury and their Diocese* (Oxford, 2000), pp. 95–9; Jeffrey S. Chamberlain, *Accommodating High Churchmen: The Clergy of Sussex, 1700–1745* (Urbana, 1997).

[22] Stephen Taylor, 'Sir Robert Walpole, the Church of England, and the Quakers Tithe Bill of 1736', *The Historical Journal*, 28/1 (1985): pp. 51–77.

[23] Horace Walpole, *Memoirs of King George II*, ed. John Brooke (3 vols, New Haven, 1985), vol. 1, p. 238; David S. Katz, *The Jews in the History of England, 1485–1850* (Oxford, 1994), p. 240; T.W. Perry, *Public Opinion, Propaganda, and Politics in Eighteenth-Century England: A Study of the Jew Bill of 1753* (Cambridge, MA, 1962); G.A. Cranfield, 'The "London Evening-Post" and the Jew Bill of 1753', *The Historical Journal*, 8/1 (1965): pp. 16–30. For a discussion of the gendered nature of anti-semitic attacks on the Jewish Naturalisation Bill see Dana Rabin, 'The Jew Bill of 1753: Masculinity, Virility, and the Nation', *Eighteenth-Century Studies*, 39/2 (2006): pp. 157–71.

[24] Ian Haywood and John Seed (eds), *The Gordon Riots: Politics, Culture and Insurrection in Late Eighteenth-Century Britain* (Cambridge, 2012).

[25] Tony Claydon and Ian McBride (eds), *Protestantism and National Identity: Britain and Ireland, c. 1650–c. 1850* (Cambridge, 1998); Andrew C. Thompson, *Britain, Hanover and the Protestant Interest, 1688–1756* (Woodbridge, 2006); S.J. Connolly, *Religion, Law and Power: The Making of Protestant Ireland 1660–1760* (Oxford, 1992).

[26] Tony Claydon, *Europe and the Making of England, 1660–1760* (Cambridge, 2007).

expansionism of Louis XIV's France. In recent decades efforts have also been made to place an emphasis on religion as a pillar of Scottish national identity in the eighteenth century.[27]

Alongside this religiously inflected approach to late seventeenth and early to mid-eighteenth-century British political history has come the reappraisal of religious life and activity. The caricature of the eighteenth-century Church of England as intellectually and pastorally torpid has come under steady challenge.[28] English Catholicism in this period has been shown to be theologically dynamic and outward-looking.[29] Most influentially (and controversially), J.C.D. Clark's study of *English Society, 1660–1832*, the first edition of which was published in 1985, insisted upon foregrounding religious commitment as a key to understanding the political and social life of this period, regarding England as a 'confessional state' and refusing to 'treat religion as a specialised activity within the realm of private opinion'.[30] The keynote of Clark's analysis is continuity with the confessional age, and several subsequent studies (while not enslaved to his historiographical agenda) have explored the theme of an enduring culture of 'popular' piety, linking it to contemporary intellectual developments and social history.[31]

However, it is also clear that this period saw a shift in the very concept of religion itself, so that the theological authority, moral discipline and political influence of an established Christian Church was contested as never before. This mental breakthrough had much to do with a growing awareness of world cultures, as well as the internal divisions and controversies of the British religious landscape. At a time when British horizons were ever-expanding – when exotic new tastes and habits were being imported from its colonial settlements, when Protestants were acquiring a fresh sense of the global responsibility of Christian mission, and when philosophical questions were turning to ever more fundamental and daring themes – religion, it has been argued, became an *object* of thought,

---

[27]   Richard J. Finlay, 'Keeping the Covenant: Scottish National Identity', in T.M. Devine and J.R. Young (eds), *Eighteenth Century Scotland: New Perspectives* (East Linton, 1999), pp. 121–33.

[28]   John Spurr, *The Restoration Church of England, 1646–1689* (New Haven, 1991); John Walsh, Colin Haydon and Stephen Taylor (eds), *The Church of England, c. 1689–c. 1833: From Toleration to Tractarianism* (Cambridge, 1993); Gregory, *Restoration, Reformation and Reform*; Andrew Starkie, *The Church of England and the Bangorian Controversy, 1716–1721* (Woodbridge, 2007).

[29]   Gabriel Glickman, *The English Catholic Community, 1688–1745: Politics, Culture and Ideology* (Woodbridge, 2009).

[30]   J.C.D. Clark, *English Society 1660–1832: Religion, Ideology and Politics during the Ancien Regime*, 2nd edn (Cambridge, 2000), p. 29. For a response to Clark, see Joanna Innes, 'Review Article: Jonathan Clark, Social History and England's "Ancien Regime"', *Past and Present*, 115 (1987): pp. 165–200.

[31]   See, for example, Jane Shaw, *Miracles in Enlightenment England* (New Haven, 2006); W.M. Jacob, *Lay People and Religion in the Early Eighteenth Century* (Cambridge, 1996).

subject to comparative scrutiny and rational critique.[32] While the theory of secularization no longer seems as persuasive for this period as it once did, there is clearly a degree of cultural displacement – even bereavement – associated with this objectification of religion. Charles Taylor locates within the late seventeenth and eighteenth centuries the 'inception' of 'the narratives of modernity', whereby a great 'disembedding' of the sacred from traditional structures led to spiritual pluralism and a radically subjective religious attitude.[33] If the ideological and cultural transformations of this period did not equate to a decline of belief, they certainly involved the relocation of spiritual authority. It might be suggested that the anxiety that what was once guaranteed and secure seemed provisional and unstable encouraged women, among other unauthorized persons, to involve themselves in both conservative and subversive religious discourse.

Moreover, the relationship between religion and Enlightenment has also come under intense scrutiny in recent historiography, especially in the British case. The very language of 'Enlightenment' itself is highly controversial: was there such a thing as a unitary, iconoclastic movement fundamentally subversive of the ecclesiastical *ancien régime*? For Jonathan Israel, Radical Enlightenment, 'an anti-theological and ultimately democratic emancipatory project – though not necessarily always anti-religious provided ecclesiastical authority is sufficiently curbed', holds the key to retaining a unified vision.[34] English radicals, exemplified by John Toland and Anthony Collins, take an honoured place in this narrative alongside Spinoza, as precocious freethinkers who laid the basic intellectual groundwork for a secular Enlightenment before 1740. Or, as John Robertson suggests, should we think in terms of a coherent Enlightenment project focused on the means of advancing the progress of society?[35] Or, in the end, is it better to imagine multiple and diverse Enlightenments? J.G.A. Pocock recommends that we drop the definite article, and present intellectual developments in this period as a 'family of Enlightenments', characterized by national context or theological and philosophical orientation.[36] This problem is particularly acute in the British context, where piety and clericalism were central to intellectual life.[37] In the

---

[32] See Peter Harrison, *'Religion' and the Religions in the English Enlightenment* (Cambridge, 1990).

[33] Charles Taylor, *A Secular Age* (Cambridge, MA, 2007), p. 717, pp. 146–58.

[34] Jonathan Israel, 'Enlightenment! Which Enlightenment?', *Journal of the History of Ideas*, 67/3 (2006): pp. 528–9.

[35] John Robertson, *The Case for the Enlightenment: Scotland and Naples 1680–1760* (Cambridge, 2005).

[36] J.G.A. Pocock, *Barbarism and Religion: The Enlightenments of Edward Gibbon, 1737–1764* (Cambridge, 1999), vol. 1, p. 9.

[37] See Roy Porter, 'The Enlightenment in England', in Roy Porter and Mikuláš Teich (eds), *The Enlightenment in National Context* (Cambridge, 1981), p. 6; J.G.A. Pocock, 'Clergy and Commerce: The Conservative Enlightenment in England', in R. Ajello et al. (eds), *L'Età dei Lumi: studi storici sul Settecento europeo in onore di Franco Venturi* (2 vols, Naples, 1985), vol. 1, pp. 524–62.

rational religion of the latitudinarians, the tolerationist rhetoric of John Locke and William Warburton, and George Berkeley's idealism, it seems that theology was not in opposition to the claims of Reason.[38] Despite some excellent recent studies of gender and the Enlightenment, there is also considerable scope to develop questions about the responses of women to the forces of Enlightenment and Counter-Enlightenment, particularly as increasing numbers of female writers, among them Damaris Masham, Anne Conway, Mary Astell, and later Catherine Talbot, gained confidence in handling theological and moral subjects.[39]

While a strongly secular emphasis has characterized much of the recent social and cultural analyses of the early to mid-eighteenth-century Britain – 'almost to obliterate religion as a major cultural component', as B.W. Young has remarked – nevertheless, the significant religious dimensions to eighteenth-century British society are starting to be appreciated.[40] Print culture, politeness and the reshaping of the urban environment (important features of studies of long eighteenth-century Britain and the growth of the public sphere) provide here some stimulating points of departure.

Tony Claydon has critiqued accounts of the public sphere that focus on the new, as represented by the coffeehouse and the periodical press, at the expense of older forms. 'Sermons, although a very traditional product, played a vital role in creating and sustaining the public sphere after 1660', he has argued.[41] As Claydon has shown, published sermons remained immensely popular with the late seventeenth-century reading public, and not just those by firebrands like Sacheverell.[42] The works of celebrity preachers, in particular John Tillotson, archbishop of Canterbury, went through many, very affordable, editions and were a significant part of the late seventeenth-century and eighteenth-century book trade. Tillotson's much admired prose style (praised in *The Spectator* and *The Tatler*, both of which deployed the language of moral and religious reform) had a

---

[38] See B.W. Young, *Religion and Enlightenment in Eighteenth-Century England: Theological Debate from Locke to Burke* (Oxford, 1998); David Sorkin, *The Religious Enlightenment: Protestants, Jews and Catholics from London to Vienna* (Princeton, 2008).

[39] See Sarah Knott and Barbara Taylor (eds), *Women, Gender and Enlightenment* (2005; Basingstoke, 2007); Phyllis Mack, *Heart Religion in the British Enlightenment: Gender and Emotion in Early Methodism* (Cambridge, 2008).

[40] For Young's comment see B.W. Young, 'Religious History and the Eighteenth-Century Historian', *The Historical Journal*, 43/3 (2000): p. 859. See also Robert G. Ingram, '"The Trembling Earth is God's Herald": Earthquakes, Religion and Public Life in Britain during the 1750s', in Theodore E.D. Braun and John B. Radner (eds), *The Lisbon Earthquake of 1755: Representations and Reactions* (Oxford, 2005), pp. 98–100.

[41] Tony Claydon, 'The Sermon, the "Public Sphere" and the Political Culture of Late Seventeenth-Century England', in Lori Anne Ferrell and Peter McCullough (eds), *The English Sermon Revised: Religion, Literature and History, 1600–1750* (Manchester, 2000), p. 211.

[42] Ibid., pp. 213–15.

lasting impact on late seventeenth-century and eighteenth-century literature more widely.[43]

Religious writers not only brought new life to the more traditional forms of religious communication, however. They also keenly embraced new literary genres, such as the periodical essay. The Dissenting periodicals, the *Occasional Paper* (1716–18) and the *Old Whig* (1735–38), for instance, gave prime place in each issue to an essay (often in defence of Protestantism or Dissenting interests), and the *Old Whig*'s contents were frequently noted in the mainstream *The Gentleman's Magazine*.[44] As *The Gentleman's Magazine*'s interest in the *Old Whig* indicates, periodicals might mingle the religious with the secular for their readers. Elizabeth Rowe (as Elizabeth Singer) made her print debut in 1691 in the pages of John Dunton's intellectually wide-ranging *Athenian Mercury* (a periodical sympathetic to Dissent), asking whether 'Songs on Moral, Religious or Divine Subjects, compos'd by Persons of *Wit* and *Virtue*, and set to both grave and pleasant Tunes, wou'd not ... make good Impression of Modesty and Sobriety on the Young and Noble ... and prepare their minds for the design'd *Reformation*?' As well as considering how secular literary and musical genres could be used to make religion more appealing, Rowe published several religious and political poems in the periodical over the course of the 1690s.[45]

The idiom of politeness and polite sociability which, by 1700, was increasingly influential in shaping how men and women analysed and interpreted social communication, also had religious inflections, with Christianity being viewed as instrumental in creating true, benevolent politeness and easing denominational conflict.[46] From the outset, women were recognized as integral to the 'polite' world, since it was through their social interactions with men that polite behaviour, conversation and taste might be formed and diffused. Consequently, the fundamental significance that proponents of politeness placed on polite hetero-sociability provided women with a new cultural legitimacy.[47] Male and female writers were

[43]   Isabel Rivers, *Reason, Grace, and Sentiment: A Study of the Language of Religion and Ethics in England, 1660–1780* (2 vols, Cambridge, 1991), vol. 1, pp. 49, 56–7; Rosemary Dixon, 'The Publishing of John Tillotson's Collected Works, 1695–1757', *The Library*, 8/2 (2007): pp. 154–81; Philip Carter, *Men and the Emergence of Polite Society, Britain, 1660–1800* (Harlow, 2001), p. 60.

[44]   Andrew C. Thompson, 'Popery, Politics, and Private Judgement in Early Hanoverian Britain', *The Historical Journal*, 45/2 (2002): pp. 336–8.

[45]   Sarah Prescott, 'Elizabeth Singer Rowe: Gender, Dissent, and Whig Poetics', in David Womersley, Paddy Bullard and Abigail Williams (eds), *Cultures of Whiggism: New Essays on English Literature and Culture in the Long Eighteenth Century* (Newark, 2005), pp. 174–5. See also Helen Berry, *Gender, Society and Print Culture in Late-Stuart England: The Cultural World of the Athenian Mercury* (Aldershot, 2003).

[46]   Carter, *Men and the Emergence of Polite Society*, pp. 42–4; Emma Major, *Madam Britannia: Women, Church, and Nation, 1712–1812* (Oxford, 2011), p. 10.

[47]   Lawrence E. Klein, 'Gender, Conversation and the Public Sphere in Early Eighteenth-Century England', in Judith Still and Michael Worton (eds), *Textuality and*

quick to point to how polite sociability with virtuous women could bring about religious and moral reform. In 1694 Mary Astell had urged women to introduce religious topics into drawing-room conversation. 'Not the Follies of the Town, but the Beauties and the Love of JESUS wou'd be the most polite and delicious Entertainment. 'Twould be thought as rude and barbarous to send our Visitors away uninstructed, as our foolishness at present reckons it to introduce a pertinent and useful Conversation'.[48] Richard Steele famously lauded 'Aspasia' – reputedly referring to Lady Elizabeth Hastings, the later Anglican benefactor – in a similar way in *The Tatler* in 1709. Possessed of an 'unaffected Freedom, and conscious Innocence', Aspasia's 'Mien carries much more Invitation than Command, to behold her is an immediate Check to loose Behaviour, and to love her, is a liberal Education ... a Regard for *Aspasia* naturally produces Decency of Manners, and good Conduct of Life, in her Admirers'.[49] Later, in the mid-eighteenth century, polite sociability was one of the ways in which Lady Elizabeth Hastings's sister-in-law, Selina Hastings, countess of Huntingdon, attempted to evangelize amongst her own social circle, including establishing chapels in the 1760s in the fashionable spa towns of Bath and Tunbridge Wells.[50]

The creation of prominent public secular spaces in Britain's towns and cities, such as the assembly room and the square, were a crucial feature of the new (polite) urban streetscape of the late seventeenth century and eighteenth century. But it must be remembered that religious buildings were also a significant aspect of this reshaped urban environment (and used as arenas for polite socializing) in a period that saw, as Peter Borsay has remarked, 'the first serious wave of urban ecclesiastical building since the Reformation'.[51] The churches of Sir Christopher Wren, Nicholas Hawksmoor, Thomas Archer and James Gibbs were designed to meet the needs of post-1660 Anglican worship, their furnishings, such as altarpieces, making a visually striking, confrontational, theological statement.[52]

Sexuality: Reading Theories and Practices (Manchester, 1993), pp. 100–15; Michèle Cohen, *Fashioning Masculinity: National Identity and Language in the Eighteenth Century* (London, 1996), esp. pp. 29–34, 50–53; Carter, *Men and the Emergence of Polite Society*, esp. pp. 66–70.

[48]   Mary Astell, *A Serious Proposal to the Ladies* (London, 1694), p. 145. See also William Kolbrener's chapter in this volume.

[49]   Anne Laurence, 'Lady Betty Hastings (1682–1739): Godly Patron', *Women's History Review*, 19/2 (2010): p. 201; Donald F. Bond (ed.), *The Tatler* (3 vols, Oxford, 1987), vol. 1, pp. 301–2, 349. The original Aspasia was famed in the ancient classical world as a conversationalist.

[50]   Alan Harding, *The Countess of Huntingdon's Connexion: A Sect in Action in Eighteenth-Century England* (Oxford, 2003), pp. 34, 44, 51–3.

[51]   Borsay, *English Urban Renaissance*, pp. 110–12.

[52]   Paul Jeffery, *The City Churches of Sir Christopher Wren* (1996; London, 2007); Vaughan Hart, *Nicholas Hawksmoor: Rebuilding Ancient Wonders* (2002; New Haven, 2007), pp. 131–85; Kenneth Fincham and Nicholas Tyacke, *Altars Restored: The Changing Face of English Religious Worship, 1547–c. 1700* (Oxford, 2007), pp. 305–51; Haynes,

The Dissenting meeting-houses that were officially licensed after the Toleration Act of 1689 were noticeable within the urban landscape too, and not only by their newly legalized presence. Drawing on the neo-classical vocabularies so popular with secular and Anglican architectural projects, Dissenting meeting houses in urban areas could be fairly large, elaborate structures that projected a statement about the strength and permanence of post-1689 Dissent.[53]

The role that women played in contributing to the erection and ornamentation of religious buildings in this refashioned urban landscape merits further analysis; commissions provide insights into the way in which women might sponsor and shape their religious communities, as well as into religious belief and practices. Such an assessment is often problematized by the surviving source material. 'Merely identifying women's commissions is difficult, especially those of married women in the early modern period, since the presumption is always that the work was done for the husband who paid the bills', Anne Laurence has remarked more generally of women's building activities, and this is also the case with regard to religious buildings.[54] In 1692 a purpose-built Independent meeting house was constructed in St Saviourgate, York. It is likely that support for this was a joint initiative between Sir John Hewley and his wife Dame Sarah Hewley; one biographer of John Hewley attributed the commission to him, despite the fact that Sarah Hewley was equally, if more, committed to nonconformist causes and her inheritance provided the basis both for the couple's wealth and her major charitable endowments.[55] Henry Rogers left a large sum in 1672 for the rebuilding of a City of London church, and, some years later, the archbishop of Canterbury, William Sancroft, duly acknowledged Rogers's 'pious benevolence' in a commemorative inscription in St Mary Aldermary, London, which Rogers's money helped to rebuild. What Sancroft considered memorializing, but eventually decided otherwise, was the key role that Rogers's niece, Anne Rogers, played in instigating the reconstruction of St Mary Aldermary between 1679 and 1681. It was primarily owing to Anne Rogers that her uncle's bequest was implemented. She launched a legal case to retrieve the sum which he had left for this purpose

Pictures and Popery; Terry Friedman, *The Eighteenth-Century Church in Britain* (New Haven, 2011).

[53] Borsay, *English Urban Renaissance*, pp. 111–12; Christopher Stell, *An Inventory of Nonconformist Chapels and Meeting-Houses in South-West England* (London, 1991), pp. 68, 107, 118; Christopher Stell, *An Inventory of Nonconformist Chapels and Meeting-Houses in the North of England* (London, 1994), pp. 6, 112–13, 256–8; Christopher Stell, *An Inventory of Nonconformist Chapels and Meeting-Houses in Eastern England* (Swindon, 2002), pp. 142, 180, 186, 256, 260.

[54] Anne Laurence, 'Women Using Building in Seventeenth-Century England: A Question of Sources?', *Transactions of the Royal Historical Society*, 6th ser., 13 (2003): p. 293.

[55] C.V. Wedgwood, 'Sir John Hewley, 1619–1697', *Transactions of the Unitarian Historical Society*, 6/1 (1935): p. 13. For a reappraisal see Richard Potts, *Dame Sarah's Legacy: A History of the Lady Hewley Trust* (York, 2005), pp. 22–31, 34–5, 37–8.

after his other executors had misappropriated it for themselves, and she decided which church was rebuilt and authorized payments for its construction. Another female benefactor, Dame Jane Smith, paid for the church's altarpiece.[56]

The construction and ornamentation of religious buildings had long been a focus of female religious activity before 1660 of course. But did the nature and pattern of such patronage differ in the long eighteenth century in comparison to earlier and later periods, and how did gender intersect with religious trends in this context? To what extent did location – urban or rural – influence the ways in which women were involved? After all, the sponsorship of an urban project was a more publicly visible act and statement of belief, which potentially had an impact on how men and women of a similar social rank to the donor worshipped. By contrast, a rural project could be construed in a paternalistic light, its impact primarily felt by social inferiors, thus potentially giving the donor greater freedom of action.[57]

II

Poised awkwardly, but formatively, between historians' conceptions of 'early modern' and 'modern' epochs, the period from 1660 to 1760 is often interrupted in studies of British religion. This is unfortunate, for the cultural disturbances in the realm of the sacred in this period deserve more sustained examination, particularly where they interact with gender and female experience. Over the past couple of decades, we have learnt much about gender roles and gendered experiences in the long eighteenth century. The concept of separate spheres has become increasingly problematized, with scholars pointing to the need to look beyond or re-examine prescriptive texts to explore how gender roles were practiced on a day to day basis.[58] Such research has particularly focused on the activities of elite women, who stepped beyond the private sphere of the home to participate in the political world, to defend and advance their family's parliamentary interests, to push for patronage and advocate political causes, although the activities of socially more

[56]   Howard Colvin, 'The Church of St Mary Aldermary and Its Rebuilding after the Great Fire of London', *Architectural History*, 24 (1981): pp. 27–31.

[57]   For examples of women commissioning urban and rural religious buildings, alterations and furnishings throughout this period see K.A. Esdaile, 'Cousin to Pepys and Dryden: A Note on the Works of Mrs. Elizabeth Creed of Tichmarsh', *The Burlington Magazine*, 77/448 (July 1940): pp. 24–7; Basil F.L. Clarke, *The Building of the Eighteenth-Century Church* (London, 1963), pp. 52–9, 64–7, 70–73, 76, 81, 85, 87; Jacob, *Lay People and Religion*, pp. 197, 212–17; Laurence, 'Women Using Building', pp. 295–6; Friedman, *Eighteenth-Century Church*, pp. 27, 57, 66–7, 152.

[58]   Hannah Barker and Elaine Chalus, introduction to Hannah Barker and Elaine Chalus (eds), *Gender in Eighteenth-Century England: Roles, Representations, and Responsibilities* (Harlow, 1997), pp. 24–5; Kathleen Wilson, *The Island Race: Englishness, Empire, and Gender in the Eighteenth Century* (London, 2003), pp. 92–3.

marginal women – printers, hawkers and Whig conspirators of the 1680s – have been considered too.[59] Scholars have also illuminated the careers of female writers, such as Aphra Behn, Mary Astell, Delariviere Manley and Susanna Centlivre who wrote for and about specific political matters.[60] Yet, more often than not, the main emphasis of much of this work on women and politics has been secular in approach; indeed recent writing on women and politics has been critiqued as 'Namierite' for its focus on 'kinship and connection in which ideology vanishes'.[61]

Among so many other watersheds, the century from 1660 to 1760 has also been identified with the development of the concept of gender difference and the consolidation of modern patriarchy. Following Thomas Laqueur, Michael McKeon has argued that the new insight in the later seventeenth and early eighteenth centuries that there were two distinct sexes, not a unitary male norm, restructured the conceptualization of gender along the lines of natural, incommensurable sexual difference.[62] This leads to the claim that 'the early modern shift from a sexual system of hierarchy to one of difference may be seen as a shift to the system of heterosexuality, reciprocally inseparable from its dialectical antithesis, homosexuality – which is therefore also a crucial part of the system'.[63] While this conclusion may depend rather too heavily on Laqueur's debatable narrative of hegemony of the 'one-sex model', it is certainly observable that contemporary commentators were exercised to an unprecedented extent by the question of women's status in marriage, law and education and, in a period where heterosexuality and masculinity were increasingly conjoined, perturbed by male same-sex sexual relations, as manifested by fears over the proliferation of 'molly-houses' in early eighteenth-century London.[64] As one commentator

---

[59]   Rachel Weil, 'The Female Politician in the Late Stuart Age', in Julia Marciari Alexander and Catharine MacLeod (eds), *Politics, Transgression, and Representation at the Court of Charles II* (New Haven, 2007), pp. 177–91; Elaine Chalus, *Elite Women in English Political Life, c. 1754–1790* (Oxford, 2005); Elaine Chalus, 'Ladies Are Often Very Good Scaffoldings': Women and Politics in the Age of Anne', *Parliamentary History*, 28/1 (2009): pp. 150–65; Paula McDowell, *The Women of Grub Street: Press, Politics, and Gender in the London Literary Marketplace, 1678–1730* (Oxford, 1998), pp. 265–7; Melinda Zook, 'Nursing Sedition: Women, Dissent, and the Whig Struggle', in McElligott (ed.), *Fear, Exclusion and Revolution*, pp. 189–203.

[60]   For introductions to the ever-growing literature on women's writing see Sarah Prescott and David E. Shuttleton (eds), *Women and Poetry, 1660–1750* (Basingstoke, 2003); Susan Staves, *A Literary History of Women's Writing in Britain, 1660–1789* (Cambridge, 2006).

[61]   Wilson, *Island Race*, p. 93.

[62]   Michael McKeon, 'Historicizing Patriarchy: The Emergence of Gender Difference in England, 1660–1760', *Eighteenth-Century Studies*, 28/3 (1995): pp. 295–322.

[63]   Ibid., p. 307.

[64]   On the question of women's status, see, for example, Hilda L. Smith, *Reason's Disciples: Seventeenth-Century English Feminists* (Urbana, 1982); Amy M. Froide, *Never Married: Singlewomen in Early Modern England* (Oxford, 2005); Patricia Springborg,

notes, historians 'posit this period as the century of change in the ways in which bodies were understood, sexuality constructed, and sexual activity carried out'.[65] If there was indeed a shift towards the heterosexual organization of the genders, we might expect to see a complex set of negotiations between this new model of sexual differentiation and traditional theological discourse about male and female nature, as well as customary sexual roles. Such a process would have implications for women's self-understanding and the reception of patriarchal doctrines about femininity. In fact, some of the most stimulating work on gender for this period has centred around the evolution of British masculinities, and within that, masculinity and religion.[66]

In this volume, we have chosen 'women' rather than 'gender' as our organizing category, because we have unapologetically focused our attention on hitherto neglected female identities and experiences. We also want to make space to consider the contributions of individual women to religious discourse and practice and the different social realities to which women were subject as a result of the changing religious landscape, and not only to consider change from the perspective of gender construction. This responds both to the challenging recent assertions that this was a century of discontinuity for religious mentalities and gender relations, and to the apparent lack of concern for the placement of women within these narratives. As a consequence of the turn to religion in late seventeenth-century, eighteenth-century and Enlightenment studies, historians have systematically analysed the ways in which (male) politicians, clergymen, preachers and writers sponsored and reacted to religious change. Women's contributions have, however, been somewhat overlooked by scholars of the period, who have tended to focus either on the impact of (secular) Enlightenment and social change on female lives, or on clerical politics.[67] By contrast, literary studies of women's writing after the Restoration, while sometimes privileging intellectual concerns such as the emergence of feminism or sexual identities over religious content, have

---

Mary Astell: Theorist of Freedom from Domination (Cambridge, 2005). On same-sex relations see Emma Donoghue, *Passions Between Women: British Lesbian Culture, 1668–1801* (London, 1993); George E. Haggerty, *Men in Love: Masculinity and Sexuality in the Eighteenth Century* (New York, 1999); Tim Hitchcock, *English Sexualities, 1700–1800* (Basingstoke, 1997).

[65] Karen Harvey, 'The Century of Sex? Gender, Bodies, and Sexuality in the Long Eighteenth Century', *The Historical Journal*, 45/4 (2002): p. 900.

[66] See, for example, Cohen, *Fashioning Masculinity*; Tim Hitchcock and Michèle Cohen (eds), *English Masculinities 1660–1800* (London, 1999); Stephen H. Gregg, '"A Truly Christian Hero": Religion, Effeminacy, and Nation in the Writings of the Societies for Reformation of Manners', *Eighteenth-Century Life*, 25/1 (2001): pp. 17–28.

[67] Earlier and later periods are better served. See, for example, Crawford, *Women and Religion in England*; Sue Morgan (ed.), *Women, Religion and Feminism in Britain, 1750–1900* (Basingstoke, 2002).

nonetheless done much to reveal the textures of female piety.[68] The essays in this volume aim to build on such work and illustrate the enriching potential of interdisciplinary study in this area.

This collection seeks to deploy, as well as reconnect with, some of the approaches central to more general historiographies of this period and integrate female religious experiences, and religion itself, back into them. How, for instance, did women's religious beliefs inform their political preoccupations and thus their political commitments? In what ways did women use the agencies of authority, influence and patronage – understandings of which have been crucial to complicating our appreciation of eighteenth-century gender roles – to privately and more publicly contribute to, and intervene and adjudicate in, their religious communities and with what results? The volume will probe how features of late seventeenth-century and early to mid-eighteenth-century society, which have been identified as characteristic of the period, in particular, the emerging public sphere and the print culture which was an indisputable part of it, presented women with new opportunities for religious expression and advocacy, along the way further illuminating the public sphere's religious dimensions. An additional aim of the volume is to contribute to refocussing scholarly approaches to the history of gender, marriage and especially the history of feminism, by locating the British writers often characterized as early feminists, such as Mary Astell or Damaris Masham, within their theological, spiritual and confessional traditions.[69]

III

In the volume's opening chapter, Alison Searle offers an insight into the different meanings of marriage for women in dissenting communities facing persecution. She compares the domestic experiences and public interventions of two types of female exemplar in Protestant nonconformity: the minister's wife and the prophetess. Both Margaret Charlton, wife of the supremely influential Presbyterian Richard Baxter, and Anne Wentworth, a Baptist visionary, encountered hostility to their public activity. For Charlton, marriage provided the space to exercise her gifts in energetic voluntarism; paradoxically, for Wentworth, repression in the household became the stimulus for an oppositional prophetic ministry which challenged state, church and husband. Wentworth's visionary discourse was distinctively that of both Dissenter and abused wife. Sarah Apetrei's chapter continues this

---

[68] For example, Carol Barash, *English Women's Poetry, 1649–1714: Politics, Community, and Linguistic Authority* (Oxford, 1996); Kathryn R. King, *Jane Barker, Exile: A Literary Career, 1675–1725* (Oxford, 2000); Anne Kelley, *Catharine Trotter: An Early Modern Writer in the Vanguard of Feminism* (Aldershot, 2002); Susan Staves, 'Church of England Clergy and Women Writers', *Huntington Library Quarterly*, 65/1–2 (2002): pp. 81–103; Prescott, 'Elizabeth Singer Rowe'.

[69] For a similar approach see William Kolbrener and Michal Michelson (eds), *Mary Astell: Reason, Gender, Faith* (Aldershot, 2007).

exploration of the links between women, marriage and religion. Apetrei recovers early Enlightenment discussions of the question of female celibacy, showing how a debate over the religiously devoted single life evolved and polarized opinion in the post-Reformation. In particular, Apetrei argues, women's purposeful abstinence from marriage carried several controversial implications: it could signify sexual perversity and hypocrisy, like the papist celibates; it might mean a disavowal of the worldly concerns and dedication to public reform; or, most subversively, it might stand as a protest against tyranny in marriage. While Restoration wits were extolling the virtues of the bachelor lifestyle, there was also a serious defence of celibacy underway and the female vocation to singleness was a matter of considerable religious concern.

In the following chapter, Alasdair Raffe reminds us of the British scope of our study and draws attention to another vocational space for women, pointing out that women's roles in Scottish Presbyterianism in the years after the Restoration have rarely been examined. Like Searle, his focus is on the response to the experience of dissent and oppression, and the opportunities which paradoxically opened up for women through their community's marginal position. Participating actively in the underground networks which kept Presbyterian commitments alive during the period in the wilderness, women came to exercise considerable spiritual authority, to the extent that the Kirk was attacked for the status it gave to women after its restoration in 1690. Raffe's account indicates that women's experiences are far from marginal to the history of early modern religion, and that the survival of one of the most important Protestant traditions in Britain owed much to its female faithful. Claire Walker's chapter demonstrates that women were also instrumental in sustaining English Catholicism and the Jacobite cause when both were facing intense pressure at home. Through the communication and patronage networks fostered by English convents in mainland Europe during this period, a strong sense of social and spiritual cohesion was upheld among Catholics on both sides of the Channel. However, Walker illustrates the growing independence and self-determination of these communities of single women as they developed distinctive political and missionary priorities in their separation from English concerns.

After these case studies of women as dissenters and religious exiles, Melinda Zook takes us right to the heart of the establishment. This chapter brings into focus the personal influence of Mary II on the Church of England at a formative point in its history. A queen regnant without executive power, married to a man who did not share her devotion to the Church of England, Mary II's religious commitments were shaped and restrained by her marriage. Like Walker, Zook situates English religious politics within a continental European landscape (a salutary nod to the agenda set by Jonathan Scott and Tony Claydon). Zook links Mary II's religious reformism to her identification with international Protestantism, a product of the 12 years that she spent as princess of Orange in the United Provinces. Zook argues that Mary II preferred clergymen with latitudinarian inclinations as a consequence of her encounters with Counter-Reformation aggression in Europe. Through a careful analysis of her patronage choices, Zook presents Mary II, with William III, very much as part of a 'Protestant International' which shaped the character of the English Church in the 1690s.

Writing in the decade after the Revolution of 1688–89, Damaris Masham and Mary Astell have come to symbolize the female contribution to the Anglican Republic of Letters. At rather different points in the philosophical spectrum, these two women stimulated and responded to the religious controversies of the early English Enlightenment. In the chapters which follow, Sarah Hutton and William Kolbrener assess their respective contributions and, in doing so, offer new insights into the structure of their thought. Hutton reconsiders the religious content of Damaris Masham's writings, and especially her letters to such major Enlightenment figures as Locke and Leibniz. The religious undercurrents of Masham's philosophical thought have not received much scholarly attention, and Hutton's chapter highlights the centrality of religious topics in the debates which absorbed Masham's interest. Likewise, emphasizing the enduring vitality of theological discourse in the age of Enlightenment, William Kolbrener provides a new interpretation of Astell's works. He suggests that Astell's Anglican apologetic is not retrogressive, but draws creatively and tactically on Enlightenment themes to construct an innovative vision of a Christian public sphere. Reconceiving conversation as a space free from masculine party interest and political posturing, Astell advocated polite intercourse in the public sphere as a vehicle for moral and theological edification and championed the role that women could play in furthering this end.

Responding to a widespread interest in distinctively 'Tory feminists' such as Mary Astell, Hannah Smith readjusts the focus in her chapter on Susanna Centlivre's 'Whig feminism', reminding us that women were closely linked to the Tory and Jacobite agenda by eighteenth-century contemporaries as well as by more recent commentators. Smith shows how the Whig Centlivre tried to persuade her female readers of the benefits of the Revolutionary settlement, and attacked the Tory hold on women's religious sensibilities through domineering clergy and scaremongering about the 'Church in danger'. The personal agency and public profile of an individual Anglican woman, the 'Bluestocking' Catherine Talbot, is the subject of the final essay in this volume by Emma Major. Talbot's letters, journals and published works are mined for clues to illuminate her reputation as a moral exemplar and model of femininity. Major considers the significance of this public construction of Talbot and asks why this individual life came to embody the religious and ethical priorities of her generation.

IV

This volume presents a series of windows into the lives of women which reveal the character and extent of female involvement in the formative processes of religious renewal, reform, revolution and reaction. Such contributions were distinctive because of the social, cultural and biological factors that constrained women.

Every religious denomination barred women from exercising formal ministerial authority over congregations; the majority banned them from publicly preaching. Women of all social groups had more limited access to educational resources than their male peers. They were denied the opportunity to make and receive material wealth in the same way as men because of trade regulations and customary inheritance and employment practices. Married women enjoyed no separate legal identity from their husbands. Frequent child-bearing and -rearing absorbed women's time and exhausted and imperilled their physical health. Obvious as these observations may seem, it is important to reiterate them here, since their impact on women's religious involvement and activities were profound. The women whose religious beliefs and experiences are analysed in the following chapters are all 'exceptional' women; exceptional in that they could record what they thought and did; exceptional because their activities were prominent enough to prompt others to document them; and exceptional in that few of them bore children or had childcare commitments that devoured the time they had to write and act. Their exceptionalism renders them atypical, and any conclusions must keep this in mind.

What emerges from the chapters in this volume is the degree of continuity over the course of the period. There is some shifting ground: the print culture of the eighteenth century presented women with an increasing range of opportunities for religious expression, advocacy and authority, as did the growing respectability of female authorship. These extended opportunities had their roots in women's participation in the public sphere of the mid-seventeenth century, but our period saw important evolutions. If Anne Wentworth and Mary Astell can be situated within existing traditions of women's religious writing and publishing through their use of the pamphlet or tract to articulate their views, Susanna Centlivre can be viewed as embracing newer forms, such as the newspaper. These genres, along with the novel, became integral to women's (and men's) religious writing as the eighteenth century progressed. As Norma Clarke has remarked, 'woman's reflections and fictions, offered in a form which drew attention to spiritual matters, provided opportunities for leadership'.[70] 'Distinctions between genres such as the periodical essay, the published sermon, devotional writings, moral tales and realistic and fanciful fictions were fluid'.[71] Perhaps most striking in this respect was Elizabeth Rowe who, in the 1720s and 1730s, used the form of the romance to elevate piety and virtue, with popular success and public approbation.[72] Yet while the early to mid-eighteenth century saw the proliferation of print and the genres which it took, the continuing significance of scribal circulation and publication for women and men should be noted. The 'politics of religion' informed and inspired women's commitments and activities; the extent and nature of their involvement

---

[70] Norma Clarke, 'Bluestocking Fictions: Devotional Writings, Didactic Literature and the Imperative of Female Improvement', in Knott and Taylor (eds), *Women, Gender and Enlightenment*, p. 461.

[71] Ibid.

[72] Ibid., pp. 466–7.

were shaped by their own, and others, conceptions of gendered norms. Some of the women considered in this volume – the English Protestant Dissenters Margaret Charlton and Anne Wentworth; the radical Scottish Presbyterian Coat-Muir Folk Margaret Harley, Grisell Spritt and Mary Spritt; the Catholic nuns Mary Knatchbull, Mary Caryll and Mary Rose Howard; and the Anglicans Mary Astell and Susanna Centlivre – were all forward in defending their religious beliefs and confessional or denominational standpoints in ways which drew them into conflict with particular political regimes or those of different religio-political views. Religious belief remained central to women's political involvements after 1760, and particularly during the French Revolutionary and Napoleonic Wars, as the lives and works of Hannah More, Mary Wollstonecraft and Anna Laetitia Barbauld notably and amply demonstrate.[73]

Such similarities are most marked in terms of the impact of religious beliefs and concerns on gender politics. Without doubt, the contexts for late eighteenth-century gender politics were different to those of circa 1700. As Emma Major has remarked, 'a hundred years of women writers, of feminised commerce, and a proliferating print culture, meant that there were more writers, more genres, more readers, and more critics'. 'Women writing about women found championing their sex simultaneously more difficult and easier'.[74] But the convictions and fears that had motivated late seventeenth-century women writers to publish remained, primarily their anxieties over female education. The tenor of Astell's religious arguments for educating women in the 1690s was echoed a century later by writers as politically dissimilar as Hannah More and Mary Wollstonecraft.[75]

Yet while gender was instrumental in determining the nature of female religious practices and the scope of opportunities, socio-economic circumstances were fundamentally important in an *ancien régime* society. Elite and royal women had, of course, the networks, status, authority and material resources to act as religious patrons and pursue more personal initiatives which poorer, socially more marginal women and men lacked. It is no coincidence that possibly the most influential patron of the Evangelical Revival – Selina Hastings, countess of Huntingdon, who both founded and gave her name to a movement within the Church of England, the 'Countess of Huntingdon's Connexion' – was aristocratic, comparatively well off (with generous friends) and a widow. As a peeress she had the right to maintain private chapels, thus allowing the Connexion to circumvent the Toleration Act's requirement that religious meeting places be registered, and to attempt to evade

---

[73]   See Anne Stott, *Hannah More: The First Victorian* (Oxford, 2003); Barbara Taylor, *Mary Wollstonecraft and the Feminist Imagination* (Cambridge, 2003); Major, *Madam Britannia*, esp. pp. 233–303.

[74]   Major, *Madam Britannia*, pp. 275–6.

[75]   Ibid.; Barbara Taylor, 'The Religious Foundations of Mary Wollstonecraft's Feminism', in Claudia L. Johnson (ed.), *The Cambridge Companion to Mary Wollstonecraft* (Cambridge, 2002), pp. 99–100.

hostility by presenting the Connexion's chapels as the countess's.[76] Queens regnant – Mary II and Anne – and queens consort – Mary of Modena and Caroline of Ansbach – acted as important sponsors of religious groups, causes and piety. Again, this conception of queenship persisted into the post-1760 period, with George III's queen, Charlotte of Mecklenburg-Strelitz, taking on such a role.[77] Indeed, Hannah More hoped in 1805 that George III's granddaughter and a likely future queen of Britain, Princess Charlotte of Wales, would see her duties in a similar light and praised Mary II and Caroline of Ansbach to her as exemplary Protestant queens.[78]

It would be misleading, however, to conclude from this evidence that the only female culture which mattered in British religion in this period was that of rich and powerful female patrons or published women writers. Another thread which links the essays in this volume is the emphasis on the gendered character of religious reform, often associated with a culture of sensibility in which women's manners, domestic virtues and religious sentiments were exemplary.[79] It is, perhaps above all, in this sense that one can speak of a 'feminization of religion' between 1660 and 1760. Phyllis Mack's recent exploration of gender and emotion in the Methodist movement illustrates beautifully how women, sometimes even ordinary women, were able to give eloquent voice to the passionate piety which so powerfully resonated with considerable swathes of eighteenth-century British society at the time of the Evangelical Revival. In particular, the 'iconic roles played by Methodist women leaders' – as 'the Fallen Woman redeemed by faith', or as the 'Ardent Virgin' or 'venerable Mother in Israel' – captured something essential about the spirit of evangelical reform. Mack reminds us that these ideal types 'are as old as Christianity itself', but as their many parallels in this volume indicate, they held fresh significance for a Christian society gripped with anxiety, however unjustified, about sexual morality and spiritual decay.[80]

---

[76]   Harding, *Countess of Huntingdon's Connexion*, pp. 163–4, 315.

[77]   Clarissa Campbell Orr, 'The Late Hanoverian Court and the Christian Enlightenment', in Michael Schaich (ed.), *Monarchy and Religion: The Transformation of Royal Culture in Eighteenth Century Europe* (Oxford, 2007), pp. 317–42.

[78]   Stott, *Hannah More*, pp. 260–65.

[79]   See G.J. Barker-Benfield, *The Culture of Sensibility: Sex and Society in Eighteenth-Century Britain* (Chicago, 1992).

[80]   Mack, *Heart Religion*, p. 128.

Chapter 2
Women, Marriage and Agency in Restoration Dissent

Alison Searle

When Parliament passed the Act of Uniformity in 1662, one unintended consequence was the marriage of Margaret Charlton and the controversial divine, Richard Baxter. Baxter believed that celibacy was preferable for ministers; his ejection from the Church of England after he refused to conform to the 1662 Act thus enabled him to marry Margaret Charlton. But Charlton's decision to marry Baxter was also driven by her beliefs. As Baxter later noted, Charlton thrived in an environment of persecution and political opposition; had he accepted the bishopric of Hereford, which he was offered, 'it would have alienated her much from me in point of esteem and love'.[1] Charlton (1636–81) was a relatively wealthy woman, and her personal income and passion for the gospel led her to facilitate Baxter's ministry, indefatigably to hire and build venues for him to preach in throughout London, to fund other preachers and to set up schools. This activity on the part of a nonconformist woman in the public sphere provoked criticism. However, Baxter not only defended her, but commented: 'It was not mine which she gave, but her own.... I am not ashamed to have been much ruled by her prudent love in many things'.[2]

Marriage offered Margaret Charlton emotional security and opportunities for personal interventions in the public sphere; for Anne Wentworth (1629/30–93, though this latter date is uncertain) it meant 'fierce looks, bitter words, sharp tongue, and cruel usage'.[3] In 1670 she experienced a divine healing from the physical and spiritual infirmities that had plagued her for years. This led to a religious awakening and transformed her from an oppressed wife to a prophet determined to proclaim God's word publicly. Anne Wentworth had to contend with both the political powers of the state, which warily tracked her apocalyptic predictions in the years immediately preceding the Exclusion Crisis,[4] and the patriarchal authorities in her local Particular Baptist community. Unlike Margaret

---

[1]   Richard Baxter, *A Breviate of the Life of Margaret, The Daughter of Francis Charlton ... Wife of Richard Baxter* (London, 1681), G4v.

[2]   Ibid., K1v.

[3]   Anne Wentworth, *A Vindication of Anne Wentworth Tending to the Better Preparing of All People for her Larger Testimony, which is Making Ready for Publick View* (London, 1677), p. 5.

[4]   The National Archives, Kew (TNA), SP 29/398, fol. 175.

Charlton, she intervened in the public sphere through a deliberate rejection of her husband and ministers, asserting a spiritual authority that was conveyed by direct communion with and revelation from God. This found expression in her prophetic utterances and the dissemination of her writings through the medium of print. The contrasting histories of Charlton and Wentworth demonstrate the ways in which female piety was shaped by the religious settlement of 1660 and the vividness, breadth and influence of such piety within English culture before 1689. Gender and dissent each inflect the ways in which women like Charlton and Wentworth were able to engage in the public sphere following the re-establishment of the monarchy and state church that defined them as nonconformists.

Recent scholarship has attempted to map the extent to which the interrelationships between radical religion, gender and the public sphere were re-negotiated following the Restoration. Patricia Crawford postulated that '[e]nthusiastic religion was no longer a common cultural ground between men and women', and that 'elite men distanced themselves from lower-class men as well as women'. Rationalism, informed by scientific debate, became a male characteristic, while females continued to be defined in terms of emotion and instability.[5] It is necessary, however, to avoid the dangers inherent in telling historical narratives where 'women begin with a public role and end up by being banished into domesticity', as David Norbrook has remarked.[6] Norbrook's revisionist account of the English public sphere incorporates the multiple ways in which women were involved in the republic of letters and the impact of radical Protestant religion. Although '[n]arratives of seventeenth-century women's disappearing into a private sphere do draw our attention to important constraints' they also 'run the risk of patronizing a period of extraordinary energy and creativity'.[7] Kevin Pask argues, similarly, that a new concept of the literary public sphere emerged in England during the 1650s and 1660s, in which writing women played a central role. That which had previously been regarded as private and quotidian became essential to an understanding of one's social self and a collective public identity. This transformation transcends traditional period distinctions between the Interregnum and the Restoration and is exemplified in the love letters of Dorothy Osborne – particularly her manipulation of the marriage market – and the diary of Samuel Pepys.[8] As Norbrook observes, '[s]ome women in the seventeenth century did indeed assume that certain spheres of discourse were universal, rather than specifically masculine, and hence vigorously claimed inclusion'.[9]

---

[5]   Patricia Crawford, *Women and Religion in England 1500–1720* (London, 1993), p. 185.

[6]   David Norbrook, 'Women, the Republic of Letters, and the Public Sphere in the Mid-Seventeenth Century', *Criticism*, 46/2 (2004): p. 224.

[7]   Ibid., p. 235.

[8]   Kevin Pask, 'The Bourgeois Public Sphere and the Concept of Literature', *Criticism*, 46/2 (2004): p. 251.

[9]   Norbrook, 'Women, the Republic of Letters', p. 224.

Dissenting women, however, felt the tensions experienced by other women and disenfranchised men who engaged in this republic of letters even more acutely due to their double alienation from the public sphere on the grounds of gender and religious affiliation.[10]

This chapter focuses on female agency within dissenting marriage in the Restoration era. It explores the extremely different, yet creative and influential ways in which individual women responded to the difficulties presented by a hostile government and state church after 1660 through new opportunities in the public sphere. Richard Baxter's *Breviate of the Life of Margaret ... Baxter* presents one option available to dissenting women: companionate marriage as an interdependent partnership, facilitating gospel ministry in the public sphere. Anne Wentworth's pamphlets offer a different model: radical protest against her husband, church and elements of London society through an appeal to her mystical marriage to Christ. The historical sources which form the basis of these case studies are inevitably partial and offset each other in important ways. Margaret Charlton's marriage is depicted primarily in the words of her husband; though he incorporates much of her own writing in the *Breviate*, it is preselected and framed by his own account. The reverse is the case with Anne Wentworth: her marriage is portrayed in typographical and vivid terms in her own words, and any indication of her husband's perspective is mediated through her representation of his behaviour and language. It is crucial to keep the absence of these two voices in mind when considering the different pathways and opportunities that marriage – physical and mystical – offered these two dissenting women from both mainstream nonconformity and the more radical sectarian fringe in Restoration England.

Joanne Bailey has noted that historiography treating the institution of marriage from the medieval to the Victorian periods inclines to either an optimistic or pessimistic model in its assessment of the role and agency of women. She argues that it is better to think about agency in marriage in terms of interdependency, as 'a more convincing model of the causes of conflict can be built on the contrast between reality and ideals in marital roles'. This is because it was 'issues in which both spouses had a vested interest, like child care and upbringing and finances' that 'were those most likely to create power struggles, leading men to express and attempt to implement patriarchal ideals'.[11] Frances E. Dolan explores the way in which these tensions resulted from the marriage advice provided to men and women in the sixteenth and seventeenth centuries, in particular, 'the persistent dilemma of reconciling spiritual equality and social hierarchy, the erotic melding into one and the tension between two potential heads of this shared body'.[12] Naomi Tadmor has traced the intimate relationship between early modern English Bible

---

[10]   Pask, 'Bourgeois Public Sphere', p. 253.

[11]   Joanne Bailey, *Unquiet Lives: Marriage and Marriage Breakdown in England, 1660–1800* (Cambridge, 2003), pp. 198–9.

[12]   Frances E. Dolan, *Marriage and Violence: The Early Modern Legacy* (Philadelphia, 2008), pp. 28–9.

translations that 'served to naturalise in the text a monogamous idiom of marriage, which was also further hammered in through adjacent commentaries and notes' and 'the standardisation of marriage laws and their vigorous enforcement ... by both church and state'.[13] Moreover, Rachel Weil has demonstrated that the close relationship between the family and politics, or marriage and the state, continued to flourish in late Stuart England.[14]

Bailey's model of marriage as interdependency is important: it offers an opportunity to explore the relationships detailed in this chapter in terms that are not limited to the dichotomy of patriarchal authority and submission or subversion. It is also necessary to recognize the tensions implicit in the ideology of marriage that developed in post-Reformation England between the assertion on the one hand of spiritual equality between men and women and the reiteration on the other of hierarchies of gender and class that undercut this. Couples negotiated the implications for their marriages in different ways. Richard Baxter and Margaret Charlton combined a passionate commitment to the same religious convictions with an equally strong respect for their individual right to act autonomously. Anne Wentworth and her husband separated from one another due to their inability to unite a sense of religious vocation with a rigid understanding of male headship in marriage. The broadly shared conviction – that hierarchy and order in the family was a microcosm which reflected the stability and distribution of power in the state and church – meant that the organization of these personal relations inevitably made an impact upon the ways in which dissenting women engaged with the public sphere.

This developing ideology of marriage was constructed alongside a parallel exploration of divorce and celibacy. Roni Berger notes that while divorce was technically illegal, the ideas about divorce that John Milton articulates in his *Doctrine and Discipline of Divorce* (1644) had already been circulating throughout England for at least a century.[15] Tim Stretton also emphasizes that private separations were not a sudden innovation developed during the 1650s. 'It is undeniable that in that decade, when the jurisdiction of the church court was abolished with no immediate thought given to its replacement, estranged spouses had to seek alternative ways to separate', but in turning to private settlements by deed or conditional bond, 'they were drawing on a tried and tested mechanism familiar since at least the time of Queen Elizabeth'.[16] The common law had

---

[13]   Naomi Tadmor, *The Social Universe of the English Bible: Scripture, Society and Culture in Early Modern England* (Cambridge, 2010), pp. 53, 69.

[14]   Rachel Weil, *Political Passions: Gender, the Family and Political Argument in England 1680–1714* (Manchester, 1999), pp. 1–3.

[15]   Ronit Berger, *Legalizing Love: Desire, Divorce, and the Law in Early Modern English Literature and Culture* (Saarbrücken, 2007), p. 2.

[16]   Tim Stretton, 'Marriage, Separation and the Common Law in England, 1540–1660', in Helen Berry and Elizabeth Foyster (eds), *The Family in Early Modern England* (Cambridge, 2007), p. 39.

allowed couples from Elizabethan times to work around the limited legal options available in order to ensure that married partners who were no longer able to live together had pragmatic solutions open to them:

> the complex web of consultation, negotiation and compromise, and the consent and approval (willing, tacit or begrudging) of different members of the community, that preceded marriage did not suddenly evaporate once a couple became husband and wife. This rich mix of family, neighbourly and political surveillance continued to play a key role in maintaining (or where necessary in breaking) marital bonds throughout the duration of marriage.[17]

The community involvement, religious guidance and pragmatism that characterized the approach of early modern men and women to marriage relationships, divorce and celibacy, both prior to and during the Interregnum continued to shape the nature and practice of marriage relationships in a communal context after the Restoration.

The issue of female agency within dissenting marriage and the impact of marriage upon women's role in the home, their religious communities and the public sphere will be examined through two detailed case studies. Firstly, I will analyse the experience of Margaret Charlton primarily as it has been recorded in the posthumous biography written by her husband, Richard Baxter, a noted cleric who can be loosely categorized as Presbyterian, though he strenuously resisted any labels other than that of Christian. Secondly, I will consider the apparently more radical nonconformist context offered by the Calvinistic or Particular Baptists.[18] The *Church Book of the Bunyan Meeting* records cases of congregational discipline which demonstrate the inconsistencies between prescriptions and practice that characterized dissenting marriages in the Baptist church led by John Bunyan;[19] this can also be seen in the autobiographical account of one of the female members of his congregation, Agnes Beaumont.[20] These instances offer an informative context for considering in detail the marriage experience and writings of the estranged Particular Baptist and prophet, Anne Wentworth.

---

[17]   Ibid., p. 38.

[18]   John Bunyan, unlike most Calvinistic Baptists, held open communion principles. This meant that he was willing to accept adults into his congregation who had not been baptized a second time. See Anne Dunan-Page, *Grace Overwhelming: John Bunyan, The Pilgrim's Progress and the Extremes of the Baptist Mind* (Bern, 2006), pp. 22–3.

[19]   Monica Furlong (ed.), *The Trial of John Bunyan and the Persecution of the Puritans* (London, 1978), p. 119; G.B. Harrison (ed.), *The Church Book of Bunyan Meeting, 1650–1821* (London, 1928), fols 96, 100.

[20]   Vera J. Camden (ed.), *The Narrative of the Persecutions of Agnes Beaumont* (East Lansing, 1992).

I

Baxter's *Breviate* of his wife's life has been edited and republished several times since its first publication in 1681.[21] Ann Hughes observes that this biography 'openly displays the ambiguities of Puritan marriage'. By praising Margaret Charlton, Baxter could be seen to be validating his 'own authority and influence' or acknowledging his failure to be 'master' in his marriage.[22] Baxter, however, undercuts these traditional dichotomies between mastery and submission, public and private, by reconstructing the debate in terms of gospel imperatives for godly zeal:

> There are some things charged on her as faults, which I shall mention. 1. That she busied her head so much about Churches, and works of Charity, and was not content to live privately and quietly. But this is just what prophane unbelievers say against all zeal, and serious godliness.[23]

This, as Hughes notes, causes Baxter to critique his wife for her conformity to the stereotype of the silent woman: 'My dear wife was faulty indeed in talking so little of Religion in Company'. It resulted from her desire to avoid hypocrisy.[24] Baxter consistently advised godly women to speak more openly and freely to others. His chief female correspondent during the 1650s, a Derbyshire gentlewoman, Katherine Gell, concluded after reading Baxter's classic, *The Saints' Everlasting Rest* (1650):

> wherin you earnestly presse the helping others to your rest & in particular by admonishing I was soe clearly convinced of my neglect & unaptnes to it & my uselessnes in my family that way; that I have drawne this conclusion from it that I am not in a state of grace & that upon this account that whoever lives in the

---

[21] Richard Baxter, *A Breviate of the Life of Margaret, the Daughter of Francis Charlton ... and Wife of Richard Baxter, Etc* (London, 1826); Richard Baxter, *Richard Baxter and Margaret Charlton ... Being the Breviate of the Life of Margaret Baxter ... With Introductory Essay, Notes and Appendices by John T. Wilkinson, Etc.* (London, 1928); Richard Baxter, *A Grief Sanctified: Passing Through Grief to Peace and Joy; J.I. Packer Presents Richard Baxter's Memoir of his Wife's Life and Death* (Leicester, 1998).

[22] Ann Hughes, 'Puritanism and Gender', in John Coffey and Paul C.H. Lim (eds), *The Cambridge Companion to Puritanism* (Cambridge, 2008), pp. 296–8. For a fuller discussion of the genre of the *Breviate* within the Puritan literary tradition see Alison O'Harae, 'Theology, Genre and Romance in Richard Baxter and Harriet Beecher Stowe', *Religion and Literature*, 37/1 (2005): pp. 69–91.

[23] Baxter, *Breviate*, I4v.

[24] Ibid., O2, L4. Neil Keeble has noted a similar instance in Christiana's response to Mrs Timorous in Part 2 of *The Pilgrim's Progress*: Neil Keeble, '"Here is Her Glory, Even to be Under Him"': The Feminine in the Thought and Work of John Bunyan', in Anne Laurence, W.R. Owens and Stuart Sim (eds), *John Bunyan and his England, 1628–88* (London, 1990), pp. 136–7.

constant omission of a known duty or commission of a know[n] sin is not in a state of grace but I have done \therefore/ & c: this hath cost me much sorrow for indeed sir I have indeavored it very much since & could speake but for a naturall foolish bashfullnes that attends me in all other matters hindering me much from doing or receiving good.[25]

She is inclined to melancholy, but Baxter's spiritual counsel directs her away from introspection and privacy:

Sit not at home as if you had no body to looke after but yourselfe; but step out now and then to your poore tenants, or send for them to you, and deale with them about the matters of their salvation. And you may find that, compassion to them, and such holy discourse in the worke of God, will do more to enliven you, then much Sorrow Striving with your heart will do.[26]

Baxter's pastoral advice was given to Gell while he was still a bachelor on 7 June 1656. His own experience of marriage to Margaret Charlton, however, confirmed him in it. He observes in his biographical account of her life (1681):

When we were married, her sadness and melancholy vanished; counsel did something to it, and contentment something; and being taken up with our houshold affairs, did somewhat. And we lived in inviolated love, and mutual complacency, sensible of the benefit of mutual help.[27]

Baxter's and Charlton's relationship is one of the best exemplifications of the model of 'companionate marriage' that it is argued Puritan theology produced.[28] He comments further:

These near nineteen years I know not that we ever had any breach in point of love, or point of interest, save only that she somewhat grudged that I had persuaded her for my quietness to surrender so much of her Estate, to a disabling her from helping others so much as she earnestly desired.[29]

According to Baxter, the assurance of faith, security and spiritual comfort that Margaret Charlton gained through the pastoral care of and marital relations with her husband helped to liberate her from the religious anxieties and corrosive introspection that marked her conviction of sin, doubts and depression around the time of her conversion and a serious illness. Indeed, the combination of

---

[25]   Dr Williams's Library, London, MS 59.V.216. I am grateful to the Trustees of Dr Williams's Library for permission to quote from the manuscripts in their possession.

[26]   Dr Williams's Library, MS 59.V.217.

[27]   Baxter, *Breviate*, G4.

[28]   See, for example, B.J. Sokol and Mary Sokol, *Shakespeare, Law, and Marriage* (Cambridge, 2003), pp. 8–90.

[29]   Baxter, *Breviate*, G4.

marriage and persecution by external authorities seems to have positively enabled Charlton's transformation from an introspective, melancholic young woman into an energetic, redoubtable and highly intelligent nonconformist patron and activist during the 1660s and 1670s. Baxter clearly indicates that prior to their marriage he and Charlton concluded a prenuptial agreement that gave them both a remarkable degree of economic and personal freedom within their relationship.[30] Their nonconformity repeatedly exposed them to persecution and removal, but Charlton arranged and managed each transition with care and wisdom.[31] She also energetically promoted Baxter's nonconformist pastoral activities following the Act of Uniformity. He notes that she 'prepared her house [at Acton] for the reception of those that would come in, to be instructed by [him], between the morning and evening public assemblies, and after'.[32] When he was imprisoned for teaching, 'she cheerfully went with [him] into Prison; *she brought her best bed thither*, and did much to remove the removable inconveniences of the Prison. I think she scarce ever had a pleasanter time in her life than while she was with me there'.[33] The Five-Mile Act (1665) forced them to move from Acton to Totteridge, where she found an apprenticeship for the son of her poor landlady.[34] Following the Declaration of Indulgence (1672), which gave nonconformists 'leave to build Meeting-places, and preach', once other ministers were settled, Charlton strongly encouraged Baxter to return to London for the exercise of his ministry, taking a 'most pleasant and convenient house in *Southampton-Square*'.[35]

Margaret Charlton's facilitation of Baxter's ministry went further, however. In London, seeing him 'too dull and backward', she 'fisht out of [him] in what place [he] most desired more Preaching'; he replied, 'St. *Martins* Parish, where are said to be forty thousand more than can come into the Church, especially among all the new buildings in St. *Jameses*, where Neighbours many live like *Americans*, and have heard no Sermon of many years'.[36] She managed to hire 'some capacious Room there' and when on one occasion the building almost collapsed under the weight of the roof, she found a carpenter who was able to prop up the beam, thus protecting Baxter's auditors from harm.[37] She also built a chapel in Oxenden Street, set up a school for poor children in St James's, hired another chapel in

---

[30]   Baxter notes that they agreed to the following conditions prior to their marriage: '1. That I would have nothing that before our Marriage was hers; that I (who wanted no outward supplies) might not seem to marry her for covetousness. 2. That she would so alter her affairs, that I might be intangled in no Law-suits. 3. That she would expect none of my time that my Ministerial work should require' (Baxter, *Breviate*, G4).

[31]   Baxter, *Breviate*, H1.

[32]   Ibid., H1v.

[33]   Ibid., H2.

[34]   Ibid., H2–H2v.

[35]   Ibid., H2v.

[36]   Ibid., H3v.

[37]   Ibid., H3v–H4.

Swallow Street and encouraged Baxter to travel to Southwark, when due to his notoriety as a prominent nonconformist he was no longer able to preach in the chapels she had founded.[38]

Margaret Charlton's public ministry was not limited to physical and material initiatives. Baxter unreservedly praises her quick apprehension in various cases of conscience, noting the 'excellency of her reason', which 'lay not so much in the speculative, as the *prudential practical part*'.

> [I]n this I never knew her equal: In very hard cases, about what was to be done, she would suddenly open all the way that was to be opened, in the things of the Family, Estate, or any civil business. And to confess the truth, experience acquainted her, that I knew less in such things than she; and therefore was willing she should take it all upon her.... *Except in cases that require Learning, and skill in Theological difficulties, she was better at resolving a case of conscience than most Divines that ever I knew in all my life....* Insomuch that of late years, I confess, that I was used to put all, save secret cases, to her, and hear what she could say.[39]

This was extraordinary praise from one of the most respected English casuists of the seventeenth century. Something of Margaret Charlton's broad education, patience, practicality and tact in dealing with and advising those within her circle of patronage can be seen in her surviving correspondence with her husband's second cousin and heir, William Baxter.[40] Charlton was the one who ensured that his education was provided for financially; she wrote to him personally with advice as to his professional training, suggesting that he should not become a nonconformist minister,[41] and she sought to establish him as a doctor or as a lawyer depending on his own inclination. Richard Baxter disarmingly concludes: 'I was naturally somewhat tenacious of my own conceptions, her reasons and my experiences usually told me, that she was in the right, and knew more than I'.[42]

II

The complex pastoral, theological and congregational concerns that shaped the understanding of marriage amongst non-denominational nonconformists such as Margaret Charlton and Richard Baxter were also integral to the communal life and writings of the Particular Baptists. One of the most challenging elements from the perspective of pastoral care and oversight was the attempt to resolve problems resulting from a mixed marriage (the union of a believer with a nonbeliever) or

---

[38]   Ibid., H4v–I2.

[39]   Ibid., K2–K2v.

[40]   N.H. Keeble and Geoffrey Nuttall, *Calendar of the Correspondence of Richard Baxter* (2 vols, Oxford, 1991), vol. 2, pp. 192–3.

[41]   Dr Williams's Library, MS 59.V.170, MS 59.V.234.

[42]   Baxter, *Breviate*, K2.

domestic abuse, which could lead to a hardening or radicalization of the beliefs and practices of the perceived offender. Several such cases are recorded in the *Church Book of the Bunyan Meeting* at Bedford, and John Bunyan also presents the dangers and problems inherent in this kind of troubled marriage in his pseudo-novel *The Life and Death of Mr Badman*. This situation also arose amongst the London Baptist congregations led by Hanserd Knollys and Nehemiah Cocks in the 1670s to which Anne Wentworth belonged. Wentworth appears, in Elaine Hobby's words, to have been a 'battered woman'.[43] She was married to a man whom she accused of maintaining an outward show of piety, without possessing the inner reality.[44] Unlike Mr Badman's exemplary first wife, however, Wentworth was not prepared to endure this situation patiently. When the church officers in a disciplinary meeting accepted and endorsed her husband's character, authority and version of events, she resisted vociferously. However, the justification she provided for her separation from the Baptist community and the divine authorization of her prophecies was marriage to her heavenly bridegroom, Christ. Her subjugation in this heavenly union absolved her of all responsibilities to her earthly husband, whom she accused of spiritual hypocrisy and a desire to murder her, reducing the experience of this earthly relationship to nothing more than an eschatological signifier of the judgement to come.

Dolan argues that Wentworth understood 'her husband's metaphorical death as the precondition of her own union with Christ and consequent salvation'; this was not a unique position for female prophets in seventeenth-century England.[45] 'Wentworth adopts violent metaphors that conflate her bodily and spiritual experience.... [She] imagines that her husband's metaphorical death is necessary for her to be able to commit herself to a new spiritual union; yet she construes this new marriage as equally violent, its violence is again a matter of bowing her will, breaking to pieces, becoming nothing'.[46] Wentworth's position on marriage is almost identical to Bunyan's views, as described by Thomas Luxon, though she was driven by different gender concerns and external pressures:

> for Bunyan, marriage remains an insistently bodily matter, confined to this world of corruption. In the next world, the glorious bodies and souls of Christians belong utterly to Christ.... Bunyan does not say so explicitly ... but to enter fully into the marriage supper of the lamb [he] implies one must be separated from the wife of one's corruptible flesh.[47]

[43]   Elaine Hobby, *Virtue of Necessity: English Women's Writing, 1649–1688* (London, 1988), p. 51.

[44]   Wentworth, *Vindication*, pp. 3–4.

[45]   Dolan, *Marriage and Violence*, pp. 59–60.

[46]   Ibid.

[47]   Thomas H. Luxon, 'One Soul Versus One Flesh: Friendship, Marriage, and the Puritan Self', in Vera J. Camden (ed.), *Trauma and Transformation: The Political Progress of John Bunyan* (Stanford, 2008), p. 89.

For Wentworth, separation from the husband of her corruptible flesh occurred in the present, earthly realm, not the future kingdom of God. Elizabeth Clarke has noted that more work needs to be done on

> how this kind of spirituality intersected with women's experience of earthly marriage in the seventeenth century, but it is clear that the relationship is a conflicted one, the spiritual discourse often compensating for or comparing favourably with a less than ideal relationship with earthly husbands. When these kind of direct comparisons were made ... the absolute distinction between the discourse of divine love and that of human sexuality which allegorical interpretations of the Song of Songs demanded became untenable.[48]

If Margaret Baxter's life is compared with that of Anne Wentworth, the dramatically different lives and experiences of nonconformist women during the Restoration can be readily illustrated. Wentworth and her husband were both members of the London Baptist community led by Hanserd Knollys and Nehemiah Cocks.[49] Initially, it appears that Wentworth was respected and admired by Knollys. In 'An Admonition to the Reader' attached to Wentworth's final publication, *England's Spiritual Pill* (1679), an anonymous supporter (A.B.) writes:

> but that thou mayst know, what kind of woman Mrs. *Wentworth* is, and not misjudge of her with others, let me present thee with a description, given to some persons of quallity and my self by Mr. *Hansward Knoylls*, upon our first acquaintance with Mrs. *Wentworth*, which is above two years agone. We went to him to inquire, what she was, and to get his assistance to procure Mrs. *Wentworths* Book of experience and other papers out of her Husbands hands. This latter he waved, but as to the fotmer [*sic*], he was neer an hour describing her, and gave such a character of her, from her child-hood, for her nature, humility, modesty and Christianity, that I never heard a better of any creature! He said, whereever she lived, she adorned the Gospel, and made all the families, where she came, in love with religion; and moreover, was of so tender a spirit, that a child might domineer over her, nay a stamp of her husbands foot was enough, to make her swound; and much more he added, which made us all desirous of her acquaintance; wherein I have continued ever since.[50]

Once Wentworth started writing and prophesying in a way that publicly indicted her husband, relatives and the leaders of the Baptist congregations for their behaviour

[48] Elizabeth Clarke, *Politics, Religion and the Song of Songs in Seventeenth-Century England* (Basingstoke, 2011), p. 169.

[49] Anne Wentworth, *The Revelation of Jesus Christ Just as he Spake it in Verses at Several Times, and Sometimes in Prose, unto his Faithful Servant Anne Wentworth, who Suffereth for his Name* ([London], 1679), p. 20. The most recent biography of Hanserd Knollys does not mention Anne Wentworth at all: Dennis C. Bustin, *Paradox and Perseverance: Hanserd Knollys, Particular Baptist Pioneer in Seventeenth-Century England* (Milton Keynes, 2006).

[50] Anne Wentworth, *Englands Spiritual Pill* (London, 1679), p. 34.

towards her, their attitude changed; she may well have been excommunicated.[51] In *A True Account* (1676) Wentworth states:

> let now *Thomas Hicks* and *William Dix* draw up their Bill, and all the rest of my Husbands brethren what it is they have to charge me with of all they have against me in misbehaviour in life and conversation, or neglect of my duty to their Brother, in not obeying of him from the first day of my Marriage unto the day of my healing, compleat 18 years the third of *January*, 1670.[52]

Wentworth believed that the male church hierarchy favoured her husband's testimony over her own, due to an inbuilt gender bias. She writes of how they represented her 'as a *Proud, Passionate, Revengeful, Discontented* and *Mad* Woman, and as one that has unduly published things to the prejudice and scandal of my Husband; and that have wickedly left him'.[53] This may have led them, perhaps inadvertently, to legitimize abusive patterns of behaviour through their adherence to a particular form of male headship in marriage. Wentworth describes her husband's 'fierce looks, bitter words, sharp tongue, and cruel usage'.[54] She comments further: 'I … spent out all my natural strength of body in obedience to satisfy the unreasonable will of my earthly Husband, and laid my body as the ground, and as the street for him to go over for 18 years together'.[55] However, on 3 January 1670, Wentworth claimed to have been dramatically healed from her debilitating meekness and physical infirmities. This transformed the silent woman who had been oppressed and abused for so many years.[56] She subsequently became convinced that she was called to testify to God's goodness and to prophesy in his name. Unsurprisingly, her husband was not pleased at the prospect of being exposed publicly through his wife's prophetic activity and 'in a most cruel manner' he hindered Wentworth 'from performing' the commands of her heavenly bridegroom by 'seizing, and running away with [her] Writings'.[57] She criticized the Particular Baptist community for a false typological reading of Scripture which led them to view her husband as 'the patient, meek Lamb', defining her in contrast as 'an impudent Hussy…. deluded by a lying Spirit'.[58]

---

[51]   Catie Gill, 'Wentworth, Anne (1629/30–1693?)', *Oxford Dictionary of National Biography*, http://0-www.oxforddnb.com.catalogue.ulrls.lon.ac.uk/view/article/67075, accessed 12 April 2011.

[52]   Anne Wentworth, *A True Account of Anne Wentworths Being Cruelly, Unjustly, and Unchristianly Dealt with by Some of Those People Called Anabaptists* (London, 1676), p. 16.

[53]   Wentworth, *Vindication*, p. 2.

[54]   Ibid., p. 5.

[55]   Wentworth, *True Account*, p. 8.

[56]   Ibid., p. 10.

[57]   Wentworth, *True Account*, p. 3.

[58]   Wentworth, *Revelation of Jesus Christ*, p. 20.

While Wentworth wrote letters of warning to the lord mayor of London and Charles II and foretold of coming judgement upon England,[59] her prophetic publications were firmly rooted in and primarily directed at the Particular Baptist congregations of London. She wrote: 'From the house of my abode this ten years in *Kings-Head Court* in *White-Cross-street* neer *Cripple-Gate*'.[60] And, in *The Revelation of Jesus Christ* (1679), she referred directly to her husband and other members of the Baptist community by name, pronouncing God's judgement upon them:

> Therefore all that they have done, and do so, shall feel the Rod of an angry God, as there is *Hanserd Knolys* with his Church, and *Nehemiah Cocks*, my Husbands Pastor, *Thomas Hicks, William Dicks, Philip Barder*, my Relations, and hundreds more, that have a hand in setting my Husband against me, so that he will not own me: And then they go on to blame and defame me, and say, that I am run away from him![61]

Wentworth's abusive marriage, sectarian persecution and sense of divine calling precipitated an entirely different engagement in the public sphere to that undertaken by Margaret Baxter. Wentworth interpreted her broken relationship with her husband as a typological signifier of God's relationship with his church in the world. She developed a hermeneutic common to radical sects of the earlier seventeenth century, of reading according to the Spirit, rather than the letter of God's word, drawing particularly upon the Song of Songs. Erica Longfellow observes:

> [M]ystical marriage was one way of negotiating this paradox [between an injunction to silence and the requirement to live a godly life].... [M]ystical marriage mediated between human and divine relationships in which gender was ultimately irrelevant, a mere construct.... The sacrificial love of Christ served as a model of gendered behaviour that was not oppressive to women. His unimpeachable authority provided a means to authorise their conventionally silenced voices.[62]

Sharon Achinstein has noted that Wentworth's prophetic interpretation of the Song of Songs radicalizes divine romance and leads to an 'assault upon patriarchal

---

[59]   TNA, SP 29/395, fols 118–23.

[60]   Wentworth, *True Account*, p. 22.

[61]   Wentworth, *Revelation of Jesus Christ*, p. 20. Despite Knollys's high view of Wentworth's character, his presence on one of the occasions when Anna Trapnel was prophesying, and his willingness to write a prefatory letter endorsing Katherine Sutton's more discreet prophecies (Bustin, *Paradox and Perseverance*, pp. 304–5), he was not prepared to countenance Wentworth's rebellion against her husband in the name of obedience to Christ, or on the grounds of self-defence.

[62]   Erica Longfellow, *Women and Religious Writing in Early Modern England* (Cambridge, 2004), p. 13.

marriage' in her 'Revelations'.[63] Katharine Gillespie suggests further that the 'pastoral ideal of marriage, which was to end every social plot with the virginal woman's rupturing submission ... was both reified and frustrated through the separatist displacement of 'marriage' on to the eternally 'chaste' and enclosed relationship that every individual enjoyed with God as a self-sufficient 'couple' of one'.[64] Longfellow concludes that women could exploit 'the contradictions inherent in early modern gendered morals, using the seemingly limiting model of the prophetess who was not herself when she spoke in order to emphasise the divine origins of her speech.... The paradigm enabled ... women prophets to deflect attacks against themselves onto God himself'.[65]

Wentworth drew a sharp distinction between the body and the spirit or soul, complemented by a clear differentiation between her earthly husband and her spiritual or heavenly bridegroom. She must be removed from the former, if she was to remain faithful to the latter. Her authorial persona was thus a dizzying juxtaposition of extreme self-abnegation and triumphant spiritual exaltation: Wentworth's language shifts as she moves from describing her earthly marriage to her mystical union with Christ, eliding the real impact that the life of the spirit has on the life of the body. However, this was balanced by her detailed attention to the material ways in which her mystical bridegroom provided tangibly for her physical needs – housing, food and furniture. Her vision of a spiritual union with Christ was concretely realized through providence in this world, as well as in the world to come.

Wentworth developed a broader sense of the prophetic and religious significance of her experiences and sufferings by fusing her autobiographical account with a typological hermeneutic, attributing both to God's direct revelation:

> my *oppressions* and *deliverance* had a *Publick* Ministry and *meaning* wrapt up in them, and that it must be seven years before I could perfect that writing, and the Lord would bring forth his end in all this, and give an open Testimony to the world that he had chosen and called me to write and glorifie him.[66]

Her prophetic attempts to use her own experience of domestic abuse and oppression as a signifier of God's attitude towards England and, more specifically, as a loaded message to hypocritical professors amongst the Baptists, foundered due to a resolute refusal on the part of her audience either to read her life in this way, or to accept her reinterpretation of traditional biblical images, such as the

---

[63]   Sharon Achinstein, 'Romance of the Spirit: Female Sexuality and Religious Desire in Early Modern England', *English Literary History*, 69/2 (2002): p. 422.

[64]   Katharine Gillespie, *Domesticity and Dissent in the Seventeenth Century: English Women's Writing and the Public Sphere* (Cambridge, 2004), p. 7.

[65]   Longfellow, *Women and Religious Writing*, p. 162.

[66]   Wentworth, *Vindication*, p. 12.

'meek Lamb'.[67] She saw the support given by the male pastors and members of her family to her husband's headship and authority in the marriage, at the expense of her own physical safety and spiritual freedom, as the inevitable result of their inherent gender bias and wilful spiritual blindness.

Gillespie has commented that sectarian women like Wentworth developed an 'internalized sovereignty that often manifested itself most fully ... in a state of crisis'; 'a secure and stable sense of self that acted as a counter to ... pressures – and that was the God-within'.[68] Wentworth responded to the resistance of her husband and pastors by identifying herself more closely with her divine bridegroom, proclaiming judgement as God's mouthpiece. The additional, initialled authors who contributed to *England's Spiritual Pill* indicate that Wentworth had some support from believers who were willing to promote her message and, presumably, helped her to publish her prophecies. Wentworth's anonymous friend claims that God established the truth of her words by returning her to the home on White-Cross Street, from which her husband had evicted her, and providing her with 'Beds ... Chairs, Tables, and all manner of useful Things' from strangers.[69] Wentworth indicts her husband for his failure to conform to traditional conceptions of masculinity as a crucial justification for her decision to enter the public sphere and appeal to a broader audience for support. It is important to recognize that her prophetic activity in this respect was far from radical in origin.[70] However, her clear and consistent vision of the ways in which her mystical union with Christ providentially transformed her physical, material and spiritual condition in this world and acted as a justification for her denunciation of the state of the nation does make her stand out amongst nonconformist female writers in the 1670s.

Unlike Margaret Charlton, though, Wentworth did not have a supportive husband or pastor to publicize and justify her ministry to posterity, nor was she commemorated amongst the pious women memorialized by the industrious compiler Samuel Clarke. In his introductory letter 'To the Reader' prefacing *The Lives of Sundry Eminent Persons in this Later Age* by his friend, Clarke, Baxter explicitly set out his views on the value of biography. This collection included short lives of divines, and the nobility and gentry of both sexes, like Baxter's wife, Margaret. Baxter argued that these biographies helped to convince those who had not known people of holy character that it was possible to attain a high

---

[67] Wentworth, *Revelation of Jesus Christ*, p. 20. Objections to a politicized reading of the Song of Songs were not limited to a male audience. Elizabeth Clarke traces Jane Lead's dislike of the apocalyptic specificity with which Wentworth interpreted the trope of mystical marriage: Clarke, *Politics, Religion and the Song of Songs*, p. 168.

[68] Gillespie, *Domesticity and Dissent*, p. 171.

[69] Wentworth, *Revelation of Jesus Christ*, p. 21.

[70] Warren Johnston, 'Prophecy, Patriarchy, and Violence in the Early Modern Household: The Revelations of Anne Wentworth', *Journal of Family History*, 34/4 (2009): pp. 344–68.

level of sanctification. It is crucial that 'the Faithful' are truly represented in the face of Satan's lies in order to vindicate 'Gods Image upon them'.[71] But more than this: 'Nature is delighted in History … And the true History of exemplary Lives, is a pleasant and profitable recreation to young persons; and may secretly work them to a liking of Godliness and value of good men, which is the beginning of saving Grace: O how much better work is it, than Cards, Dice, Revels, Stage-Plays, Romances or idle Chat'.[72] Baxter disarmingly confessed that he had not had an opportunity to read the volume he has been asked to introduce. However, his own knowledge of the persons and histories recounted convinced him that 'the Reader will have no cause to question the Historical truth'.[73] The life of Joseph Alleine, he noted, 'I had a hand in Publishing and Prefacing heretofore: And O that I could reach that heavenly frame of mind, by which they lived and died in triumphant joy and praise to God!'[74] Baxter models the affective response that he desires to evoke in Clarke's readers and offers a glimpse of how he would have liked to similarly package and publish the short biographies that he had penned in a variety of other genres:

> I have in Funeral Sermons and Epistles described truly many excellent persons, whose Examples would be useful to this depraved Age; were it not for the charge of Printing, I would wish them Bound all together as these be, viz. Mrs. *Bakers* of Worcester, Mrs. *Coxes*, Mrs. *Hamners*, my Wives Mother, Alderman *Ashhursts*, Mr. *Waddesworth*, Mr. *Stubbs*, Mr *Corbets*, &c.[75]

Significant in Baxter's list is the number of exemplary women – Wentworth, however, is not amongst them. Her commemoration is limited to the testimony of her initialled supporters, included in her own publications. These, unlike Baxter's *Breviate* of his wife, have not been consistently republished. To some extent this testifies to the fragility of narratives told by men and women in the early modern period when not legitimated by a supportive, authoritative patron. It may also reflect anachronistic preconceptions regarding the genres of biography, autobiography and self-revelation and a pragmatic commercialism on the part of those republishing that led them to focus on what they knew would sell. Baxter, despite his prescriptive emphasis on the uses of biography, was preoccupied with the idiosyncrasies of his subjects in a way that pre-empts the concerns of modern biographers. Wentworth's self-revelations – a mixture of first-person narration,

[71] Baxter, 'To the Reader', *The Lives of Sundry Eminent Persons in this Later Age* (London, 1683), a3.

[72] Ibid., a3v.

[73] Ibid., a4.

[74] Ibid., a4; see also Richard Baxter, introduction to *The Life and Death of that Excellent Minister of Christ Mr. Joseph Alleine, Late Teacher of the Church of Taunton in Somerset-Shire, Assistant to Mr. Newton* (1671), B1r–C1v. It is worth noting that Baxter here endorses the narrative account provided in part by Alleine's wife, Theodosia.

[75] Baxter, 'To the Reader', a4v; see also Baxter, *Breviate*, A3–A4.

poetry, biblical commentary and prophecy – do not conform; they are part of 'a culture of life-writing whose very inclusivity and taxonomical strangeness demand[s] that [we] revisit many of [our] assumptions about autobiographical forms'.[76] Much, in fact, as Margaret Charlton's papers must have looked before they were rearranged into a chronological and didactic account by Baxter after her death.[77]

Richard Baxter's admiration for his wife's abilities, refusal to benefit from her personal income and advocacy of the gospel imperative to live 'as fruitfully to the Church and others, as we can do in the world'[78] enabled him to defend, support and encourage her various endeavours to further the gospel in the public sphere and to manage the practical aspects of their mutual spiritual endeavours. By contrast, the Calvinistic Baptist communities in Bedford and London demonstrate the social conservatism characteristic of dissenting denominations in the Restoration often perceived to be radical and subversive. The prescriptive advice enshrined in Bunyan's *Life and Death of Mr Badman* illustrates his pastoral concern over the dangers of marriage between a believer and an unbeliever. While the first, pious wife of Mr Badman is commended for her courage in resisting his evil influence and for her desire to stay at home and order things wisely, she is condemned for her failure to seek godly counsel prior to contracting her unsuccessful marriage. Badman's second wife is loud, sexually licentious and indicted for her tendency to spend time outside, rather than keeping her home. The *Church Book* of the Bunyan meeting reveals that cases of discipline for such mixed marriages were not uncommon. Anne Wentworth's prophetic writings demonstrate in detail what such a mixed marriage looked like. Despite the glowing testimonial provided by Knollys to Wentworth's character and his earlier support for Katherine Sutton whose 'writings voiced teachings of a prophetess in a very public forum',[79] neither he, nor his fellow minister Nehemiah Cocks, nor Wentworth's relatives were willing to support or defend her when she claimed that her husband had failed to fulfil his role as provider, and they threatened her life after she began to prophesy.

Understanding marriage as an interdependent relationship helps to illustrate the threat that Wentworth posed to her husband's reputation and standing both within the Baptist community and, more generally, amongst their neighbours in London and politically through her letters to the lord mayor of London and Charles II. Her husband's refusal to return her writings and decision to bar her from their home left her physically vulnerable and in great need. Her family and church's endorsement of her husband's position illustrates the importance of community in policing violence and sustaining marriage unions or, alternately, pragmatic separations. Wentworth's response to her unsatisfactory relationship

---

[76] Adam Smyth, *Autobiography in Early Modern England* (Cambridge, 2010), p. 1.
[77] See, for example, Baxter, *Breviate*, B3–B4, C1v–D3v, E1v–E4, F4v–G2, M1–N1.
[78] Ibid., K3.
[79] Bustin, *Paradox and Perseverance*, p. 305.

with her earthly husband was also expressed in the language of marital union: her divine spouse, Christ, authorized her agency in the public sphere as a prophet and writer. The disintegration of her human union became a typological signifier of God's judgement on the Baptists and Restoration England. Though the cases of Charlton and Wentworth are by no means exhaustive, they demonstrate the diverse and creative ways in which individual dissenting women exercised agency in the public sphere, from which they were excluded twice on the grounds of religion and gender, in and through the institution of marriage.

Chapter 3
Masculine Virgins:
Celibacy and Gender in Later Stuart London

Sarah Apetrei

In many religious traditions, not least in Western Christianity, celibacy has been regarded as a means for women to transcend their gender. Through sexual self-denial, the lascivious and sensual aspects of female nature could be overcome, and virgins become 'manly and perfect'.[1] Based on a patristic reading of Matthew 22:30 ('For in the resurrection they neither marry, nor are given in marriage, but are as the angels of God in heaven': AV), Christian celibates were thought to share instead in the mysterious nature of angels, an existence that was abstracted, incorporeal, and devoted to the service of God. After the Reformation, it has often been observed, even this ambivalent emancipation was no longer available: women in Protestant societies were defined solely by their reproductive and supportive role, while Catholic authorities policed ever more closely the communities of virgins so vulnerable to sexual temptation.[2] The period 1660–1760 has been identified with a watershed in gender theory leading to even sharper delineations of relations between the sexes, especially in England – one of the nations in Europe where celibacy, of course, was no longer a vocation recognized institutionally for men or women.[3] According to some recent narratives, masculine and feminine identities became more deeply opposed and embedded than ever during this century, as shifts in medical discourse reconceptualized sexual difference as immutable and dimorphous, and 'Enlightened' tastes contrasted manly reason to the brutish, effeminizing passions.[4] It has also been argued that the late seventeenth and eighteenth centuries witnessed an intense moralistic crisis in British society, focused precisely on upholding marriage and heterosexual values, which would ultimately give way to an essentially private, libertarian conception of sexual

---

[1] Clement of Alexandria, cited in Grace Jantzen, 'Mystics, Martyrs and Honorary Males', in Grace Jantzen, *Power, Gender and Christian Mysticism* (Cambridge, 1995), p. 53.

[2] See, for instance, Merry Wiesner-Hanks, *Christianity and Sexuality in the Early Modern World: Regulating Desire, Reforming Practice* (London, 2000), pp. 63–4, 106.

[3] Michael McKeon, 'Historicizing Patriarchy: The Emergence of Gender Difference in England, 1660–1760', *Eighteenth-Century Studies*, 28/3 (1995): pp. 295–322.

[4] Genevieve Lloyd, *The Man of Reason: Male and Female in Western Philosophy* (London, 1984).

morality.[5] Translations of gender identity, once made conceivable by doctrines of angelic celibacy and the Galenic 'one sex' model, were profoundly transgressive in this environment.[6]

This chapter examines meanings of female virginity and celibacy in England, as these anxieties about sexual identity and public morality heightened. Against the grain of dominant Protestant rhetoric, alternative programmes for a celibate life were conceived in some High Church circles and groups stigmatized as 'enthusiasts', which I argue formed part of the current of reforming moralism but also articulated a protest against rigid gender categories and the tyranny of women's domestic servitude. The chapter takes three parts. The first analyses the Protestant and rationalistic critiques of female celibacy, which placed an increasing emphasis on the ethics of sociability, always harnessed to anti-Catholic sentiment and English patriotism. In the second, I look at political discourse in Protestant England, which linked sexual purification with national godliness and apocalyptic fulfilment and heightened the tension between anti-ascetical currents and utopian reform. The third part examines ventures to revive celibacy in London, in the context of the religious societies which emerged in the 1680s and 1690s. My argument is that in returning to celibacy, such reformers were not merely reacting to moral decline. In a culture that was increasingly monolithically heterosexual, their apocalyptic imagination allowed them to conceive of human society and spiritual vocations outside the structures of the gender order. While such experiments did not amount to a broad social movement, radically alternative schemes of this sort as well as literary utopias were a familiar feature of the period after 1689, reflecting both the relative openness and, paradoxically, the repressiveness of the religious environment.[7]

I. Celibacy and Sociability

The impact of the structures and doctrines of sociability on women have been widely explored, in relation to the masculinity of the public sphere, for instance; or in the increasing attention to education for girls as a hallmark of a truly enlightened and thoroughly sociable civilization.[8] Marriage, however, was the basic unit

---

[5]   See Faramerz Dabhoiwala, 'Lust and Liberty', *Past and Present*, 207 (2010): pp. 89–179.

[6]   Thomas Laqueur, *Making Sex: Body and Gender from the Greeks to Freud* (Cambridge, MA, 1992), ch. 5; Randolph Trumbach, *Sex and the Gender Revolution*, Volume 1: *Heterosexuality and the Third Gender in Enlightenment London* (Chicago, 1998).

[7]   See Gregory Claeys (ed.), *Restoration and Augustan Utopias* (New York, 2000).

[8]   See, for instance, Brian Cowan, 'What Was Masculine about the Public Sphere? Gender and the Coffeehouse Milieu in Post-Restoration England', *History Workshop Journal*, 51 (2001): pp. 128–9; Evelyn Gordon Bodek, 'Salonières and Bluestockings: Educated Obsolescence and Germinating Feminism', *Feminist Studies*, 3/3–4 (1976):

of Protestant and enlightened sociability as far as women were concerned: a microcosm of social harmony, a bulwark against rampant individualism and a secure outlet for the feminine virtues: modesty, sensibility, discretion and industry. The charity schools for girls founded in London and beyond from the 1690s were not designed to make women intellectually sophisticated, but rather to train them up in precisely these virtues, to be 'happy Wives and holy Mothers'.[9] Reading, writing and arithmetic took second place to catechism, needlework and domestic labour.[10] Preparation for an auxiliary role in the household, the sole imaginable environment for women's flourishing, was the ultimate purpose of female formation. Single women might be tolerated as cases for charity, but there was no positive concept of female celibacy. Yet in reality women married late, and nearly one in four English adults were never-married by the later seventeenth century, many of them women: perhaps as many as a third of all adult females in Southampton in 1696. Although, as Amy Froide has shown, economic options remained limited for never-married women in England in the later seventeenth century, opportunities for independent trading were improving in a growing market economy.[11] The emerging status of professional female writer was, of course, overwhelmingly reserved to single women (either widows or celibates), but it was a scarce and hard-won privilege.[12] Demographic evidence suggests that urban development prior to 1750 tended to attract more female migrants, which may partially account for the trend towards celibacy among adult women. Froide links this trend to a vicious backlash in popular culture against old maids as 'nasty, rank, rammy, filthy Sluts' or 'She-Cannibals'.[13]

Such stigmatizing of single women sprang in part from a patriotic, as well as a confessionally Protestant, distrust of celibacy. Popery, sexual corruption, religious hypocrisy and social weakness were closely associated in seventeenth-century English minds. In 1664, in a discourse described as 'one of his major theological works', the Platonist philosopher Henry More attacked Catholic religious orders from a social and economic point of view, exclaiming:

185–99; Karen O'Brien, *Women and Enlightenment in Eighteenth-Century Britain* (Cambridge, 2009).

[9] White Kennett, *The Excellent Daughter. A Sermon for the Relief of the Poor Girls Taught and Cloathed by Charity within the Parish of St. Botolph Aldgate* (London, 1708), p. 21.

[10] M.G. Jones, *The Charity School Movement* (Cambridge, 1938), pp. 94, 241, 345.

[11] See Amy M. Froide, *Never Married: Singlewomen in Early Modern England* (Oxford, 2005); David R. Weir, 'Rather Never than Late: Celibacy and Age at Marriage in English Cohort Fertility, 1541–1871', *Journal of Family History*, 9/4 (1984): pp. 340–54.

[12] See Ruth Perry, 'The Veil of Chastity: Mary Astell's Feminism', in Paul-Gabriel Boucé (ed.), *Sexuality in Eighteenth-Century Britain* (Manchester, 1982), p. 151.

[13] *A Satyr upon Old Maids* (London, 1713), p. 9; see also Froide, *Never Married*, p. 175.

> The multiplied *Convents* therefore of such Angelical Fraternities, how can they
> but be so many Fish-ponds digged out for the draining of the Wealth of the
> respective Nations and Provinces wherein they are made?[14]

During the reign of James II, there were intense debates over marriage and the
rule of celibacy, as one of the most visible differences between Anglican and
Roman Catholic church discipline.[15] As well as the usual arguments surrounding
the dangers of incontinence and scriptural precedent and prohibition, a growing
emphasis on patriotic values characterized Anglican apologetics. The Whig bishop
William Lloyd warned that the increase of popery would promote the 'Celibate or
single life', threatening 'the Wealth and flourishing of the Kingdom' by draining the
population of its sons and daughters 'in the Nation which already has too few'.[16] At
around the same time, Sir Peter Pett claimed that 'the Progress of the Reformation
hath vastly encreased the value of our Land and proportion of our Commerce', and
calculated in careful detail how far monastic celibacy had restrained demographic
growth, thus demonstrating 'what *Depopulators* or dispeoplers of the Kingdom
the Monks were'.[17]

Female celibacy, in particular, was viewed with scornful suspicion by many of
the most luminous wits in the Augustan public sphere. Overwhelmingly, these were
Whigs, often Dissenters and freethinkers. When Mary Astell published *A Serious
Proposal to the Ladies* in 1694, her scheme for a celibate female community or
Anglican convent, she was savaged by Grub Street. Jonathan Swift lampooned
her 'Protestant Nunnery' as a seedbed of hypocrisy and sexual promiscuity.[18]
Daniel Defoe was convinced that 'nothing but the heighth of Bigotry can keep up
a Nunnery: Women are extravagantly desirous of going to Heaven, and will punish
their *Pretty Bodies* to get thither'.[19] Instead, Defoe set out his alternative vision of
an academy for women which had nothing to do with religion, but rather marriage

---

[14]   Henry More, *A Modest Enquiry into the Mystery of Iniquity* (London, 1664), p. 73;
Richard H. Popkin, 'The Spiritualistic Cosmologies of Henry More and Anne Conway', in
Sarah Hutton and Robert Crocker (eds), *Henry More (1614–1687): Tercentenary Studies*
(Dordrecht, 1989), p. 108.

[15]   The printed polemics on this subject included *Sodom Fair* (London, 1688); Francis
Atterbury, *Answer to Some Considerations on the Spirit of Mart. Luther, and the Original
of the Reformation* (Oxford, 1687); George Tully, *An Answer to a Discourse Concerning
the Celibacy of the Clergy* (Oxford, 1688); Henry Wharton, *A Treatise of the Celibacy of the
Clergy* (London, 1688); R.H. [Abraham Woodhead], *A Discourse Concerning the Celibacy
of the Clergy* (Oxford, 1687), see also Bodleian Library, Oxford, Bod. MS Univ. Coll.
D. 183.

[16]   William Lloyd, *Seasonable Advice to Protestants Shewing the Necessity of
Maintaining the Established Religion in Opposition to Popery* (London, 1688), p. 25.

[17]   Peter Pett, *The Happy Future State of England* (London, 1688), p. 111.

[18]   Jonathan Swift, *The Tatler, Or, The Lucubrations of Isaac Bickerstaff Esq.*, Tuesday
21 June to Thursday 23 June 1709, no. 32 of 271 (London, 1709), pp. 231–4.

[19]   Daniel Defoe, *An Essay upon Projects* (London, 1697), p. 286.

and society: as he put it, 'I wou'd have Men take Women for Companions, and Educate them to be fit for it'.[20] A discussion in one of John Dunton's popular periodicals in October 1695 is revealing of this anti-ascetical trend, which was situated squarely in the emerging discourse of sociability. A female correspondent wanted to know whether a contemplative life, withdrawn from 'the delights of Society and Conversation', was not venerated 'in the times of the Primitive fathers' and permissible for those endowed with 'an extraordinary gift from God'? She wanted to know what should be done if 'a young Lady shou'd have a desire to enter into such a course of Life, and to retire from the Follies of this ungrateful age'. The response from the editors was unequivocal. 'A Solitary Life' was not 'a State of Life which God has designed for mankind. He has made us Sociable, and required us to be so, and to be assistant to one another, which how shou'd we be without Conversation?' Asceticism for its own sake was anti-social, inhumane and superstitious, for

> what rational man can believe that St Anthony, for example, ever pleas'd God the more for his lying so long upon the ground, and eating nothing but a few dates for several days, or Simeon Stylites, by being Spitch-cockt a top of a Pillar I know not how many years, in the scorching sands of the Eastern Nations[?]

As for the desire to withdraw into a contemplative life, the editors observed that 'she can find no such place unless she flies to a Popish Nunnery, where sometimes they have more company, and not better, than while abroad in the world'.[21]

II. The Virgin Bride

However, theirs was not the only possible vision for sociability in an Enlightenment characterized by J.G.A. Pocock as overwhelmingly conservative and Anglican.[22] The concept of society was not, indeed, the invention of the English Enlightenment. Moreover, it is distorting to regard Karen O'Brien's more precise notion of 'benevolence' – understood as 'the selfless, well-meaning disposition we have towards fellow members of society' – as a distinctively eighteenth-century preoccupation.[23] Christians had always thought in corporatist terms both politically and spiritually, or in terms of a 'commonwealth' subject to decline and improvement, in which every member was responsible to the whole and to their neighbour. In union with Christ, as his living body on earth, individual

---

[20] Ibid., pp. 302–3.

[21] *The Athenian Gazette, Or Casuistical Mercury*, Tuesday 1 October 1695, no. 23 of 465 (London, 1695).

[22] See, for instance, J.G.A. Pocock, 'Clergy and Commerce: The Conservative Enlightenment in England', in R. Ajello et al. (eds), *L'età dei Lumi: studi storici sul settecento europeo in onore di Franco Venturi* (2 vols, Naples, 1985), vol. 2, pp. 523–68.

[23] O'Brien, *Women and Enlightenment*, p. 3.

Christians were profoundly and intimately bound together. Division and hatred were signs of apostasy from Christ; one of the principal reasons why, for some Anglican theologians, dissent from the national church was a matter of such profound pastoral and spiritual as well as political concern.[24] For Catholic and Calvinist alike, this social bond was embodied in the sacraments, in which the whole congregation enjoyed union with Christ and one another.[25] The sacerdotal view of kingship implied that social cohesion was ultimately guaranteed in both the person of the bishop and that of the monarch. Such an integrated and mystical conception of the Christian kingdom survived the Reformation to some extent, and was scrupulously resurrected by Charles II and his regime's Anglican apologists after the traumas of the republican episode, though it suffered a grave blow again in 1689.[26] Nonetheless, J.C.D. Clark has characterized eighteenth-century English society as ideologically Anglican and monarchist.[27]

Within a religious understanding of the social body, there were competing interpretations of the relationship between church and nation. In *Irenicum*, his controversial Erastian treatise of 1661, Edward Stillingfleet identified the political nation with the Church, without strictly defining the nature of ecclesiastical government: 'a National Society incorporated into one civil Government, joyning in the profession of Christianity'.[28] The Nonjuror controversy, in which clergymen were deprived on royal authority for their refusal to swear allegiance to William III, exposed profound dissent within the Anglican establishment about the nature of Christian society. For the nonjuring party, which regarded the deprivations as unjust and schismatic, the society which must be preserved intact was not the national commonwealth, but the universal Christian Church. This 'Spiritual Body' was 'not only the Church of one place or Country, wherein all the Members may Embody and Associate under the same Governors; as the Church of Rome, Alexandria, or Antioch. But the collection of all particular Christian Societys, or the whole number of independent Churches, Existing in all times, and diffused

---

[24]   See John Spurr, 'Schism and the Restoration Church', *The Journal of Ecclesiastical History*, 41/3 (1990): pp. 408–24.

[25]   The quest for mystical, sacramental underpinnings to society by no means died out along with the totalizing claims of the established Church. Some of the religious societies promoted the revival of the daily eucharist, as part of their quest for national unity. See Eamon Duffy, 'Primitive Christianity Revived: Religious Renewal in Augustan England', in Derek Baker (ed.), *Renaissance and Renewal in Christian History*, Studies in Church History, 14 (Oxford, 1977): pp. 291–2.

[26]   See Robert Zaller, 'Breaking the Vessels: The Desacralization of Monarchy in Early Modern England', *The Sixteenth Century Journal*, 29/3 (1998): pp. 757–78.

[27]   J.C.D. Clark, *English Society 1688–1832: Ideology, Social Structure and Political Practice During the Ancien Regime* (Cambridge, 1985), p. 6.

[28]   Edward Stillingfleet, *Irenicum A Weapon-Salve for the Churches Wounds, Or The Divine Right of Particular Forms of Church-Government* (London, 1661), p. 156.

through all places'.[29] Catholicity in the church was a higher value than political and social cohesion. Dissenting commentators, meanwhile, seem to have identified very strongly with the spiritual nation, notwithstanding their disavowal of the established church. In a powerful sense, the Dissenters' protest against Anglican forms of liturgy and government represented their desire to preserve England as a chaste, Reformed society uncorrupted by Roman vices.

The image of the nation or church as a spotless virgin was also deeply established and remained a powerful motif in English Protestant patriotism, both Anglican and nonconformist. Traditionally, the analogy had worked both ways. Since the earliest generations of Christianity, celibates – female virgins in particular – were regarded as embodying the Church's apocalyptic, corporate identity as the virgin bride of Christ. While male religious underwent the same rigours of self-denial, it was female virgins who, from the fourth century onwards, came to represent bridal intimacy, in a literal-minded application of the nuptial metaphor.[30] As influential Latin theologians like Jerome became fixated on Mary's perpetual virginity, women were also regarded as the natural successors of the original and pristine Virgin.[31] By the late Middle Ages, the concept of virginity was gendered almost exclusively as female, and enclosed convents had become the supreme emblems on earth of the Church's mystical marriage to its lover and Lord.[32] Such enclosure represented the transcendent, angelic life to which all Christians were eventually called. Trust in vicarious merit, derived by the church from the self-denial of the religious elite, also helped to establish female celibacy as a sinew of the social body. Consecrated virginity is not a universal element in religious societies: as an ideal it is almost entirely absent, for instance, from Islamic teaching (as one Restoration travel writer noted, comparing strict Muslims to Puritans on this point);[33] but it was a central pillar of Western Christian society before the Reformation.

The events of the sixteenth century, however, disrupted not only the tradition of clerical celibacy, but this entire, embedded metaphorical system in which virginal women symbolized the universal society of the Church and heaven. For

---

[29] John Kettlewell, *Of Christian Communion to be Kept on in the Unity of Christs Church and Among the Professors of Truth and Holiness* (London, 1693), p. 3.

[30] See Peter Brown, *Body and Society: Men, Women, and Sexual Renunciation in Early Christianity* (New York, 1988), p. 271; Elizabeth Castelli, 'Virginity and its Meaning for Women's Sexuality in Early Christianity', *Journal of Feminist Studies in Religion*, 2/1 (1986): pp. 61–88; Elizabeth A. Clark, 'The Celibate Bridegroom and His Virginal Brides: Metaphor and the Marriage of Jesus in Early Christian Ascetic Exegesis', *Church History*, 77/1 (2008): pp. 1–25; John Bugge, *Virginitas: An Essay in the History of a Medieval Ideal* (The Hague, 1975), esp. chs 3–4.

[31] See Maurice Hamington, *Hail Mary?: The Struggle for Ultimate Womanhood in Catholicism* (London, 1995), pp. 63–5.

[32] Bugge, *Virginitas*, p. 4.

[33] Lancelot Addison, *West Barbary, Or, A Short Narrative of the Revolutions of the Kingdoms of Fez and Morocco* (Oxford, 1671), p. 180.

Protestants, these lilies among thorns had usurped the status of bride of Christ, which belonged to all believers. Reformers complained that *human* marriage had been debased by the Western Church's privileging of *mystical* marriage, and many Protestants concluded that celibacy vows had inverted the created order, spawning incontinence and hypocrisy. It was believed that celibacy vows were, for most adults, ultimately impossible, and would lead to perjury and fornication. Marriage, as one Calvinist English bishop wrote in 1688, was 'the *Means* appointed by God to preserve Chastity, and where that is forbidden (as in the Church of *Rome* it is) abominable pollutions will be the fatal consequence'.[34] Far from being Christ's innocent bride, the Church had made itself Satan's whore: sexually corrupt and spiritually deformed. Early modern doctrines of society continued to link individual virtue, especially that of the monarch, to the spiritual health of the whole community. Sexual restraint, in particular, was regarded as a social and personal requirement essential to sustaining the Christian commonwealth. Yet Protestant England reserved no special place for dedicated celibates. Nonetheless, paradoxically, all adults were expected to live effectively as celibates outside of marriage.

Sexuality and society were thus woven together by fine symbolic threads in Christian theology, deeply problematized by the mental revolutions effected by Reformation. Spirit and flesh, church and state, were ever more complex category distinctions. It became conventional for Protestants either to interiorize or to politicize chastity and the bridal imagery associated with the church. As Elizabeth Clarke has recently shown, the allegorical currents of the Song of Songs ran deep in the veins of seventeenth-century Reformed theology, and carried strong political as well as spiritual overtones.[35] The Song evokes in poetic dialogue form a love story and its nuptial consummation, and orthodox interpreters had found in it a metaphor of Christ's union with his virgin bride, the Church. For many radical and nonconformist readers, the true bride was the unblemished Protestant who had not compromised with Antichrist either in inward piety or outward ceremony. The Song of Songs thus became a personal romance in which every pure-hearted or 'virginal' believer was directly united in a mystical marriage with Christ. By contrast, high church polemicists like William Sherlock interpreted the allegorical bride in institutional terms, and he accused nonconformists of making Christ a polygamist in their belief that he courted every individual soul.[36]

Although this interior allegory implies a trend towards individualism, there remained a perceived correspondence between the personal soul and the political body, heightened by the millenarian hopes unleashed by the Civil Wars and Interregnum. Some religious radicals developed an appetite for political (and

---

[34] Thomas Barlow, *A Few Plain Reasons Why a Protestant of the Church of England Should Not Turn Roman Catholick* (London, 1688), p. 48.

[35] Elizabeth Clarke, *Politics, Religion and the Song of Songs in Seventeenth-Century England* (Basingstoke, 2011).

[36] Ibid., pp. 186–7.

gendered) performances of asceticism during the 1650s, with female virgins like Anna Trapnel and Sarah Wight undergoing feats of fasting as a sign of bodily transcendence, and emancipation from the tyranny of the temporal order.[37] As John Rogers has shown, the complex ideal of sexual abstinence, with its connotations of mystical union and self-determination, found new resonance among the religious and political radicals of this period.[38] The early Quaker preacher Richard Hubberthorne complained in 1654 that some of those involved in the movement had begun to 'divide and separate between the husband and the wife, and he that is bound to a wife amongst you, seek to be loose, and then you say you are separated from the beastly lust'.[39] In 'A Treatise on Virginity', the anonymous author of *A Looking-Glasse for the Ranters* (a self-consciously 'Ranter' text) quoted Jerome on the virgin life, and encouraged young readers to 'abstain from fleshly lusts, which fight against the soul, not caring to marry, as worldly men and women do'. The 'end of that discipline' was not only transcendence of the flesh, but also the 'birth' within themselves of '*Immanuel*, or Christ, who cannot be born of any but Virgins', and thus such chaste virgins could 'attain the divine nature'.[40]

This doctrine of regeneration was an idea that had spiritual, political and social dimensions. Gerrard Winstanley, seeking far-reaching social and spiritual reformation, wrote of a virginity of the heart, a 'plaine heartednesse without envie or guile', which 'is the Virgine-state of Mankinde; And this Virgine is she that must beare a sonne, and call his name *Emanuell*, God with us'. Through the birth of divinity within the virginal human spirit, 'the Sonne of righteousnesse will arise, and take the man into union with himselfe; he rules as King, and Mankinde, the living soule is freely subject with delight'.[41] For many millenarians, the virgin bride was synonymous with the English nation, the supreme candidate for the New Jerusalem on earth. The army preacher William Erbery wrote to Oliver Cromwell in July 1652, advocating justice for the poor as an expression of the Christian purity of the English people. As he put it,

> If this Virgin Commonwealth could bee preserved chast and pure, if the oppressed, the prisoner & the poore might bee speedily heard & helped, how would the most high God bee praysed, & men pray for you.[42]

---

[37] See Jane Shaw, 'Fasting Women: the Significance of Gender and Bodies in Radical Religion and Politics, 1650–1813', in Timothy Morton and Nigel Smith (eds), *Radicalism in British Literary Culture, 1650–1830* (Cambridge, 2002), pp. 101–15.

[38] John Rogers, 'The Enclosure of Virginity: The Poetics of Sexual Abstinence in the English Revolution', in Richard Burt and John Michael Archer (eds), *Enclosure Acts: Sexuality, Property and Culture in Early Modern England* (Ithaca, 1994), pp. 229–50.

[39] Richard Hubberthorne, *A True Separation Between the Power of the Spirit, and the Imitation of Antichrist* (London, 1654).

[40] *A Looking-Glasse for the Ranters* (London, 1653), part 2, pp. 16–22.

[41] Gerrard Winstanley, *Fire in the Bush* (London, 1650), pp. 50–51.

[42] Society of Antiquaries of London, London, MS 138, fol. 158, William Erbery, 29 July 1652.

The popular legend of St George, reworked for post-Reformation England in Spenser's *The Faerie Queene* and in seventeenth-century ballads, had also linked Protestant religion with the pure virgin church which England had defended and preserved intact, opening a gateway to the New Jerusalem.[43]

The Dissenters' (as well as many Anglicans') hope of a socially visible, national reformation did not fade altogether after the Restoration. Fuelled by apocalyptic dread, this was precisely the impetus behind the movement for the Reformation of Manners which built up a head of steam under William and Mary. Sex was at the heart of this social rite of purification.[44] The campaign was inspired by repressive legislation against sexual immorality and drunkenness in neighbouring Reformed states during the late seventeenth century, among them Scotland and the Dutch Republic. The appetite for policing sexual behaviour did not collapse with the ecclesiastical courts in the 1640s: if anything, moral reformers sought harsher forms of discipline, by parliamentary statute.[45] As Faramerz Dabhoiwala has recently argued, sexual and spiritual discipline were closely linked in early modern minds.[46] Heretics, the Ranters and the papists alike, were stigmatized as sexual deviants. While Anglican reformers sought to use the same strategies against Dissenters as they had employed against moral transgressors, many Dissenters accused the established Church under Charles II and James II of persecuting the true Reformed church while tolerating sexual laxity. In both cases, the defence of the mystical bride synchronized exactly with regulating sex.

III. Asceticism, Gender and Freedom

Protestant freedom was at stake, alongside English masculinity, in the drive for sexual purification: continence, rather than prowess, was a defining characteristic of the Protestant male, and the zealous godly contrasted this self-discipline to the slavish lust of the papists. Daniel Defoe linked Reformation history to the moral state of the nation, accusing the later Stuart kings of encouraging 'Lewdness and all manner of Debauchery' as part of their deviation from Protestant religion and liberty.[47] Pulpits resounded in the 1690s with condemnation of 'the effeminacy of the last two reigns'; a strategy, of course, to amplify William III's credentials as the champion of Protestantism and the one who would 'revive the Military Courage of the Nation'.[48] One account of the reign of Charles II suggested that he had

---

[43]   See *A Most Excellent Ballad of S. George for England and the Kings Daughter of Aegypt* (London, 1658).

[44]   See Faramerz Dabhoiwala, 'Sex and Societies for Moral Reform, 1688–1800', *Journal of British Studies*, 46/2 (2007): pp. 290–319.

[45]   Ibid., pp. 292–3.

[46]   See Dabhoiwala, 'Lust and Liberty', pp. 89–179.

[47]   Daniel Defoe, *The Poor Man's Plea* (London, 1698), pp. 3–6.

[48]   Vincent Alsop, *Duty and Interest United in Prayer and Praise for Kings and All That Are in Authority from 1 Tim. II. 1, 2* (London, 1695), pp. 25–6. See also Stephen H.

learned during exile 'that undoubted Maxim of Tyranny, that the only way ... to introduce Slavery and Popery, the support of Thraldom, was to weaken and make soft the Military Temper of the People by Debauchery and Effeminacy, which generally go hand in hand together'.[49] Promiscuity in the courts of the later Stuarts was not only emasculating, introducing luxury and softness into the very seat of political power, but also led to oppression and the enslavement of the people. The horror of effeminacy in government and society, and the hazard it posed to English national identity, has often been highlighted by historians of the late seventeenth and eighteenth centuries.[50]

It thus becomes evident why celibacy may have held a fresh appeal within such a climate. The word 'celibacy', derived from the Latin *cœlibatus*, refers to a state of being alone, or unmarried. It carries the connotation of abstinence from sex, but its primary meaning is exclusion (voluntary or otherwise) from a particular unit of society. Some anthropologists regard celibacy as a 'specific example of sociality', associated in diverse cultures with sacred status and the exemption of select individuals from ordinary procreative arrangements, in order that they might be released to perform a special service to the community.[51] This separation, in early Christian thought, signified a foretaste of spiritual liberation from the burdens of this world and an altogether alternative and dissenting vision of society. As Peter Brown puts it,

> In Christian circles, concern with sexual renunciation had never been limited solely to an anxious striving to maximize control over the body. It had been connected with a heroic and sustained attempt, on the part of thinkers of widely different background and temper of mind, to map out the horizons of human freedom. The light of a great hope of future transformation glowed behind even the most austere statements of the ascetic position. To many, continence had declared the end of the tyranny of the 'present age'. In the words of John Chrysostom, virginity made plain that 'the things of the resurrection stand at the door'.[52]

In her study of female celibacy in three utopian religious communities in nineteenth-century America, Sally Kitch suggests that sexual abstinence among

---

Gregg, '"A Truly Christian Hero": Religion, Effeminacy, and Nation in the Writings of the Societies for Reformation of Manners', *Eighteenth-Century Life*, 25/1 (2001): pp. 17–28.

[49]   John Phillips, *The Secret History of the Reigns of K. Charles II and K. James II* (London, 1690), p. 26.

[50]   See Michèle Cohen, introduction to *Fashioning Masculinity: National Identity and Language in the Eighteenth Century* (London, 1996); John Spurr, *England in the 1670s: 'This Masquerading Age'* (Oxford, 2000), p. 202; Kathleen Wilson, *The Sense of the People: Politics, Culture and Imperialism in England, 1715–1785* (Cambridge, 1995), pp. 185–9.

[51]   See Elisa Janine Sobo and Sandra Bell (eds), *Celibacy, Culture and Society: The Anthropology of Sexual Abstinence* (Madison, 2001), pp. 3–28.

[52]   Brown, *Body and Society*, p. 442.

women underscored both a spiritual conception of sociability and the kind of emancipation which Brown describes. She shows how the celibate's separation from worldly corruption and sexuality was thought to enable her to attain 'unity with divine reason and the spiritual domain', escaping the mental prison of women's lives on earth.[53]

Notwithstanding the tastes of rational Dissenters, the absence of celibacy as a pathway to transcendence and freedom, as well as a kind of purifying outlet for the community, seems to have left a cultural vacuum. A yearning for the visible 'life of angels' on earth can be detected in some English spiritual writings of the late seventeenth century, both Anglican and nonconformist.[54] As the Church of England asserted its kinship with primitive Christianity, many of its apologists were uneasily aware that the discipline of celibacy, institutionally renounced during the Henrician and Edwardian Reformations, had an ancient pedigree in church history.[55] Venerable fathers of the church, not to mention Jesus Christ and the apostle Paul, had never married. Perhaps the most popular Anglican devotional writer of the Restoration period, Richard Allestree, echoed the patristic view that a consecrated life of virginity constituted 'one of the nearest approaches to the Angelical State' that could be achieved on earth. He wished that the reformers had chosen 'to rectify and regulate' the celibate religious orders, rather than 'abolish them', allowing women to embrace their 'spiritual bridegroom' rather than be bound to worldly anxieties and obligations. He mused,

> But tho there be not among us such societies, yet there may be *Nuns* who are not Profest. She who has devoted her heart to God, and the better to secure his interest against the most insinuating rival of Human Love, intends to admit none, and praies that she may not; does by those humble purposes consecrate her self to God, and perhaps more acceptably, then if her presumtion should make her more positive, and engage her in a vow she is not sure to perform.[56]

The editor of *The Ladies Dictionary* (1692), probably John Dunton, paraphrased Allestree's commendation of the 'virgin state' as 'the divinest, as coming nearest to that of Angels and blessed Spirits, who live free and unincumbred'.[57]

This rather utopian view of unsupported spinsterhood appealed to some ladies of quality, of various political and confessional inclinations. Several female writers

---

[53]   Sally Kitch, *Chaste Liberation: Celibacy and Female Cultural Status* (Urbana, 1989), p. 82.

[54]   See B.W. Young, 'The Anglican Origins of Newman's Celibacy', *Church History*, 65/1 (1996): pp. 15–27.

[55]   See Jean-Louis Quantin, *The Church of England and Christian Antiquity: The Construction of a Confessional Identity in the 17th Century* (Oxford, 2009).

[56]   Richard Allestree, *The Ladies Calling* (Oxford, 1673), pp. 144–6.

[57]   N.H., *The Ladies Dictionary, Being a General Entertainment for the Fair-Sex: A Work Never Attempted Before in English* (London, 1694), p. 440. See John Considine and Sylvia Brown (eds), introduction to *N.H., The Ladies Dictionary (1694)* (Farnham, 2010).

such as Mary, Lady Chudleigh, Mary Astell and Jane Barker also promoted 'the single life' as a route to religious freedom, whereby the liberated woman might spend her days 'in Prayers, and Hymns and Psalms' as 'Chief Commandress of her Will and Mind'.[58] Astell, as we have seen, was most closely associated with the rejection of marriage as the highest calling for women. Her seraphic vision of Christian society, rooted in Platonism and an attraction to early church models of holiness (or 'the antient Spirit of Piety'), was in profound tension with the sociable values of her Grub Street critics. It was a monastic vision, as she admitted, in which she imagined an emancipation from the irrational customs, divisions and vanities of the world by building a celestial community among the living:

> this happy Society will be but one Body, whose Soul is love, animating and informing it, and perpetually breathing forth it self in flames of holy desires after GOD, and acts of Benevolence to each other.[59]

Abstention from conventional forms of sociability should not be a deterrent to women seeking this ascetic freedom, since 'no Company can be so desirable as GOD's and his holy Angels'.[60] Friendships, in Astell's 'little emblem' of 'Heav'n, that region of perfect Love', would be disinterested, sympathetic, charitable and equal – quite the opposite of the worldly unions which she describes in her later *Reflections upon Marriage*, in which, frequently, 'Folly and Ignorance tyrannize over Wit and Sense'.[61]

Astell and her scheme have been widely studied, but less well-known are the sympathetic contemporary echoes found in the moralizing, psalm-singing religious societies which formed across England and especially in London in the last decades of the seventeenth century, which sometimes took the form of lay monasticism.[62] In 1695, the Anglican lawyer and moral crusader Edward Stephens, who would eventually become a Nonjuror and then break communion with all parties, established a 'Religious Society of Single Women', which he hoped would supply 'some Devout Women, with such mean, but convenient Habitation, Work, Wages and Religion, that they may have Time and Strength for the Worship of GOD, both in Publick and Private, and Freedom of Mind for

---

[58] Jane Barker, 'The Preference of a *Single Life* before *Marriage*. Written at the Request of a Lady', in Jane Barker, *Poetical Recreations Consisting of Original Poems, Songs, Odes, &c* (London, 1688), pp. 102–3. See also Mary, Lady Chudleigh, 'To the Ladies', in Mary Chudleigh, *Poems on Several Occasions* (London, 1703).

[59] Mary Astell, *A Serious Proposal to the Ladies* (London, 1694), pp. 59, 60, 97–8.

[60] Mary Astell, *A Serious Proposal to the Ladies*, Part II (London, 1697), p. 13.

[61] Astell, *Serious Proposal*, Part I, pp. 137–41; Mary Astell, *Reflections upon Marriage*, 3rd edn (London, 1706), p. 4.

[62] See Hannah Smith, 'Mary Astell, *A Serious Proposal to the Ladies* (1694), and the Anglican Reformation of Manners in Late-Seventeenth-Century England', in William Kolbrener and Michal Michelson (eds), *Mary Astell: Reason, Gender, Faith* (Aldershot, 2007), pp. 31–48.

Meditation, and Religious Exercises'. Stephens supplemented his proposal with a discourse on the 'Antiquity, Divine Approbation, and high Esteem, which hath always been had in the Catholick Church, of a Religious Life Abstracted from the World'. It formed part of a moralizing worldview according to which he lived 'not only in a Wicked World, but in a more than ordinary degenerate Age, and wicked Generation, wherein not only the Manners, but the Sentiments and Notions of Men ... are greatly corrupted'.[63] He believed that the Society would spiritually enrich the women themselves, and that 'the Church and Nation may be benefited by their constant Prayers'. For Stephens, even a small association of persons dedicated to an abstracted, purely spiritual existence on earth would provide a living gateway between the English people and the kingdom of heaven, creating closer communion with the angelic sphere. As he put it:

> This is indeed to lay up Treasure in Heaven, and to make us Friends there; to make the Favourites of Heaven upon Earth, and their Angels in Heaven our Friends; and the God of Heaven himself, if we do not otherwise offend him.

Stephens chose to focus on women rather than men in his vision of a celibate society for three reasons outlined in his proposal: first, because 'of that Sex we find most Devout People'; second, because women's occupations enable them to attend regular acts of devotion; and finally, interestingly, because they 'do most need it; for whereas Men can ordinarily Earn 2s. or 2s. 6d. per day, most Women cannot Earn above 6d. or 4d. or not so much'.[64] Even a mystic like Edward Stephens needed a utilitarian argument to justify his project, in the sophisticated metropolis of the late seventeenth century. But at the heart of Stephens's as well as Astell's reforming visions was the conviction that promoting piety and moral purity in this way would open up the lines of communication between heaven and this world. The society he wanted to strengthen, and for which he wanted to reform English manners, was the whole communion of Christ's eternal kingdom.

Within the context of the religious societies, the symbolic associations of celibacy with spiritual freedom and communion also found fresh expression among the English 'Behmenists', or interpreters of Jacob Boehme, the controversial Lutheran mystic whose thought so profoundly influenced the German Pietist renewal movement. According to Boehme, sexual difference was a consequence if not the essence of the Fall of humankind, and the first Adam enjoyed a 'Holy Virgin state' which 'exempted him from those impure, deformed, bestial Members for Propagation': namely, his sexual organs. Adam's androgynous condition represented the harmony which existed in Paradise, and his division into two sexes embodied the fracturing of human society. Death in Christ, taught Boehme, would restore the soul to its sublime original condition, and eliminate all distinctions between individuals:

---

[63]   Edward Stephens, *A Letter to a Lady* (London, 1695), pp. 2, 8.

[64]   Edward Stephens, *The More Excellent Way: Or, A Proposal of a Compleat Work of Charity* (London, c. 1695), pp. 1–3.

As *Adam* slept to the Holy Paradisical Virgin state, and awaked to the bestial World's Adulterous state: so the true Christian's Death is a sleeping to that sleep of his, *viz.* The filthy, sickly, cumbring, prophane, Elementary Life, and an awaking to the pure, holy, triumphant, dear, sweet child-like, angelical, Endless Life; it transfers him out of the howling Wilderness of Temptation into Eternal *Canaan:* out of a Dungeon into the glorious Liberty of the Sons of God: out of the *Turba* of perplexing Multiplicity and restless wrestling of contrary Properties, into the equal Temperature and Calm harmonious complete Unity, the private Self being extinct he entreth the Universal sacred Freedom of the Lord's Redeemed ones.[65]

There was some ambiguity in Behmenist circles, however, as to how far this prelapsarian virginity referred to a physical or a spiritual condition. In the 1650s John Pordage, one of Boehme's more notorious readers, was accused (among other things) of condemning marriage and procreation.[66] Yet this charge may have stemmed from a confusion about the language of virginity which he drew upon to frame his doctrine of sanctification: the 'Virgin Life, or the Life of Purity and Righteousness in its perfection' did not necessarily inhere in sexual innocence. As he put it in some early writings, 'meerly to abstain from the concupiscible lustings of *Venus* under the Spirit of this great World, is but the Life of outward Chastity'. Instead, true virginity consisted in the passivity of the soul and its entire submission to the divine principle, the 'essential Essence of Love', so that 'the pure Life of God can come to be all in all'.[67] It is possibly significant that Pordage, the leader of prophetic communities first at Bradfield in Berkshire and then in Holborn, also had a reputation for sexual libertinism, though of course this was, as we have seen, a conventional charge against heresiarchs.[68] After the Restoration, some of Pordage's closest associates certainly prescribed abstinence from the married state, and even chastity within it. His companion Thomas Bromley wrote that in 'the heavenly Community' of saints on earth, 'those that have Wives, are as though they had none, returning from Idolizing, and desiring the Woman of the World'. He praised those that 'follow the Example of Christ, who lived and died in Virginity', and 'made themselves Eunuchs for the Kingdom of Heaven'.[69]

---

[65] Edward Taylor trans., *Jacob Behmen's Theosophick Philosophy Unfolded* (London, 1691), pp. 82–3, 192.
[66] See B.J. Gibbons, *Gender in Mystical and Occult Thought: Behmenism and its Development in England* (Cambridge, 1996), pp. 106–13.
[67] 'Doctor Pordage his Relation of the wonderful Apparitions, Visions, and Unusual Things which were Seen in his Family, in the Year, 1649', in Matthew Hale, *A Collection of Modern Relations of Matter of Fact, Concerning Witches & Witchcraft Upon the Persons of People*, part 1 (London, 1693), pp. 17–18.
[68] John Pordage, *Innocencie Appearing through the Dark Mists of Pretended Guilt* (London, 1655), pp. 13, 70.
[69] Thomas Bromley, *The Way to the Sabbath of Rest* (London, 1678), p. 19.

The visionary Jane Lead described Pordage as her 'Companion and Fellow-Labourer in the *Paradisiacal* Husbandry', who shared her edifying visions of heaven and communion with 'the Angelical Society' of 'God's Houshold and Family' among the living saints.[70] Lead had been married, but during the final years of her husband's life and subsequently her widowhood, she settled in Pordage's Holborn community and later became a founding member of the Philadelphian Society in the same district: a millenarian group dedicated to heralding a new dispensation of the Holy Spirit, which made itself public in 1697. Essential to these communities was a commitment to celibacy and other forms of abstinence. The Philadelphians thought of themselves as a new generation of 'Nazarites': a reference to Numbers 6, in which certain men and women among the Israelites took a special vow to separate themselves from the community, and live an undefiled life of holiness. To her readers, Lead advocated a life of 'Single Chastity', free from 'all low amorous entangling Loves', imitating Christ who had made himself 'a pure Nazarite and Eunuch for the Kingdom of Heaven's sake'. Instead, a higher, universal love detached from a particular human object but rooted in Christ's mystical body was 'the true and right Marriage, of which the first was but a Type'; in her words, 'to one only Mate we must for ever cleave'.[71]

The mystics of the Philadelphian Society inherited much of the Interregnum radicals' apocalyptic anthropology, with whom they shared the belief that a celibate life would generate new incarnations of Christ. In her diaries, deemed too elevated and 'seraphick' for publication, Ann Bathurst wrote rapturously:

> O the mysterie of conception! O the unconceivableness of the Love of God & the incarnating of his Son in us, his revealed love! O the wonder-Man, when God came to join himselfe to him in the womb of a virgin! O the virgin womb which God comes again into, to impregnat with holy powers from his Holy Spirit![72]

Richard Roach, an Anglican minister and founding Philadelphian, predicted that in this fresh appearance of Christ, 'an Honour of the Like Nature, with that to which the Blessed Virgin was Advanc'd in her Day, will be indulg'd to Numerous Virgins ... for the Conception and bringing forth Christ Triumphant, in Spirit in them: and in their being made actually the Blessed Spouses of Christ'.[73] Roach was particularly interested in the role played by female virgins in the second coming. He was fascinated by the Pietist women who were at the centre of a raging

---

[70]   Jane Lead, *A Fountain of Gardens* (3 vols, London, 1697), vol. 1, p. 143; Jane Lead, *A Living Funeral Testimony: Or, Death Overcome, and Drown'd in the Life of Christ* (London, 1702), pp. 36–7.

[71]   Lead, *Fountain of Gardens*, vol. 1, pp. 159, 184, 325.

[72]   Bodleian Library, MS Rawl. D. 1,262, fol. 3, Ann Bathurst's diaries. On Bathurst's writings, see Richard Roach, *The Great Crisis: Or the Mystery of the Times and Seasons Unfolded* (London, 1725), p. 115.

[73]   Roach, *Great Crisis*, pp. 160–61.

controversy in the early 1690s in the duchy of Magdeburg. The women were known locally as the 'Begeisterte Mägde', or 'ecstatic maids', and they were all unmarried and illiterate. In the course of intense fasting they experienced visions and manifested miraculous supernatural signs in their bodies: Anna Eva Jacobs sweated blood, and raised letters appeared on her hands; while Anna Margaretha Jahn would crow like a cockerel and moo like a cow.[74] Roach wrote that these women were 'Illustrious Females in this Age', spiritual heirs of the 'Famous Abby of Women' at Quedlinberg in Magdeburg.[75] It was primarily in holy women like these, thought Roach, that a new dispensation would unfold:

> And hence Favours will be indulged to the Females of this Day, both Virgins and others, of a like Nature with that to the Virgin Mary; but in a more Internal and Spiritual Way: Whereby the Holy Ghost shall come upon them, and the Power of the highest shall overshadow them; and that that Holy Thing which shall be born in them, not in Flesh but in Spirit, shall be called the Son of God; not in his Humiliation, but in his risen and triumphant State.... For as Male and Female in Me are One; so it must be in every Soul thus made One with Me.[76]

Through sexual union with the Holy Spirit, consecrated female spirits (not only, but perhaps especially virgins) would be impregnated with Christ's nature.

Gender was central to the Philadelphians' ascetic and mystical thought. In a reversal of the Fall, described as the 'Disgrace of the Female Sex', women were invited by Christ the 'Restorer of All' into communion with the divine, and through that sanctifying encounter were made sacred wives and mothers of God. As a result, they were released from the constraints and bonds of human love: they 'neither Marry, nor are given in Marriage, ie. in Way of Particular Appropriation, as on Earth, as both enjoying Consummate Love in Themselves, and ranging at Liberty, as Birds of Paradise, in Universal Communion'.[77] Once the 'Carnall Desire is Conquerd', the only risk was that those who shared the 'Spiritual Union' with Christ and creation might develop an 'Inordinate & fleshly desire of ye Spirituall Unions wth Persons in whome they are opend', which could lead to 'Idolatry Pollution & Adultery in Spirit'.[78] Drawing on Boehme's teachings about the androgynous Adam as well as St Paul's maxim that in Christ 'there is neither male nor female' (Galatians 3:28, KJV), Roach also envisaged a radical

---

[74]   See Judd Stitziel, 'God, the Devil, Medicine, and the Word: A Controversy Over Ecstatic Women in Protestant Middle Germany 1691–1693', *Central European History*, 29/3 (1996): pp. 309–37.

[75]   Francis Lee and Richard Roach (eds), *Theosophical Transactions*, no. 5 (London, 1697), p. 294.

[76]   Richard Roach, *The Imperial Standard of Messiah Triumphant* (London, 1727), p. 186.

[77]   Roach, *Great Crisis*, pp. 95–6.

[78]   Bodleian Library, MS Rawl. D. 833, fol. 5, papers of Richard Roach.

dissolution of gender. In the resurrection state, 'both Male and Female are United' and 'the Perfected Saints, are Virginiz'd or made Masculin Virgins'.[79]

This doctrine of a union of genders was cast in various forms. An anonymous manuscript document among some papers of the Philadelphian Society (bound with unpublished visions of Jane Lead) contains reflections on the query, 'whether ther shall be Any Women so Raysed And So To Remaine in Eternity, in ye Two Determinated Places, Heav'n & Hell'. The author took the remarkable and original view, certainly heretical among the Philadelphians, not only that human marriage was 'made in Heav'n', but that each individual woman was created 'for a Peculiar Certain Husband' with whom they would be united in one body at the general resurrection. It was a tragedy, according to this Philadelphian writer, that:

> Ther are so very Few marriages Rightly made; more being made for Interest or By-Ends, viz: Money or Lust &c Than for Pure Affection & Love: So yt ye True Naturall Yoak-Fellow, is very seldom mett with, chosen, or Thought on.

However, even unmarried women who had never met their 'Peculiar Natural second-halves' would enjoy this incorporation in eternity. The form of the resurrection body would be 'Wholly Masculine, & yet wthout any Memberly Distinction such as we now Carry about us'.[80] The gendered eschatology of the Philadelphian Society also provided the inspiration for an extraordinary Pietist sect founded in January 1700 in Hesse, in expectation of the millennium. Led by the charismatic Eva von Buttlar, a community of around 70 radical Pietists pursued mystical marriage with divinity through ritual purification: for men, this involved sexual intercourse with 'Mother' Eva herself; while women underwent an excruciating form of circumcision.[81] It is possible to see the potential in Philadelphian thought both for women's authority and for the repression of female identity through the practices of this controversial separatist group.

IV. Conclusions

Female celibacy has carried complex, and sometimes paradoxical, symbolic burdens throughout Christian history, and not least in the English post-Reformation. Virginity has represented a distinctively feminine form of holiness which women could inhabit in a unique way as brides of Christ and successors of the Virgin Mother. However, it might also signify the transcendence of gender and the rejection of female identity, in favour of what was regarded as a higher, masculine spirituality. In this chapter, I have explored how the concept of consecrated virginity

---

[79]   Roach, *Great Crisis*, p. 143.

[80]   British Library, London, Sloane MS, 2,569, fols 70r–76r, 'Concerning Man's Eternall-Forme And what it is Like to be &c'.

[81]   See Barbara Hoffmann, *Radikalpietismus um 1700. Der Streit um das Recht auf eine neue Gesellschaft* (Frankfurt, 1996).

found particular expression among certain mystical and millenarian groups, during a period of British history which historians have characterized as increasingly narrow in terms of formulations of sexual difference, and increasingly obsessed with gender transgressions. Isolated as these celibate communities may have been in fashionable London society, they manifest symptoms of wider anxieties and cultural tensions: reflecting not merely a morally repressive impulse, but concern about social cohesion after the decline of discipline, and perhaps equally centrally a protest against the inhibitions placed on the female sex as a result of their domestic containment and economic dependency. In promoting both outward and inward virginity, these reformers sought to create a higher form of sociability with the invisible society of heaven and its angels in which traditional gender distinctions and institutions such as marriage were no longer of any significance. Rather than being seen as eccentric episodes in English religion, the imaginative visions of celibate community in the later seventeenth century should be viewed as illuminating, by their very oppositional character, the mainstream trends which would ultimately provoke far more fundamental reactions and transformations.

Chapter 4
Female Authority and Lay Activism in Scottish Presbyterianism, 1660–1740

Alasdair Raffe

The Reformation was a mixed blessing for Scotland's women. John Knox denounced female rule, and the downfall of Mary, Queen of Scots seemed to vindicate his views.[1] Protestant ideas fuelled the Scottish witch-hunt, a campaign that saw over 3,800 people accused, 84 percent of them women.[2] And the Reformers launched a war against sin that often had female sexual transgression in its sights. In the century and a half after 1560, Brian Levack contends, '[e]fforts to prosecute sexual offenders in the secular courts were more intensive and successful in Scotland than in any other European country'.[3] Kirk sessions, the local church courts, also interrogated suspected fornicators and adulterers, administering fines and ordering those convicted to perform public penance. Because the sessions' financial penalties were normally gender blind, they had a greater impact on women than on men, proving especially burdensome to low-paid female servants.[4] Yet sexual misdemeanours were not the only concern of kirk sessions, and women were not always cast in the role of victims. Because kirk sessions also dealt with sins such as slander, women could use the courts to defend their reputations.[5]

[1] John Knox, *John Knox on Rebellion*, ed. Roger A. Mason (Cambridge, 1994), pp. 3–47; Jenny Wormald, 'Godly Reformer, Godless Monarch: John Knox and Mary Queen of Scots', in Roger A. Mason (ed.), *John Knox and the British Reformations* (Aldershot, 1998), pp. 220–41.

[2] Julian Goodare, Lauren Martin, Joyce Miller and Louise Yeoman, 'The Survey of Scottish Witchcraft', http://www.shca.ed.ac.uk/Research/witches, accessed 4 May 2014; Julian Goodare, 'Women and the Witch-Hunt in Scotland', *Social History*, 23/3 (1998): pp. 288–308.

[3] Brian P. Levack, 'The Prosecution of Sexual Crimes in Early Eighteenth-Century Scotland', *Scottish Historical Review*, 89/2 (2010): pp. 172–93, at p. 180.

[4] Gordon DesBrisay, 'Twisted by Definition: Women under Godly Discipline in Seventeenth-Century Scottish Towns', in Yvonne Galloway Brown and Rona Ferguson (eds), *Twisted Sisters: Women, Crime and Deviance in Scotland since 1400* (East Linton, 2002), pp. 137–55.

[5] Michael F. Graham, 'Women and the Church Courts in Reformation-Era Scotland', in Elizabeth Ewan and Maureen M. Meikle (eds), *Women in Scotland, c. 1100–c. 1750* (East Linton, 1999), pp. 187–98; John McCallum, *Reforming the Scottish Parish: The Reformation in Fife, 1560–1640* (Farnham, 2010), ch. 7.

Regardless of the impact of its discipline, the Reformed Church of Scotland incubated a style of piety that was attractive to men and women alike. Based on conversion, self-examination and extemporary prayer, this spirituality offered intense emotional experiences. The devout searched their lives and prayers for evidence of their prospects of salvation, linking their feelings to the theological concepts of predestination, justification and sanctification.[6] Men and women were thought equally likely to be among the elect, and both sexes enjoyed the fruits of divine grace in their devotional experiences. Godly men valued the prayers and conversation of their female co-religionists, and this reciprocity of spiritual interest made for loving marriages and close friendships between men and women.[7] Knox, despite his sexist politics, had ardent spiritual relationships with several women.[8] About half of the letters of the mid-seventeenth-century minister Samuel Rutherford were addressed to women, and these reflect the correspondents' shared commitment to affective piety.[9] Between the late sixteenth and the mid-seventeenth centuries, spirituality of this kind was practised by Scots holding various views about authority and government in the Church. But it was most common among convinced Presbyterians. After the re-establishment of episcopacy in 1661–62, Episcopalians increasingly distanced themselves from this style of emotional piety, denigrating what they saw as dangerous 'enthusiasm'.[10] Many Presbyterian nonconformists continued to derive from their spiritual lives a sense of personal authority, stiffening their resolve to dissent from the established Church. Among these conscientious dissenters were thousands of women.

This chapter investigates female religious authority in Scottish Presbyterianism.[11] Beginning with Presbyterian nonconformity in the Restoration

---

[6]   Louise A. Yeoman, 'Heart-work: Emotion, Empowerment and Authority in Covenanting Times' (University of St Andrews PhD thesis, 1991), esp. ch. 1; David G. Mullan, *Narratives of the Religious Self in Early Modern Scotland* (Farnham, 2010), esp. chs 5, 7; Alasdair Raffe, 'Presbyterians and Episcopalians: The Formation of Confessional Cultures in Scotland, 1660–1715', *English Historical Review*, 125/3 (2010): pp. 570–98, at pp. 588–9. On affective piety in congregational worship, see Leigh Eric Schmidt, *Holy Fairs: Scotland and the Making of American Revivalism*, 2nd edn (Grand Rapids, MI, 2001).

[7]   Yeoman, 'Heart-Work', pp. 253–61; David G. Mullan, *Scottish Puritanism, 1590–1638* (Oxford, 2000), ch. 5.

[8]   Patrick Collinson, 'John Knox, the Church of England and the Women of England', in Mason (ed.), *Knox and the British Reformations*, pp. 74–96.

[9]   John Coffey, *Politics, Religion and the British Revolutions: The Mind of Samuel Rutherford* (Cambridge, 1997), pp. 97–102.

[10]   Raffe, 'Presbyterians and Episcopalians', pp. 589–92; Alasdair Raffe, *The Culture of Controversy: Religious Arguments in Scotland, 1660–1714* (Woodbridge, 2012), ch. 5.

[11]   For women in Scotland's other religious communities, see for example, Alasdair F.B. Roberts, 'The Role of Women in Scottish Catholic Survival', *Scottish Historical Review*, 70/2 (1991): pp. 129–50; Gordon DesBrisay, 'Lilias Skene: A Quaker Poet and her "Cursed Self"', in Sarah M. Dunnigan, C. Marie Harker and Evelyn S. Newlyn (eds), *Woman and the*

period, it argues that lay activists were crucial to Presbyterianism's endurance in the face of government suppression. Female activists performed important roles, organizing and attending conventicles, providing ministers with accommodation and other support. More than the established Presbyterianism of the years 1638–61 and after 1690, in which male elders, patrons and politicians were the principal lay participants in the Church's politics, Restoration nonconformity offered women influence. As John Coffey remarks of the mid-seventeenth-century Church, 'it was the conventicle rather than the committee that empowered the female sex'.[12] Moreover, in the clandestine networks of Restoration Presbyterianism, outstanding piety gave some women particular importance, especially in small prayer groups. The Presbyterian settlement of 1690 re-integrated the great majority of Scotland's Presbyterians into an established Church with male-dominated courts and a socially conservative outlook. But female spiritual energies remained a dynamic force, most notably in the lay prayer societies that paralleled the Church's parish structure. By examining the Coat-Muir Folk, a hitherto unstudied cell of lay Presbyterians who dissented from the re-established Church, this chapter suggests how female authority contributed to the departure of lay people from the Kirk in the eighteenth century and the resulting fragmentation of Scottish Presbyterianism.

I

The re-establishment of Episcopalian government at the Restoration brought about a religious crisis in Scotland, dividing the country's clergy and alienating many of the laity. At least 300 ministers – almost a third of the national total – were deprived of their parishes for refusing to comply with the settlement. In parts of the south and west of Scotland, a majority of ministers were deprived.[13] Their lay sympathizers were reluctant to attend services in the re-established Church or to countenance the conforming clergy. In these circumstances, dissenting worship took place at indoor and outdoor meetings, labelled 'conventicles' by their critics and subject to prosecution by central and local authorities. A large number of ministers preached at these gatherings, some conducting worship on an itinerant basis. They did so at considerable personal risk, enhancing their popularity with lay Presbyterians and becoming renowned for great piety.[14] Later generations of Presbyterians celebrated these famous preachers, paying little

---

Feminine in Medieval and Early Modern Scottish Writing (Basingstoke, 2004), pp. 162–77; Suzanne Trill (ed.), *Lady Anne Halkett: Selected Self-Writings* (Aldershot, 2007).

[12]   Coffey, *Politics, Religion and the British Revolutions*, p. 102.

[13]   Ian B. Cowan, *The Scottish Covenanters, 1660–1688* (London, 1976), pp. 50–55; Elizabeth Hannan Hyman, 'A Church Militant: Scotland, 1661–1690', *The Sixteenth Century Journal*, 26/1 (1995): pp. 49–74; Mark Jardine, 'The United Societies: Militancy, Martyrdom and the Presbyterian Movement in Late-Restoration Scotland, 1679 to 1688' (University of Edinburgh PhD thesis, 2009), p. 11, appendices 7.7, 7.8.

[14]   Mullan, *Narratives of the Religious Self*, ch. 2.

attention to their female supporters. Nevertheless, the Victorian minister James Anderson recognized the contribution of women, publishing short biographies of the most important female Presbyterians in his *Ladies of the Covenant* (1851).[15] More recently, David Mullan's edition of female life-writing and Louise Yeoman's account of lay prophets have deepened our understanding of women's involvement in Presbyterian dissent.[16] But the full spectrum of female activism remains to be studied.

The Presbyterians' critics in the government and the Church were well aware that women played a significant part in nonconformity. If women could be restrained from Presbyterian worship, Scotland would 'have litill trubell with conventickils', wrote Charles II's commissioner to parliament, the earl of Rothes, in 1665.[17] Nineteen years later, the Privy Council claimed that 'women were the cheiff fomenters' of dissenting worship.[18] Some representatives of the Episcopalian establishment sought to belittle the dissenting clergy by emphasizing their female following. In 1669, when he was Episcopalian minister of Saltoun, Gilbert Burnet wrote that the dissenters' rhetoric served to 'terrifie simple people', to 'triumph among women, and in your Conventicles'.[19] Alexander Rose, professor of divinity at Glasgow University, compared Presbyterians to the unholy men described in 2 Timothy 3, who 'creep into houses, and lead captive silly Women'.[20] But by presenting women as passive participants, these sources misinterpreted Presbyterian dissent.

---

[15] James Anderson, *The Ladies of the Covenant. Memoirs of Distinguished Scottish Female Characters, Embracing the Period of the Covenant and the Persecution* (Glasgow, 1851). See also D. Beaton, *Scottish Heroines of the Faith: Being Brief Sketches of Noble Women of the Reformation and Covenant Times* (London, 1909). The contribution of women in the earlier phase of the Covenanting movement is epitomized by Jenny Geddes, the probably mythical initiator of the Prayer Book riots in 1637: see Laura A.M. Stewart, 'Jenny Geddes', in Elizabeth Ewan, Sue Innes, Rose Pipes and Siân Reynolds (eds), *The Biographical Dictionary of Scottish Women: From the Earliest Times to 2004* (Edinburgh, 2006), pp. 133–4.

[16] David G. Mullan (ed.), *Women's Life Writing in Early Modern Scotland: Writing the Evangelical Self, c. 1670–c. 1730* (Aldershot, 2003); Louise Yeoman, '"Away with the Fairies"', in Lizanne Henderson (ed.), *Fantastical Imaginations: The Supernatural in Scottish History and Culture* (Edinburgh, 2009), pp. 29–46.

[17] Osmund Airy (ed.), *The Lauderdale Papers* (3 vols, London, 1884–85), vol. 1, p. 234.

[18] *The Register of the Privy Council of Scotland*, 3rd series, ed. P. Hume Brown, Henry Paton and E. Balfour-Melville (16 vols, Edinburgh, 1908–70) (hereafter cited as *RPC*, 3rd ser.), vol. 8, p. 347.

[19] [Gilbert Burnet], *A Modest and Free Conference Betwixt a Conformist and a Non-Conformist, about the Present Distempers of Scotland*, 2nd edn ([Edinburgh?] 1669), first part, p. 41.

[20] Alexander Rose, *A Sermon Preached Before the Right Honourable the Lords Commissioners of His Majesties Most Honourable Privy Council* (Glasgow, 1684), p. 29; 2 Tim. 3:6.

There was evidently a prominent female presence at dissenting conventicles. The Privy Council punished more men than women for conventicling, partly for legal reasons discussed below. But even cases in which only men were prosecuted provide evidence of women's activities. In March 1669, the council investigated a recent conventicle in Edinburgh, which had been attended by a 'multitud of persons, men and women'. The meeting had taken place in the house of a widow, known by her husband's name of Paton, and though at least three men were fined for their attendance, she was apparently not punished.[21] Other women, especially the wealthy and socially eminent, provided accommodation for Presbyterian worship. In March 1679, Margaret Stewart, wife of the commissary of Glasgow Sir William Fleming, confessed to the Privy Council that conventicles had been held in her house.[22] Wealthy women were probably also a source of funding when new buildings were constructed specifically for Presbyterian worship. After executing a government order to destroy a meeting house in Annandale in January 1679, John Grahame of Claverhouse remarked that 'the charity of many ladys' was lost.[23]

The government's use of troops to suppress field conventicles encouraged armed men to guard the meetings. But a few women were also willing to stand their ground when confronted by soldiers, perhaps expecting to be treated more leniently than their husbands and brothers. Around 1677, a field conventicle in Selkirkshire was disturbed by the neighbouring county's sheriff. According to one source, the sheriff's sister, who was with the Presbyterians, confronted her brother, taking 'his horse by the bridle, clapping her hands, and crying out, "Fye on ye, man; fye on ye; the vengeance of God will overtake you, for marring so good a work"'.[24] In 1678, troops broke up a house conventicle in Glasgow, but 'great multitudes of women' prevented them from gaining access to a locked room, where the preacher was probably hiding. Retreating to the street, the commanding officer was 'surrounded with some hundreths of women' and disarmed. The event exposed the government's weakness in the face of lay activism.[25]

The central and local authorities imposed considerable penalties on those found to have participated in illegal Presbyterian worship. Nonconformists could be fined for withdrawing from their parish church,[26] and they were liable to

---

[21]   *RPC*, 3rd ser., vol. 2, pp. 614–15, 621, 626; vol. 3, p. 2.

[22]   Ibid., vol. 6, p. 139.

[23]   George Smythe (ed.), *Letters of John Grahame of Claverhouse, Viscount of Dundee* (Edinburgh, 1826), p. 5.

[24]   Andrew Crichton (ed.), *Memoirs of the Rev. John Blackader*, 2nd edn (Edinburgh, 1826), pp. 190–91.

[25]   George Eyre-Todd (ed.), *The Book of Glasgow Cathedral* (Glasgow, 1898), p. 166.

[26]   Keith M. Brown et al. (eds), *The Records of the Parliaments of Scotland to 1707*, http://www.rps.ac.uk (St Andrews, 2007–14) (hereafter cited as *RPS*), 1579/10/23, 1661/1/345, 1663/6/19, 1670/7/14, 1672/6/51.

imprisonment and fines if they had a marriage solemnized by a deprived minister.[27] The Conventicle Act (1670) imposed a sliding scale of fines for attendance at Presbyterian services. Double fines were payable for presence at a conventicle held outdoors; male worshippers whose wives and children attended with them were also to pay extra.[28] Another act of parliament specified fines for the fathers of children baptized outwith the established Church.[29] The Privy Council sometimes ordered female Presbyterians to pay the fines incurred by their nonconformity. In 1672, the countess of Wigtown confessed to attending conventicles and was fined 4,000 merks.[30] After they were discovered at a house conventicle in Edinburgh in 1676, Mary Liddington was ordered to pay 100 merks, and her mother Mary Hepburn, Lady Saltcoats, 200 pounds Scots. The widows Margaret Hadden and Bessie Muir, arrested at the same meeting, were banished from Edinburgh, possibly under the terms of a statute against suspects who refused to answer questions under oath.[31]

But by levying financial penalties, parliament ensured that it was often men who were called to account for the nonconformity of their wives, daughters and female servants. The responsibility of male householders was underlined in 1674, when the Privy Council sought to make landowners answerable for their tenants' nonconformity, masters for that of their servants, and husbands for the conventicling of their wives.[32] The possibility that women might act independently of their husbands could make the enforcement of laws against dissent more difficult. In one instance, Presbyterians gathered at a remote house in Lanarkshire, where a minister preached and baptized several children. The sheriff of the county was frustrated in his investigation of the conventicle, in part because the children had been taken for baptism by their mothers, and their fathers had not attended the service.[33]

Other cases increased the authorities' uncertainty about demanding fines from the conforming husbands of female dissenters. In November 1683, Sir William Scott of Harden petitioned the council after he was prosecuted for several offences of nonconformity, including the refusal of his wife, Christian Boyd, to attend their parish church. Scott claimed that because he normally conformed, 'he ought to be exonered upon her account, he being alwayes ready and yet is to exhibite his wife to justice, which is all he humbly conceaves the law requires in that caice'. Scott's petition was unsuccessful, the council deciding that he had encouraged

---

27 Ibid., 1661/1/302.

28 Ibid., 1670/7/11, confirmed by 1672/6/51.

29 Ibid., 1670/7/12, also 1672/6/32.

30 *RPC*, 3rd ser., vol. 3, p. 561.

31 Ibid., vol. 5, pp. 52–3, 604; *RPS*, 1670/7/6.

32 *RPC*, 3rd ser., vol. 4, pp. 197–200, re-imposed in 1677: ibid., vol. 5, p. 196.

33 National Records of Scotland, Edinburgh (NRS), GD406/1/7601, duke of Hamilton to the earl of Arran, 2 November [1678?].

Boyd's nonconformity.[34] But as far as the wider principle was concerned, Charles II instructed the council to cancel the fines 'of such loyall husbands as are nowayes to be suspected of connivance with their obstinat wives, but are content to deliver them up to be punished'.[35] After the accession of James VII, parliament explicitly endorsed the fining of husbands for their wives' nonconformity.[36] But the practice remained controversial, and it was condemned at the revolution in the Claim of Right (1689).[37]

In addition to withdrawing from their parish churches, women were prominent in other forms of protest against the imposition of the Restoration Church settlement. Episcopalian clergy in southern and central Scotland encountered violent crowds, armed burglars in their manses, and more trivial insults and intimidation. The most serious cases of rioting occurred when a minister was being admitted to a parish for the first time.[38] Women made up a majority in several of these violent crowds, even in cases where the tumult was the product of male organization. At Kirkcudbright in 1663, the Privy Council found that John, Lord Kirkcudbright, a local landowner, and John Carsan of Sennick, formerly provost of the burgh, had connived at a largely female riot against the settling of an Episcopalian minister. Several of the women involved were sentenced to stand at the cross of Kirkcudbright on two market days, where they were to acknowledge their guilt.[39] But most female rioters seem to have escaped punishment. Sometimes this resulted from the judicial authorities' leniency towards women, a phenomenon observed by historians of eighteenth-century collective violence.[40] In other instances, it was simply difficult to find enough evidence to convict female rioters. At Kirkpatrick-Irongray, in Kirkcudbrightshire, the council's investigation found that though there had been 'a great convocation and tumult of women', there was 'no speciall probation of any persons particular miscariag'. The councillors' solution was to impose a collective punishment, quartering a party of soldiers on the parish, and imposing a bond for good behaviour on its landowners.[41]

Restoration statutes against unlawful assembly and sedition made it difficult for opponents of the crown's policies to represent their views to the authorities. Leading politicians feared anything that resembled the campaign of addressing

---

[34] *RPC*, 3rd ser., vol. 8, pp. 276 (quotation), 278.

[35] Ibid., vol. 8, pp. 366–7.

[36] *RPS*, 1685/4/23.

[37] Ibid., 1689/3/108.

[38] For a longer discussion, see Raffe, *Culture of Controversy*, ch. 8.

[39] *RPC*, 3rd ser., vol. 1, pp. 372–4, 408.

[40] Kenneth J. Logue, *Popular Disturbances in Scotland, 1780–1815* (Edinburgh, 1979), pp. 199–203; Christopher A. Whatley, *Scottish Society, 1707–1830: Beyond Jacobitism, Towards Industrialisation* (Manchester, 2000), pp. 197–200; Anne-Marie Kilday, *Women and Violent Crime in Enlightenment Scotland* (Woodbridge, 2007), ch. 6.

[41] *RPC*, 3rd ser., vol. 1, pp. 376–7.

that had launched the revolutionary Covenanting movement in 1637.[42] But in June 1674, 'because men durst not', between 20 and 30 women gathered in Edinburgh's Parliament Close to petition the Privy Council for freedom to worship. The women, who included the widows of two Presbyterian ministers and wives of gentlemen, merchants and tradesmen, succeeded in presenting their address, but were subsequently called in for interrogation. Another crowd of women assembled outside the council chamber, and attempted to prevent their friends from being imprisoned. By November, however, the council had apprehended the leading petitioners. Declaring them guilty of tumultuous convocation and submitting a 'most insolent and seditious' address, it banished 16 from Edinburgh.[43]

As we have seen, the relationship between a Presbyterian minister and a female supporter could be an intense and pious bond, an interaction between the preacher's charisma and a woman's eminent spirituality. The deprived minister Thomas Hog had several close female friends, including the sisters Katharine and Jean Collace, whose diaries reflect Hog's influence on their spiritual development.[44] The Collaces regularly corresponded with John Welwood, an itinerant preacher who exchanged spiritual advice and news reports with his female friends.[45] Presbyterian ministers greatly valued the support of elite women, even when their husbands were more cautious. At one conventicle, the commissary's wife Margaret Stewart and another woman, wife of William Anderson, a former provost of Glasgow, were allegedly 'placed on high chaires on either side of' the preacher John Welsh.[46] After the defeat of the Presbyterian rising at the battle of Bothwell Bridge (1679), one pamphleteer claimed that the 'chanting of the professing Ladies', especially in Edinburgh, had encouraged ministers to accept the crown's terms in the peace settlement. This writer, critical of the clergy's compromises, complained that under the influence of female patronage, ministers had adopted a 'laxe, partial way in the Matters of God, preaching rather to the Humors of the Hearers, than home to their Consciences'.[47]

Though women in Edinburgh enjoyed the services of many Presbyterian ministers, elsewhere preaching was less plentiful. In Fife, Jean Collace complained of the infrequency of sermons, but she and her friends were willing

---

[42]   For example, Airy (ed.), *Lauderdale Papers*, vol. 3, pp. 52–3.

[43]   James Kirkton, *A History of the Church of Scotland, 1660–1679*, ed. Ralph Stewart (Lewiston, NY, 1992), pp. 203–4, quotation at p. 203; Robert Wodrow, *The History of the Sufferings of the Church of Scotland from the Restoration to the Revolution*, ed. Robert Burns (4 vols, Glasgow, 1828–32), vol. 2, pp. 268–9; *RPC*, 3rd ser., vol. 4, pp. 258–61, 295; NRS, GD406/1/2737, James Johnston to the earl of Arran, 12 June 1674.

[44]   Mullan, *Narratives of the Religious Self*, p. 111; Katharine Collace, 'Memoirs or Spiritual Exercises', and Jean Collace, 'Some Short Remembrances of the Lord's Kindness', in Mullan (ed.), *Women's Life Writing*.

[45]   John Welwood, 'Letters', in David G. Mullan (ed.), *Protestant Piety in Early-Modern Scotland: Letters, Lives and Covenants, 1650–1712* (Edinburgh, 2008).

[46]   *RPC*, 3rd ser., vol. 6, p. 139.

[47]   *The Curate's Queries, and, the Malig[n]ant or Courtier's Answer Thereto* (n.p., [1679?]), p. 8.

to improvise their own worship. One Sunday they were interrupted by 'enemies with their dreadful blasphemies', who alleged that 'we had a minister preaching to us when there was no such thing'.[48] Collace's circle was one of many lay forums for worship in Restoration Presbyterianism. In most cases, it is difficult to document the activities of these lay prayer societies. But they were vital in fostering evangelical spirituality and keeping dissenters fixed in their opposition to episcopacy. Writing in 1717, the Presbyterian minister James Hogg recalled his 'little Share in Societies of more aged, judicious and established Christians' during the Restoration period. There he joined in prayers, and 'heard weighty and difficult Questions and Cases proposed'. Emelia Geddie, the exceptionally godly daughter of the steward clerk of Fife, thrived in these meetings. Though she was only a teenager, Geddie made 'clear and pointed Answers' to the queries under discussion, 'so close to the respective Purposes, and so well instructed from the Word, as if she had been an aged and experienced Divine'.[49]

Prayer societies were still more important after the battle of Bothwell Bridge, when few ministers preached in the fields. In 1680 or 1681, the lay activist Walter Smith compiled rules for the conduct of 'private Christian meetings, for prayer and conference to mutual edification'. Partly because of the dangers of assembling, Smith envisaged that prayer societies should contain no more than 12 members. Only individuals who made 'Conscience of secret Prayer' and were of 'an exemplary and blameless Conversation' were to be invited to join. Meetings were to last for at least four hours. Members were to begin by singing a verse or more of a psalm, before praying in turn and posing edifying questions for discussion. Though Smith warned that the societies were not to engage with complex theology, difficult passages of scripture, or controversial politics, there was clearly a risk of divisive debate.[50]

At the end of 1681, many of the societies that Smith had helped to create formed a general correspondence, known as the United Societies. The network's members adhered to the teachings and declarations of Richard Cameron and Donald Cargill, field preachers who had renounced their allegiance to Charles II and suffered violent deaths for their beliefs.[51] Only a small minority of dissenters associated themselves with the Societies, and mainstream nonconformists condemned the group's attitudes to monarchy and their separation from Presbyterians holding differing views.[52] Yet in most respects, the Societies were doctrinally conservative,

---

[48]   Collace, 'Some Short Remembrances', p. 114.

[49]   'The Publisher to the Reader', *Some Choice Sentences and Practices of Emilia Geddie, Daughter to John Geddie of Hilton in Falkland, in the Sheriffdom of Fife, from her Infancy, to her Death on the 2d of Feb. 1681. in the Sixteenth Year of her Age* (Edinburgh, 1717), p. 7.

[50]   Patrick Walker, *Biographia Presbyteriana* (2 vols, Edinburgh, 1827), vol. 2, first part, pp. 73–83.

[51]   For a detailed account, see Jardine, 'United Societies'.

[52]   Raffe, *Culture of Controversy*, ch. 3.

upholding the Westminster confession of faith, and practising the affective piety typical of Presbyterians. Indeed, by creating a structure of correspondence with regular general meetings, the Societies, like Walter Smith, perhaps intended to discipline the potentially radical force of lay spirituality, which threatened to result in increased claims for the religious authority of women.

For the founders of the Societies, the dangers of unruly female piety had been underlined by the Gibbites, a small society from the town of Bo'ness. Named after John Gibb, a sailor, the group had at its largest 30 or 40 members, most of whom were women.[53] In early 1681, they began to meet regularly to pray and sing psalms relevant to the parlous state of Presbyterianism,[54] earning the nickname 'Sweet Singers of Israel'. Gibb apparently made a trip to Lanarkshire and Renfrewshire to recruit followers, but other Presbyterians rebuked him for acting like a minister.[55] Certainly the group went beyond the bounds of a normal prayer society in its devotions; according to one account, female members were allowed to preach.[56] Moreover, some female Gibbites removed themselves from the authority of their husbands, fathers and masters, particularly when the group withdrew from Bo'ness to what one writer called 'Desert-places', to fast and lament over the country's sins.[57] The Privy Council, which imprisoned many of the Gibbites, heard evidence that one member, Margaret Stewart, had separated from her husband, the skipper John Ritchie, apparently because he paid tribute to the king for his ship.[58]

During their incarceration, several Gibbites regretted their activities with the group.[59] The friends of Janet Elphinstone, widow of an Edinburgh merchant, petitioned for her release from Edinburgh's correction house, in the hope that they could 'reclaime her' from the group's 'deluded principles'.[60] Meanwhile, Gibb and three other men issued a paper renouncing all religious authority, and claiming to be guided by the holy spirit on matters of duty 'from day to day'.[61] After their release from prison, the four men joined with two women to fast and burn the Bible. This action, a product of the Gibbites' radically individualistic spirituality, caused the group to disintegrate further.[62] Gibb and a few remaining followers

[53]   Walker, *Biographia Presbyteriana*, vol. 2, first part, p. 15; *RPC*, 3rd ser., vol. 7, p. 704; John Callow, 'Gibb, John (d.1720?)', *Oxford Dictionary of National Biography*.

[54]   Walker specified Psalms 74, 79, 80, 83 and 137: *Biographia Presbyteriana*, vol. 2, first part, p. 16.

[55]   Wodrow, *History*, vol. 3, p. 349.

[56]   *RPC*, 3rd ser., vol. 7, p. 704.

[57]   Walker, *Biographia Presbyteriana*, vol. 2, first part, pp. 16–17.

[58]   *RPC*, 3rd ser., vol. 7, pp. 123, 704–5; Robert Law, *Memorialls; Or, the Memorable Things that Fell Out within this Island of Brittain from 1638 to 1684*, ed. Charles Kirkpatrick Sharpe (Edinburgh, 1818), p. 197.

[59]   For example, *RPC*, 3rd ser., vol. 7, p. 145.

[60]   Ibid., vol. 7, p. 131.

[61]   Wodrow, *History*, vol. 3, pp. 350–53, quotation at p. 350.

[62]   Walker, *Biographia Presbyteriana*, vol. 2, first part, p. 21.

were still at large in March 1683, but they were again imprisoned.[63] In jail, their blasphemies continued to alienate other religious prisoners, further discrediting their cause at a time when Presbyterian dissent as a whole was a waning force.[64] In May 1684, the Privy Council arranged for Gibb and two other men to be transported to the American plantations.[65] Though only small numbers ever joined the Gibbites, later Presbyterians and their enemies remembered the group's unorthodox behaviour and attitudes, which served as a warning against unbridled emotional piety.[66] But as we shall see, lay activists, among them women claiming authority on the basis of their spiritual lives, remained a potentially destabilizing force within Presbyterianism.

II

The re-establishment of Presbyterian government in 1690 changed the place of lay activism in Scottish religious life. In southern and central parts of the country, where there was widespread support for the re-established Church, men who had refused to serve on kirk sessions in the Restoration period were now appointed as elders. The general assembly met for the first time since the 1650s, giving prominent men – landowners, leading merchants and professionals, especially lawyers – a say in the government of the Church. But while male control of Presbyterianism was more secure after 1690 than before, affective piety continued to give many women, and men of lower social standing, a sense of their own spiritual authority among the nation's godly. The domestic servant Elizabeth West enjoyed her formative religious experiences in the 1690s, learning to pray freely and examine her life for signs of divine favour. She gained the confidence to reprove impious fellow servants, and to form views on religious and political questions.[67]

For West and people like her, the re-established Church was far from perfect.[68] The National Covenant (1638) and the Solemn League and Covenant (1643) had an uncertain place in post-revolution Presbyterianism. Though most of the re-established Church's ministers and lay members saw these documents as oaths binding Scotland to Presbyterian principles in perpetuity, the acts of parliament settling Presbyterian government did not mention the Covenants. Instead of recognizing the restored polity's divine right, indeed, parliament justified the

---

[63]   NRS, GD406/1/3165, marquis of Queensberry to the earl of Arran, 22 March 1683.

[64]   Walker, *Biographia Presbyteriana*, vol. 2, first part, pp. 22–3; Helen Alexander, 'Passages in the Life of Helen Alexander', in Mullan (ed.), *Women's Life Writing*, p. 197.

[65]   *RPC*, 3rd ser., vol. 8, pp. 516, 709–10.

[66]   Wodrow, *History*, vol. 3, pp. 348–9; George Mackenzie, *A Vindication of the Government in Scotland during the Reign of King Charles II* (London, 1691), pp. 57–66.

[67]   Elizabeth West, *Memoirs, Or, Spiritual Exercises of Elizabeth Wast* (Edinburgh, 1724).

[68]   For a fuller discussion, see Raffe, *Culture of Controversy*, chs 3, 7.

Church settlement with reference to the popularity of Presbyterianism.[69] Fearing that Episcopalian and Anglican critics might persuade the crown to overturn the settlement, Presbyterian ministers were reluctant to express their more radical principles. To the disappointment of devout lay people, the Church failed to call for a national renewal of the Covenants and was cautious about condemning the errors of episcopacy and the policies of the Restoration regime. The crown's techniques of management prevented the general assembly from asserting its autonomous authority in religious affairs.[70] Parliament imposed the oath of allegiance on ministers; in 1712 they were also required to swear the English oath of abjuration, seen by many Presbyterians as incompatible with their principles. The Church's treatment of dissidents among its clergy alarmed some lay people. Others complained that ministers were insufficiently evangelical in their preaching, and that the temperature of Presbyterian spirituality had cooled since the revolution.

Drawing courage from their sense of a personal relationship with God, pious women were sometimes prepared to criticize their ministers or take a stand for Presbyterian principles. In 1707, Robert Wodrow read from his pulpit a sentence of the commission of the general assembly against John Macmillan, a minister deposed by the Church for criticizing its faults. Taking offence, Margaret King, one of Wodrow's parishioners, walked out of church. Referring to the scriptural text Song of Songs 1:6, she later told Wodrow that the Church's actions against Macmillan were a betrayal of the trust placed in ministers. Wodrow 'endeavoured to convince her, that the plain meaning of the place [i.e., verse] rather related to herself, as looking to the public management of Ministers, and not to her oun soul's state'.[71] Elsewhere other dissatisfied lay women spoke their minds. Elizabeth Cairns, a godly young woman in the Perthshire parish of Blackford, found the sermons of her minister unprofitable. She consulted some of the 'most experienced' Christians in the congregation, who agreed that piety in the parish was waning but were unprepared to address the problem. Cairns then confronted the minister, who dismissed her concerns, telling her that the 'World is not given to your ruling'. Rebuffed, Cairns left the parish to look for spiritual sustenance in Stirling.[72] Of course, not all female critics of the established Church were similarly knowledgeable. In November 1707, Thomas Boston, minister of Ettrick in Selkirkshire, interrogated a Presbyterian woman who refused to attend the parish church. Finding her ignorant of fundamental doctrines, Boston 'dealt with her as with a petted bairn'.[73]

[69] *RPS*, 1689/3/108, 1690/4/43.

[70] Alasdair Raffe, 'Presbyterianism, Secularization, and Scottish Politics after the Revolution of 1688–1690', *The Historical Journal*, 53/2 (2010): pp. 317–37.

[71] Robert Wodrow, *Analecta: Or, Materials for a History of Remarkable Providences* (4 vols, Maitland Club, 1842–43), vol. 1, p. 152.

[72] Elizabeth Cairns, *Memoirs of the Life of Elizabeth Cairns* (Glasgow, [1762?]), pp. 82–6.

[73] Thomas Boston, *Memoirs of the Life, Time, and Writings of the Reverend and Learned Thomas Boston*, ed. George H. Morrison (Edinburgh, 1899), p. 218.

Lay prayer societies continued to provide a focus for piety and a voice of dissent within Presbyterianism. Some societies emerged in parallel to the parochial structure, often with the blessing of ministers. One writer, probably a minister, called for 'severall societys for prayer' to be 'erected thro diverse quarters' of each parish.[74] Societies of this sort were formed in Bo'ness from the 1690s.[75] Other prayer groups were made up of scrupulous lay people reluctant to conform to a flawed establishment. These societies stood aloof from the Church and its ministers, proving that even in the southern heartlands of Presbyterianism, parish communities had been fragmented by decades of religious controversy. Some members of the United Societies joined the re-established Kirk after the revolution. But others maintained an autonomous network of societies, separating themselves strictly from all uncovenanted institutions in Church and state.[76] The Hebronites, another network of Presbyterian prayer societies, placed little faith in the mainstream ministry, instead attending services conducted by the itinerant preacher John Hepburn, from whom the group took its name. In 1713, one member published a set of rules for their gatherings. Like Walter Smith's societies, the Hebronites were to meet for at least four hours, for prayer, scriptural readings and religious discussions. Members were to eschew controversy and discussions that infringed on the work of church courts.[77] As in the period before the revolution, members of prayer societies were supposed to know their place in social and religious hierarchies. Yet this form of lay activism was again the basis for insubordinate claims of female religious authority.

Small and little-known, though unusually well-documented, the Coat-Muir Folk were a lay prayer society in which women's spiritual experiences contributed to a radical critique of the Presbyterian establishment. The group, which was probably an offshoot from the United Societies, started meeting for prayer and discussion at Coat-Muir, in the Linlithgowshire parish of Dalmeny, in 1690.[78] Investigating the Folk's leaders in 1696, the Privy Council recorded information about the group's membership. On 4 June, the Lord Advocate told the council that a committee had examined two 'Coatmuir Lads', finding them 'very Insolent and extravogant against the Government of Church and state'. The 'Lads' in question (the word suggests that they were young) were the brothers Andrew and John Harley. After

---

[74] National Library of Scotland, Edinburgh (NLS), Wod. Fol. LI, 'Reasons against forming societies for the reformation of manners', c. 1702, fol. 23r.

[75] NLS, MS. 1,668, Memoirs of John Brand, minister of Bo'ness, fol. 28.

[76] [Michael Shields], *Faithful Contendings Displayed: Being an Historical Relation of the State and Actings of the Suffering Remnant of the Church of Scotland*, ed. John Howie (Glasgow, 1780), pp. 459–80.

[77] [Gavin Mitchell], *Humble Pleadings for the Good Old-Way, Or a Plain Representation* ([Edinburgh?], 1713), appendix, pp. 13–16.

[78] *The Ravished Maid in the Wilderness, Or, A True Account of the Raise, Causes and Continuunce of the Deference between a Suffering Party of Presbyterians, Commonly Called Cotmure Folk, ond these that Follows Mr John Mackmillan, Commonly called Mountain Men* (n.p., 1708), pp. [i], 6. For the identification of Coat-Muir, see Angus Macdonald, *The Place-Names of West Lothian* (Edinburgh, 1941), p. 9.

their interrogation, as they were led back to the prison in the Canongate tolbooth, three women – Margaret Harley (the sister of Andrew and John) and the sisters Grisell and Mary Spritt – shouted in the street, denouncing the councillors as 'Bloody persecuters and persecuting Rascalls'.[79] Grisell Spritt reportedly had a spouse living in Ireland in 1696, but she and her sister probably entered irregular marriages with the Harley brothers.[80] The five Harleys and Spritts seem to have formed the core of the Coat-Muir Folk, but there were other members. Margaret Park of Bailernock was prominent in the group's early meetings.[81] Around 1698, a pious female friend of Elizabeth West announced that she would abandon the Church of Scotland and join the Coat-Muir Folk, whom she described as '*two or three singular Ones*' who had '*kept their Garments clean from all the Pollutions of the Times*'. West seems to have visited the Harleys, who were again in the Canongate tolbooth, but regretted spending a sabbath worshipping with them.[82]

Women were particularly influential among the Coat-Muir Folk. Female members seem to have provided the spiritual driving force at the earliest meetings, when the group drew up a testimony against Scotland's sins during the Restoration period and the unsatisfactory aspects of the revolution Church settlement. In their own account of events, revealingly titled *The Ravished Maid in the Wilderness* (1708), the Folk attributed their critique of religious politics to a period of spiritual anguish, experienced especially by the Spritts.[83] The Harleys described the Spritts as their 'Blessed Wifes', and allowed them considerable authority on the basis of their religious experiences.[84] Women played other significant roles in the life of the group. Grisell Spritt was sent alongside John Harley as an envoy to negotiate with the United Societies.[85] In May 1696, the general meeting of the Societies received a 'Long & Large Letter' from Margaret Park attacking the Societies for their refusal to cooperate with the Coat-Muir Folk. The letter was written in the hand of one of the Harley brothers, who acted as Park's 'clerk', but the Folk evidently considered her a suitable representative.[86]

The Coat-Muir Folk attempted to publicize their testimony against the errors of Scottish ecclesiastical politics. They submitted the document to Hugh Kennedy, moderator of the Kirk's general assembly of 1690. Like other radical Presbyterian petitions, it was not read in the assembly, but it was considered by a private gathering of ministers, and read out on the streets of Edinburgh.[87] Members of the

[79] NRS, PC1/50, Privy Council Acta, 1694–96, pp. 541, 556–7.
[80] Ibid., pp. 556–7; Wodrow, *Analecta*, vol. 1, p. 272; Walker, *Biographia Presbyteriana*, vol. 1, p. 215.
[81] *Ravished Maid*, p. 5.
[82] West, *Memoirs*, pp. 96–7.
[83] *Ravished Maid*, pp. 5–8, 39–51.
[84] Ibid., p. 33.
[85] Ibid., pp. 24–5.
[86] NRS, CH3/269/1, Conclusions of the United Societies' General Meeting, 1681–1724, p. 26.
[87] *Ravished Maid*, pp. [ii], 26; [Shields], *Faithful Contendings Displayed*, pp. 445–59.

Folk apparently protested when a Presbyterian minister was settled in Dalmeny in September 1691. They also took their testimony to Bo'ness, reading it out in the doorway of a shop belonging to William McVey, a member of the United Societies. McVey and passers-by expressed their approval of the document's contents, but McVey refused to present it to the Societies' general meeting.[88] The Folk's testimony voiced many of the same sentiments as the Societies' Sanquhar declaration of 1692,[89] but the Societies were suspicious. One of their objections was to the manner in which the Coat-Muir testimony was produced. When it became known that the Coat-Muir worshippers had begun (in their own words) 'to be something exercised with a publick Testimony', the Societies sent a series of male observers to see what was 'among' the Coat-Muir Folk. The latter thought that they were acted upon by the spirit of God; the Societies' men disagreed. Rather than joining in prayer, the Folk complained, the visitors 'mocked' their claims of spiritual experience, and behaved like the 'prophane Graceless Rable of Malignant Neighbours' who surrounded the Coat-Muir.[90] Indeed, the Societies castigated the Folk's political and religious statements as 'doating delusions'.[91] The Societies' men would probably have concurred with the Privy Councillors, who thought that the Coat-Muir prisoners were 'persons under distemper of mynd'.[92]

The Societies accused the Folk of falling into '*Gibs* errors'.[93] This was a criticism of the group's heightened emotional state and the preoccupations that resulted from it. But the Societies were presumably also referring to the place of women in the Folk. The Harleys defended the behaviour of their 'Wifes', accusing the Societies of 'great weakeness' for taking offence at the Spritts' actions. The role of the Coat-Muir women did not go beyond the limits ordinarily imposed on their activities, the Harleys argued. 'Weomen being debarred from acting so publickly in favours of a principal [*sic*] as men, their proceedings cannot be a sufficient cause of Offence when they go no furder nor what is allowed in Scripture'.[94] Nevertheless, the Presbyterian biographer Patrick Walker, who had been a member of the Societies in the 1680s, also thought that the affective, female-led worship of the Coat-Muir Folk resulted in errors. Indeed, Walker concluded that the Harleys' associates were 'overrun and overdriven with enthusiastick quakerish Notions, acted and led by *John Gib*'s Spirit'.[95]

---

[88] *Ravished Maid*, pp. 25–6.
[89] [James Renwick, Alexander Shields et al.], *An Informatory Vindication of a Poor, Wasted, Misrepresented Remnant of the Suffering* ([Edinburgh?], 1707), sigs. ¶r.–[¶¶¶3]v.
[90] *Ravished Maid*, pp. 6, 18, 13, 10.
[91] [Renwick, Shields et al.], *Informatory Vindication*, sig. [¶3]v.; *Ravished Maid*, pp. 29–31.
[92] NRS, PC1/50, Privy Council Acta, p. 541.
[93] *Ravished Maid*, p. 14.
[94] Ibid., pp. 33–4.
[95] Walker, *Biographia Presbyteriana*, vol. 1, p. 212.

III

In the early decades of the eighteenth century, then, prayer societies provided a space in which lay people could criticize the established Church. They were venues for the practice of affective piety, and fissures in the otherwise patriarchal structure of Scottish Presbyterianism, helping women to assert their views. With a few exceptions, it is hard to reconstruct the activities of these societies. Nevertheless, the twin forces of lay activism and female authority need to be restored to our understanding of Scottish Presbyterianism. This is especially true of the decades after 1707, whose Presbyterians have been studied more for their intellectual controversies than for their social dynamics.[96] Yet it was in these years that the fragmentation of Scottish Presbyterianism, begun by the separatist prayer societies of the 1680s and 1690s, and driven by lay dissent, became an irreversible trend. It is in the formation of the Secession Church in the 1730s, a movement that has been largely neglected by modern historians,[97] that the outcome of decades of lay activism can be found.

The Secession Church was the product of the separation from the Church of Scotland, in 1733, of four ministers led by Ebenezer Erskine. Their secession was the result of arguments about the exercise of church patronage and the freedom of clergy to express their disagreement with acts of the church courts. But the four ministers, who started to meet together as the 'Associate Presbytery' in December 1733, had long been critical of the Church of Scotland's political stance and theological drift. In many ways, the Secession was a populist movement, seeking among other things to involve in the selection of parish ministers all heads of households (a franchise that was predominantly, though perhaps not exclusively, male).[98] But the Secession's nineteenth- and early twentieth-century historians focused on its clerical leaders, paying too little attention to its social context.[99] The four ministers' views chimed with those of thousands of lay Presbyterians across

---

[96] Especially David C. Lachman, *The Marrow Controversy, 1718–1723: An Historical and Theological Analysis* (Edinburgh, 1988); Anne Skoczylas, *Mr Simson's Knotty Case: Divinity, Politics, and Due Process in Early Eighteenth-Century Scotland* (Montreal, 2001).

[97] But see Andrew T.N. Muirhead, 'A Secession Congregation in its Community: The Stirling Congregation of the Rev. Ebenezer Erskine, 1731–1754', *Records of the Scottish Church History Society*, 22/3 (1986): pp. 211–33; Laurence A.B. Whitley, *A Great Grievance: Ecclesiastical Lay Patronage in Scotland until 1750* (Eugene, OR, 2013), ch. 11. There is an illuminating discussion in W.R. Ward, *The Protestant Evangelical Awakening* (Cambridge, 1992), pp. 329–33. John M'Kerrow, *History of the Secession Church*, rev. edn (Glasgow, 1841) is the best of the older studies.

[98] Richard Sher and Alexander Murdoch, 'Patronage and Party in the Church of Scotland, 1750–1800', in Norman Macdougall (ed.), *Church, Politics and Society: Scotland, 1408–1929* (Edinburgh, 1983), pp. 197–220.

[99] For example, A.R. MacEwen, *The Erskines* (Edinburgh, 1900); J.H. Leckie, *Secession Memories: The United Presbyterian Contribution to the Scottish Church* (Edinburgh, 1926).

southern and central Scotland, who pored over the group's doctrinal statements[100] and sought to become affiliated to the Associate Presbytery. It responded favourably to numerous requests from lay petitioners, which asked for the ministers to preach sermons and hold fast days.[101]

In some cases, entire parishes joined the Secession, agreeing unanimously or by a vote of the kirk session to abandon the established Church.[102] It is difficult to determine how much influence women had over these decisions; the parishioners of Muckart, Perthshire, presented the Associate Presbytery with a petition of support signed by one hundred heads of families, most of them presumably men.[103] The Presbytery's failure to preserve such petitions, or to transcribe their contents and the names of their signatories, is frustrating. But the pre-eminent role of lay prayer societies in the new Church's emergence might lead us to believe that women gave their opinions for and against leaving the Kirk. The debates in lay societies sometimes went beyond the decorous limits expected by the clergy. In April 1737, the Presbytery heard that a society, meeting in Mrs Horner's house in Edinburgh, had taken part in negotiations 'more becoming a Judicatory than Societies for Prayer and Conference'. Four months later, the Presbytery warned the society to 'beware of going out of their sphere, by acting as if they were a Judicatory'.[104]

The lay people who joined the Secession Church did so in pursuit of godly worship, faithful ministers and traditional Presbyterian discipline. The Associate Presbytery soon began to appoint new ministers, and set up kirk sessions and presbyteries. Seeking normal congregational institutions, the prayer societies of Leslie and Markinch in Fife wrote that their lack of elders was not 'agreeabel to Church Diseplen' and 'good order'.[105] In Glasgow, a Secession congregation was formally inaugurated after visits by Ebenezer Erskine in April 1739 and his fellow minister William Wilson in the following February. Yet it is clear that the decision to set up a congregation had been taken at previous meetings of the local lay prayer societies.[106] The new structures of the Secession Church were thus a product of informal lay activism, in which women might well have played a part.

Like the societies of the Restoration period and the post-revolution years, the prayer groups that joined the Secession had a somewhat irregular, shadowy existence. They were bodies on the fringes of the Presbyterian establishment, with the potential to oppose it. But the male detractors of these societies often exaggerated their eccentricity. Robert Wodrow claimed that the Coat-Muir Folk

---

[100]   Especially *A Testimony to the Doctrine, Worship, Government and Discipline of the Church of Scotland* (Edinburgh, 1734).

[101]   NRS, CH3/27/1, Associate Presbytery Minutes, 1733–40.

[102]   Ibid., for example, pp. 246–8, 292, 298–9.

[103]   Ibid., p. 134.

[104]   Ibid., pp. 281, 290.

[105]   NRS, CH3/319/3, Leslie Secession Congregation Minutes, 1739–58, p. 3.

[106]   NRS, CH3/469/1, Glasgow Greyfriars (Shuttle Street) Kirk Session Minutes, 1739–55, pp. 1, 3.

'pretend to great revelations, and that one of the Spritts was to bring forth a son who was to deliver the world, and this Church in particular'.[107] Wodrow's remark recalled the birth of Christ, but also alluded to Revelation 12:5, describing a woman who 'brought forth a man child, who was to rule all nations with a rod of iron'. There is no other evidence that the Folk made claims on the basis of this text. And as we have seen, the Folk were critics of the established Church, rather than prophets of the world's end. Not even the most extreme of Scotland's female Presbyterian activists experienced eschatological visions in the manner of the 1650s English radical Joan Robins, her early nineteenth-century compatriot Joanna Southcott, or Elspeth Buchan, who founded a radical sect in south-west Scotland in the 1780s.[108] Nor were the Presbyterian women of our period inclined towards the mystical heterodoxy of their English contemporary Jane Lead.[109] Instead their activism was in the cause of a purified Presbyterianism, more true to Scotland's Covenanting heritage. It was a campaign in which women's voices could sometimes be heard over those of men.

---

[107] Wodrow, *Analecta*, vol. 1, pp. 272–3.

[108] Patricia Crawford, *Women and Religion in England, 1500–1720* (London, 1993), p. 136; Ariel Hessayon, 'Robins, John (fl.1641–1652)', *Oxford Dictionary of National Biography*; Clarke Garrett, *Respectable Folly: Millenarians and the French Revolution in France and England* (Baltimore, MD, 1975), pp. 214–16, 221; Jill Söderström, 'Buchan, Elspeth (c. 1738–1791)', *Oxford Dictionary of National Biography*.

[109] Sarah Apetrei, *Women, Feminism and Religion in Early Enlightenment England* (Cambridge, 2010), pp. 187–207.

Chapter 5
'When God shall Restore them to their Kingdoms': Nuns, Exiled Stuarts and English Catholic Identity, 1688–1745[1]

Claire Walker

In May 1688, Prioress Mary Wigmore of the English Carmelite cloister in Antwerp wrote to Queen Mary Beatrice who was in the final stages of pregnancy:

> The Divine Spirit whose fruites and Gifts adornes soe much your Royall Persone, I beseech to live [for]ever and animate the hart and soule of your Sacred Majesty, whose example and Illustrious vertues are sufficient to reduce to the waie of truth & Sanctity the whole Nation; The petitions of this Community of your majesties humble faithfull subjects are incessantly presented to the Throne of mercy beseeching the preservation of Both your Royall persons with the Benediction of the soe much wished & prayed for gift of heaven a Prince to Inherit your Crownes and vertues, to which end Madame your singular devotion to the great zelatrice of the glory of God & Salvation of soules our seraphique Mother St Teresa, will undoubtedly contribute much, whose Relique a peece of her flesh I presume to present, beseeching your Majesty to weare it in your labour, it working daylie in effect miracles giving happy deliveries & preservation of the mother & child in like cases.[2]

Mary Wigmore's letter was just one of several conveying similar good wishes for a safe delivery from abbesses and prioresses in Italy, France and the southern Netherlands. They were followed by epistles of congratulation upon the arrival of the much-awaited prince of Wales on 10 June.[3] While this correspondence can be read as female support for a woman facing confinement and its corresponding

---

[1]   I would like to thank librarians in the Barr Smith Library at the University of Adelaide and at the National Library of Australia for making accessible the microfilm of the Stuart Papers, Royal Archives, Windsor. The Stuart Papers are cited by the permission of Her Majesty Queen Elizabeth II. I likewise extend my gratitude to Westminster Diocesan Archives and St Mary's Abbey, Oulton, for permitting access to their archives.

[2]   British Library, London (BL), Add. MS 28,225, fol. 276, Letters of Royal and Other Persons to Mary, Queen of James II, 1685–88: Mary Wigmore, Carmelite at Antwerp to Mary Beatrice, 23 May 1688.

[3]   BL, Add. MS 28,225, fols 272–3, 274–5, 285–6, 293, 301–2, 306–7, 315–16.

dangers, as attested by the relic enclosed, the Carmelite prioress's letter makes it clear that this was no ordinary birth. She and her nuns hoped for a male heir to 'Inherit' his parents' 'Crownes and vertues', which, were 'sufficient to reduce to the waie of truth & Sanctity the whole Nation'. Read as a political statement, the Carmelites' prayers for the queen might be said to represent the hopes of many English Catholics for the restitution of their religion in England. In anticipating the delivery of a Catholic prince of Wales they, like James II's religious and political opponents, assumed that the king's efforts to return England to the Catholic fold would be assured. Of course, events later that year ensured this did not happen. But the birth of James Francis Edward in June and the arrival in England of the prince of Orange in November were pivotal for the identity of one particular Catholic group, the English religious houses for women in France, the Low Countries and Portugal.

This chapter is about these cloisters' relationship with the exiled Stuarts, principally James II, Mary of Modena and their son. It looks at the political ambitions of the nuns and the ways their interactions with the royal family shaped convent life and influenced pastoral strategies. The religious women abroad remained an integral part of the English Catholic community, with the cloisters maintaining schools and guesthouses and providing centres of liturgical worship for compatriots who could not access this degree of elaborate and sustained devotion at home. However, by 1688 they had put down firm roots in their continental abodes and their own sense of exile and suffering for the faith encouraged and informed their adherence to the Jacobite cause.

The allegiance of English Catholics to their rulers after 1688 continues to be debated. John Bossy's thesis that in the late seventeenth century Catholicism evolved into a moderate form of English nonconformity more or less precluded any discussion of Jacobitism and allowed for only limited influence from European Catholicism.[4] J.C.H. Aveling suggested that English Catholic loyalty to the Stuarts was in decline by 1715 and was virtually irrelevant by 1745.[5] Similarly Michael Mullett argued for the gradual 'de-politicisation of the English Catholic community' in the aftermath of 1688, finding active Jacobitism evident principally in the northern gentry while the majority of English Catholics remained politically neutral. Mullett also acknowledged the existence of 'an English Catholicism with a European orientation', noting the devotional influence of the exiled religious communities on their expatriate compatriots.[6] Gabriel Glickman's recent analysis

---

[4]   John Bossy, *The English Catholic Community 1570–1850* (London, 1975), pp. 282–92. A later discussion also suggests little Jacobite influence and focuses instead on Jansenism. See John Bossy, 'English Catholics after 1688', in Ole Peter Grell, Jonathan I. Israel and Nicholas Tyacke (eds), *From Persecution to Toleration: The Glorious Revolution and Religion in England* (Oxford, 1991), pp. 369–87.

[5]   J.C.H. Aveling, *The Handle and the Axe: The Catholic Recusants in England from Reformation to Emancipation* (London, 1976), pp. 253–5.

[6]   Michael Mullett, *Catholics in Britain and Ireland, 1558–1829* (Basingstoke, 1998), pp. 81–97, 82, 88.

of the recusant gentry and aristocracy between 1688 and 1745 has placed Jacobitism firmly at the centre of Catholic identity. Focusing on cultural and political activities, in particular the correspondence, literary output and religious treatises of leading Catholics, Glickman has argued convincingly for close links between English recusants, at home and in exile, and the international community.[7] As Glickman has demonstrated, among the recusant aristocracy and gentry, allegiance to the English state and to Rome was a complex and often contested issue. This multilateralism was reflected in the exiled English cloisters for women where the nuns' political identity and allegiance had been forged by their experience of exile from the foundation of their cloisters, and particularly from the 1640s.

I. From Royalists to Jacobites

English religious houses for women were established in the southern Netherlands and in France from 1598 when a Benedictine abbey for Englishwomen was founded in Brussels. There was already a community of English Bridgettines resident in Portugal which had survived, albeit precariously, the dissolution of Syon Abbey at Isleworth to continue their monastic life abroad.[8] Other Englishwomen had entered continental cloisters, like the Flemish Augustinian monastery of St Ursula's in Louvain. Encouraged by the support given to the Benedictines in Brussels by the Spanish crown, expatriate English recusants, and the local communities where they settled, during the following century the Franciscans, Augustinians, Carmelites, Sepulchrines and Dominicans founded female convents. Thus, by the end of the seventeenth century, 22 contemplative English houses existed abroad. Of these, half had been founded before the English Civil War, and four established after the Restoration.

The foundation of the exiled religious houses for women and their recruitment of nuns largely reflected the optimism or pessimism of England's Catholic minority.[9] It was dependent on various other factors too, like the financial strength of Catholic families and the Civil War. However, established and populated by the daughters of the gentry, the convents' formation and economic viability were often a litmus test of Catholic fortunes in England. The nuns' understanding of their vocation was similarly linked to the spiritual and political objectives of their families and friends across the channel. Constrained by their contemplative vocation and strict monastic enclosure to a life behind convent walls, the nuns could

[7]   Gabriel Glickman, *The English Catholic Community, 1688–1745: Politics, Culture and Ideology* (Woodbridge, 2009).

[8]   Claire Walker, 'Continuity and Isolation: The Bridgettines of Syon in the Sixteenth and Seventeenth Centuries', in E.A. Jones and Alexandra Walsham (eds), *Syon Abbey and its Books: Reading, Writing and Religion, c. 1400–1700* (Woodbridge, 2010), pp. 155–76, esp. pp. 157–9.

[9]   Claire Walker, *Gender and Politics in Early Modern Europe: English Convents in France and the Low Countries* (Basingstoke, 2003), ch. 1.

not participate actively in the English mission. Instead they lived as expatriate English Catholics who contributed to the mission via prayer, the preservation of monasticism for women, the education of young girls, writing spiritual works, providing accommodation and as centres of English liturgical devotion abroad for travelling or exiled compatriots.

The cloisters were therefore highly political establishments from the outset. Their avowed aim was to resettle in their homeland, once Catholicism was at least tolerated, or preferably reinstated, there. In the heady early decades of the seventeenth century, this seemed possible. It is perhaps no coincidence that the Benedictine abbey in Brussels was founded in Queen Elizabeth's final years as expectations that her heir, the son of Mary, Queen of Scots would permit Catholic toleration. In the early 1620s amid speculation surrounding the Spanish match for Prince Charles, the Bridgettine nuns in Lisbon petitioned the Infanta Maria, addressing her as the princess of Wales, and asking for consideration that they might be the first of the exiled cloisters to receive her favour.[10] As the century progressed and their hopes for Catholic toleration ebbed and flowed, they increasingly turned to the Stuarts who they saw as representing the most likely means by which their goal of returning to English soil would be achieved.

The nuns' direct connections with the royal family were limited before the Civil War. However, they were ardent royalists and decried the execution of Charles I, which the Benedictine abbess of the English abbey at Pontoise, described as 'that horrible sacrilegious murther'.[11] Ironically it was the act of regicide and the exile of Henrietta Maria and her children which were instrumental in bringing together the expatriate religious women and the Stuarts. In addition to social visits during which various members of the English royal family were entertained at convent parlour grates or within monastic enclosures, the nuns were able to offer practical assistance via access to communications networks and financial resources. I have written previously about the assistance rendered to the royalists in the 1650s by Abbess Mary Knatchbull of Ghent.[12] The hospitality the abbess afforded Charles and his supporters, combined with the royalists' obvious reliance upon her mail network, which channelled not only their correspondence but also newsletters and other intelligence, did much to cement a relationship between the convents and the Stuarts. Disappointed after the Restoration that Charles II did so little to bring about their desired return to English soil, the nuns nevertheless remained loyal

---

[10] 'The Petition to her Royal Highness the Princess of Wales whom God Preserve', in Christopher de Hamel, *Syon Abbey: The Library of the Bridgettine Nuns and their Peregrinations after the Reformation* (Otley, 1991), pp. 23–6.

[11] M.J. Rumsey (ed.), 'Abbess Neville's Annals of Five Communities of English Benedictine Nuns in Flanders, 1598–1687', in *Miscellanea V*, Catholic Record Society (hereafter cited as CRS), 6 (London, 1909), p. 31.

[12] Claire Walker, 'Prayer, Patronage and Political Conspiracy: English Nuns and the Restoration', *The Historical Journal*, 43/1 (2000): pp. 1–23; Claire Walker, 'Crumbs of News: Early Modern English Nuns and Royalist Intelligence Networks', *Journal of Medieval and Early Modern Studies*, 42/3 (2012): pp. 635–55.

to the man they had befriended. Moreover, they were hopeful that his heir might achieve what he had failed to do.

Although James did not openly admit his conversion to Catholicism until 1676, rumours abounded for several years about his allegiance to the Church of England. His first wife, Anne Hyde, converted in 1670. She was acknowledged as a generous benefactor by the Ghent Benedictines, who annually commemorated the anniversary of her 1671 death with a requiem mass.[13] James's second duchess, Mary Beatrice d'Este of Modena, was a devout Catholic who had wanted to become a nun. She was clearly nervous about life in England. In October 1673, en route to her new home and husband, she gave alms to the English cloister of Conceptionist sisters in Paris and asked them to pray 'for her prosperity in our Nation she having some apprehentions by Reason they wer of an other Religion'.[14] This simple act of patronage established a relationship between the new duchess of York and the exiled cloisters which was to last until her death in 1718.[15]

As king, James had little time to fulfil the promises he had made to the English nuns. In 1686 he had assured Mary Knatchbull that he would make good his brother's broken promises, declaring his intention 'to have your cloister, our Darling monastery, the first in my kingdom'.[16] But even he balked at installing nuns on English soil. So it was the Benedictines from Ypres who made the first move towards their homeland, but they went to Ireland where they founded what James termed 'Our chief and first Royal Monastery of Gratia Dei', stopping in London en route where they were presented to the queen at Whitehall, apparently dressed in their religious habits. The venture floundered in the aftermath of November 1688, and the Ypres sisters returned to their former monastery in 1690.[17] In 1737 the Ypres abbess, Margaret Xaveria Arthur, extolled the virtues and bountiful patronage of her cloister by James II and Mary of Modena, explaining that the latter's many favours 'engages our hearts & sincere affections in the most Strict peculiar manner' to all generations of the royal family.[18] Although disappointed,

---

[13] *Annals of the English Benedictines at Ghent, Now at St Mary's Abbey, Oulton in Staffordshire* (Oulton, 1894), pp. 43–4, 179–80.

[14] Joseph Gillow and Richard Trappes-Lomax (eds), *The Diary of the 'Blue Nuns': Or Order of the Immaculate Conception of Our Lady, at Paris, 1658–1810*, CRS, 8 (London, 1910), p. 23.

[15] Claire Walker, 'Loyal and Dutiful Subjects: English Nuns and Stuart Politics', in James Daybell (ed.), *Women and Politics in Early Modern England, 1450–1700* (Aldershot, 2004), pp. 233–6.

[16] Oulton Abbey, Stone, MS G.39, The English Benedictine Monastery at Ghent, fols 3–4.

[17] *Annals of the English Benedictines at Ghent*, pp. 46–7; Patrick Nolan, *The Irish Dames of Ypres: Being a History of the Royal Irish Abbey of Ypres Founded A.D. 1665 and Still Flourishing* (Dublin, 1908), pp. 166–207; BL, Add. MS 38,146, fol. 13, Pass to Lady Mary Butler, abbess at Dublin and her nuns from William III, 1690.

[18] Royal Archives, Windsor (RA), Stuart Papers 194/153 (M), Margaret Xaveria Arthur to James Edgar, 13 March 1737.

the nuns were confident that James, like his brother before him, would be restored to his throne. Indeed their experience of the 1650s, and the way that they had seen the assistance of women like Mary Knatchbull bear fruit in 1660, underpinned their confidence and made them ardent Jacobites. As Gabriel Glickman contended, 'Catholics would rally to the defence of the king as resolutely in 1688 as in 1641'.[19] Thus, the nuns, like their kin in England who had been staunch royalists of the Civil War and Interregnum, were committed to the Stuarts, and they easily and readily assumed the mantle of Jacobitism. For them, the Stuarts represented the surest path to the toleration of their religion and their return to English soil.

II. Nuns as Jacobites

Accordingly, upon James II's and Mary of Modena's exile in France, the cloisters resumed the prayers and patronage which had proved so efficacious during the Interregnum. In 1694 the queen thanked the elderly Mary Knatchbull of the Ghent Benedictines for the continuing prayers of her community, which she had earlier acknowledged as having long been remarkable for their 'loyal affection to the Royal family'.[20] Abbess Mary Caryll of the Dunkirk Benedictine abbey, which had enjoyed Stuart patronage since its foundation in 1662, regularly reassured her brother, who was secretary of state at the exiled court, of her nuns' prayers for a Catholic restoration.[21] In 1694 Mary of Modena gave the English Augustinian convent in Paris the relics of St Justin the Martyr, authenticated at Rome in 1675, which had previously been in her chapel at St James, as 'a testimonie of the esteeme' she held for their piety. Authorized by the archbishop of Paris to expose the relics in their church annually, lay visitors could attain an indulgence by confessing and praying for the 'extirpation of Heresie ... [and] for the health and prosperity of the sacred Parsone of his Majesty and all the Royall familie'.[22]

Cloisters located in proximity to the exiled Stuart court at St Germain-en-Laye were well placed to strengthen their ties with the royal family. The Paris Augustinians entertained James, Mary of Modena and their children on several occasions. In 1695, the nuns received James in their church where they performed various religious motets, before he breakfasted in the prioress's chambers. The following year, his son received similar hospitality and, in 1697, the queen joined the convent for prayers and music after evensong, before partaking of a light supper with Prioress Eugenia Perkins. Such visits continued into the eighteenth

[19]   Glickman, *Catholic Community*, p. 49.

[20]   *HMC 15th Report, Calendar of Stuart Papers Belonging to His Majesty the King, Preserved at Windsor Castle* (London, 1902), vol. 1, pp. 22, 90.

[21]   BL, Add. MS 28,226, Caryll Papers, fols 127, 132, Mary Caryll to John Caryll, [c. 1706], 5 June 1707.

[22]   Archives of the Archdiocese of Westminster, London (AAW), Augustinian Canonesses of Paris MS, 'A Relation of Some Remarkable Things that happened to My Lady Abbesse in her Latter Dayes', fols 169, 172, 174.

century with Mary of Modena and her daughter, Louisa Mary, attending religious services, dining with the prioresses, and participating in clothing and profession ceremonies. In August 1704, James Francis Edward visited and touched for the king's evil, after a ceremony in the church and a stroll around the garden.[23] Other houses, including the Benedictines of Ghent, Dunkirk, Brussels, Cambrai and Ypres, the Brussels Dominicans, the Rouen Poor Clares and the Bruges Augustinians, maintained similar contact. All mourned James's death in 1701 and pledged their support for 'James III'.[24]

The Paris Augustinian nuns' reaction to James II's death reflected the close alliance between the convent and the deposed monarch. When they learned that he was seriously ill, the nuns performed the Forty Hours Devotion for his recovery. Edward Lutton, the house's confessor, went to St Germain, presumably to relate their good wishes and to seek news about James's condition. Upon his return, they brought out the relics of St Justin and commenced an intensive regimen of masses and prayers. It was to no avail. On 17 September they sang a requiem mass for James, and a week later they received ten Louis d'or from Mary of Modena to pray for her deceased husband. Prioress Ann Tyldesley obtained 'a smale peece of our deceased Holly King's right Arme', which she personally embalmed and placed in a lead casket for exposition in the convent church. The nuns recited the *De Profundis* daily for his soul, and in October they held a solemn service for him in their church which was completely draped in black, save for 'a very handsome Representation' placed in the middle which was adorned with a sceptre and a crown. Later in the year, the relic of James was transferred with great ceremony to a simple monument in the wall of their choir which they explained was more in keeping with their poverty than the king's majesty.[25] They likewise performed funerary rites upon the death of Mary of Modena in 1718, expressing 'profound Respect affection & Esteem for her August and Royall Person; never to be forgott by the daughters of Sion'.[26] The queen left 300 livres each to the English Augustinians, Benedictines and Conceptionists in Paris, the Benedictines at Dunkirk, Pontoise and Ypres, and Poor Clares of Gravelines and Rouen to pray for her soul.[27] They dutifully performed their spiritual service on her behalf, and

---

[23]   AAW, 'Diurnall of the English Canonesses Regulars of St Augustin's Order established in Paris', vol. 1, fols 8–9, 12–13, 16–17, 28, 40, 56, 70, 96, 104, 106, 127, 142, 163.

[24]   *HMC 15th Report (Stuart MSS)*, vol. 1, pp. 46, 89, 90, 107, 125, 126, 149, 155; Rumsey (ed.), 'Abbess Neville's Annals', pp. 17–18; C.S. Durrant, *A Link Between Flemish Mystics and English Martyrs* (London, 1925), pp. 316–24; BL, Add. MS 28,226, fols 127, 132; F, Cédoz, *Un couvent de religieuses Anglaises à Paris de 1634 à 1884* (London, 1891), pp. 187–95; Ann M.C. Forster, 'The Chronicles of the English Poor Clares of Rouen – II', *Recusant History*, 18/2 (1986): pp. 96–7.

[25]   AAW, 'Diurnall of the English Canonesses', vol. 1, fols 72, 73, 76.

[26]   Ibid., fols 252, 254.

[27]   *Calendar of the Stuart Papers Belonging to His Majesty the King, Preserved at Windsor Castle* (7 vols, London, 1923), vol. 7, p. 699.

henceforth directed their divine petitions exclusively towards the restoration of her son, whose birthday the Paris Augustinians celebrated annually with a mixture of religious and secular festivities.[28]

Mary of Modena's death removed the nuns from the proximity of the Stuart courts. James Francis Edward had departed St Germain in 1712 and ultimately settled in the Papal States. Although the distance between Rome and the convents curtailed the royal visits previously enjoyed by certain houses, it did little to diminish their ardour for the pretender and his family, and it did not eliminate contact with him. Well-versed in a flourishing monastic epistolary culture that kept them abreast of kin's affairs in England and in regular contact with friends and associates on the continent, the religious women preserved ties with James Francis Edward using paper, quills and ink. In their letters, they consistently expressed their allegiance and their determination to assist his cause, most notably through their monastic regimen of prayer and religious services. In 1724, the Ghent Benedictine abbess, Mary Knatchbull, great-niece of her formidable namesake, assured James Francis Edward that 'the hearts and Tongues of all this family are allway [*sic*] active In importuning Heaven to preserve, encrease; and Prosper yours', as she sent him the cloister's annual New Year's tribute of 'Masses, communions, beads, acts of Pennance with many other Dayly Publick and private devotions'.[29] In 1725, the Brussels Dominican, Mary Rose Howard, assured him of her daily prayers for his family's preservation, 'the increace of the fathfull in the kingdoms and the comfort of your Magestys suffering subjects'.[30] Abbess Mary Butler of the Ypres Benedictines wrote in 1721 of her nuns' 'ardent Petions to heaven' for the restoration of James Francis Edward 'to your birth right'.[31] In 1725, Abbess Mary Crispe of the Brussels Benedictines pledged the nuns' 'continual prayers' for his 'happy Restauration which only can restore the unfortunate Kingdoms to that Happyness and Peace that theer unnatural Rebellion has so long deprived them of'.[32] Certain cloisters were still sending annual devotional tributes directed to the cause in 1745.[33]

The convents embarked on spiritual campaigns to support Jacobite military ventures. In Paris, the Augustinian nuns instituted the Forty Hours Devotion for success in the abortive attempts by James II and his son to return to their former kingdom in 1696, 1708 and 1715. A novena of masses for the same intention was also celebrated in the nuns' church for the 1708 venture, funded by the ill-

---

[28]   AAW, 'Diurnall of the English Canonesses', vol. 1, fols 253, 265, 276.

[29]   RA, Stuart Papers, 72/150 (M), Abbess Mary Knatchbull to James Francis Edward, 4 March 1724.

[30]   Ibid., 81/36 (M), Mary Rose Howard to James Francis Edward, 28 March 1725.

[31]   Ibid., 51/96 (M), Abbess Mary Butler to James Francis Edward, 27 January 1721.

[32]   Ibid., 81/47 (M), Abbess Mary Crisp to James Francis Edward, 3 April 1725.

[33]   Ibid., 263/17 (M), James Francis Edward to Mary Rose Howard, 25 Feb 1745; 263/19 (M), Edgar to Mary Rose Howard, 26 February 1745.

fated earl of Derwentwater.[34] In 1745, the convent again performed the Forty Hours Devotion, this time for Charles Edward Stuart, and held a series of other services for his preservation and prosperity during the campaign.[35] Despite repeated disappointment, they did not lose faith that eventually their prayers would be answered. In 1730 Abbess Margaret Xaveria Arthur of the Ypres Benedictines prefaced her annual offering of devotions for the Stuart cause with the wry observation that 'Tho our daily vows & [pray]ers for your Majesty & Royall famillys Restoration se[em]s In effectual', she confidently expected God to respond soon, thus 'for this effect we will renew our filial confidence in the Divin power & goodnes in not ceaseing to implore for this mercy til obtain'd'.[36] The saintly Scholastica Culcheth of the Dunkirk Benedictine abbey was so convinced that if James Francis Edward promised to erect a church in honour of the Virgin Mary, his restoration was assured, and her community was said to pray earnestly every day for this to happen.[37]

A few nuns were prepared to move beyond their monastic performance of prayer to offer more direct challenges to the English state. From Brussels, the Benedictine abbess Mary Crispe assured James Francis Edward that her abbey would joyfully celebrate the birth of his second son, Henry Benedict in 1725, despite being admonished for similar demonstrations of loyalty upon the safe delivery of Charles Edward in 1720, declaring 'wee shall always glory in being an Object of Spleen to your Majesties Enemies'.[38] Similar defiance led others to assist Jacobite military ventures. The Pontoise Benedictines, where James II's illegitimate daughter, Arabella (Dame Ignatia) Fitzjames, had in 1690 professed her monastic vows, supported the uprisings of 1715 and 1745.[39] Dame Ignatia had died in 1704, but close kinship connections between individual nuns, the exiled court and Jacobites in England encouraged direct engagement with the Stuart cause. This was most evident in the English Dominican cloister in Brussels where one of the sisters worked tirelessly for James Francis Edward.

Mary Rose Howard, the duke of Norfolk's niece, had an impeccable pedigree with several monastic and clerical kin, a cardinal uncle, and even a martyred great-uncle in William Howard, Viscount Stafford, executed during the Popish Plot. Her father, Colonel Bernard Howard, had been Master of the Horse under James II,

---

[34]   AAW, 'Diurnall of the English Canonesses', vol. 1, fols 145–6, 231; A.F. Allison, 'The English Augustinian Convent of Our Lady of Syon at Paris: Its Foundation and Struggle for Survival during the First Eighty Years, 1634–1713', *Recusant History*, 21/4 (1993): p. 484.

[35]   AAW, 'Diurnall of the English Canonesses', vol. 2 [fols 36, 38, 40].

[36]   RA, Stuart Papers, 140/72 (M), Margaret Xaveria Arthur to James Francis Edward, 6 December 1730.

[37]   Ibid., 142/31 (M), B. Strickland to James Francis Edward, 19 January 1731.

[38]   Ibid., 81/47 (M), Abbess Mary Crisp to James Francis Edward, 3 April 1725.

[39]   Peter Guilday, *The English Catholic Refugees on the Continent 1558–1795* (London, 1914), p. 271.

and he was imprisoned in the Tower after the 1696 Assassination Plot, before joining the exiled court at St Germain in 1699.[40] Professed in 1695, her dowry provided by Cardinal Howard, Mary Rose was prioress briefly from 1721 to 1724, and she evidently held other senior household offices.[41] A committed Jacobite, she obtained permission 'for receiving and transmitting letters' for James Francis Edward, and she continued corresponding with him until her death in 1747.[42] Like Mary Knatchbull in the 1650s, Howard received epistolary packets from the pretender and his ministers and forwarded the contents to their intended recipients. The nun's success in preventing her mail from falling into the wrong hands was regularly alluded to by her correspondents. To avoid detection they used local churchmen as covers for the sensitive packets. In September 1728 James Francis Edward detailed the complexities of the process when advising Howard of a new correspondent, Philip Brown. He advised her that all his mail with Brown should 'pass thro' your hands', and that it would be sent 'under a cover to you' via a cardinal in Bologna to the nuncio in Brussels. Return post should also use this conveyance. He stressed the importance of Brown's work on his behalf, asking 'I recommend to you your usual secrecy & prudence in the managem[en]t of this correspondance'. The importance of ensuring the security of his letters with Brown was reiterated in a subsequent note to the nun.[43]

For her part, Howard reassured him of her diligence in sending Brown's packets, and she regularly praised the efforts of the nuncio and others who assisted her work.[44] In October 1729, she thanked James Francis Edward for seeking preferment for the nuncio in Rome in a letter which also revealed her aptitude for espionage. She had successfully derailed the efforts of someone trying to identify Philip Brown as a Jacobite agent, after receiving intelligence about him from her contacts at the post office.[45] Likewise, she was already well aware of the earl of Mar's dubious reputation, when warned in February 1730 'you will do well to be upon your guard' not to divulge any information about the postal network to him or his associates.[46] In reply, Howard reassured James Francis Edward that she knew enough of the earl's character to have refused a meeting with him, reporting,

---

[40]   *Dominicana: Cardinal Howard's Letters, English Dominican Friars, Nuns, Students, Papers and Mission Registers*, CRS, 25 (London, 1925), p. 208; Glickman, *Catholic Community*, pp. 56, 127, 259.

[41]   *Dominicana*, pp. 204–9.

[42]   Ibid., pp. 208–9; RA, Stuart Papers, 84/5 (M), Mary Rose Howard to James Francis Edward, 11 July 1725.

[43]   RA, Stuart Papers, 120/46 (M), James Francis Edward to Mary Rose Howard, 11 September 1728; 121/31 (M), same to same, 6 October 1728.

[44]   Ibid., 122/98 (M), Mary Rose Howard to James Francis Edward, 17 December 1728; 122/134 (M), same to same, 31 December 1728.

[45]   Ibid., 131/93 (M), Mary Rose Howard to James Francis Edward, 21 October 1729.

[46]   Ibid., 134/93 (M), James Francis Edward to Mary Rose Howard, 24 February 1720.

I answered [him] I was a Religious woman, no politician, but that no visit was acceptable to me from any person that had forfeted the caracter of an honest man; be his title never so eminent in Church or stat. that I Hon:d my King, & never could valew one who forgot there duty so far as to pretend to sarve 2 masters under the nomination of Crownd heads.[47]

By her transmission of the pretender's letters, Howard had demonstrated her own loyalty to the Stuarts, and she was scathing of a man whose self-interest and lack of integrity had not only betrayed James Francis Edward but also the Hanoverians.

Such devotion to the Stuart cause came at a price, however. Dissension in the Brussels cloister over Mary Rose Howard's activism, which flouted innumerable regulations regarding the authority of the prioress and contact with the world outside the enclosure, erupted during the governance of Prioress Julia Brown. Papers were seized from Howard's cell and the prioress insisted upon her right to monitor all letters leaving and entering the cloister. Howard appealed to James Francis Edward to intervene, and the Dominican master-general ruled in her favour, permitting her to meet her kin alone in the parlour, and the unhindered transit of Jacobite mail in and out of the convent.[48] Without Julia Brown's version of the furore, it is difficult to work out exactly why she acted against Howard. She was from an Irish Dominican cloister and only temporarily in the Brussels house, despite her tenure as prioress. It is possible that she did not have Jacobite sympathies, or she may have resented the clear challenge to her authority and the statutes Howard's activities constituted. There is a suggestion that some in the community feared censure from the Habsburg authorities for Howard's activities. Whatever the factors behind the discord, the incident reveals that convents were not necessarily united in their support for the Stuarts, or at the very least, they could not agree as to the form their Jacobitism should take. In this they reflected the English Catholic community at large.

III. The Convents and English Catholic Identity

Studies of eighteenth-century Catholicism which argue that many English Catholics were becoming more pragmatic about religion and politics, and thereby sought accommodation with the state and eschewed Jacobitism, have referred somewhat disparagingly to 'the centres of pious and sentimental Jacobitism on the Continent' where 'doting nuns sought bulletins on the teething problems of Stuart infants'.[49] The convents' connections with the exiled Stuarts, their prayers and certain

---

[47]   Ibid., 134/188 (M), Mary Rose Howard to James Francis Edward, 17 March 1730.

[48]   Ibid., 152/25 (M), Mary Rose Howard to James Francis Edward, 10 March 1732; 152/53 (M), James Francis Edward to Mary Rose Howard, 14 March 1732; *Dominicana*, pp. 208–9.

[49]   Mullett, *Catholics in Britain and Ireland*, p. 95; Eamon Duffy, '"Englishmen in Vaine": Roman Catholic Allegiance to George I', in Stuart Mews (ed.), *Religion and National Identity*, Studies in Church History, 18 (Oxford, 1982): p. 346.

nuns' activism suggest that Jacobitism was important for many cloisters which did much to promote the cause of James II and his heirs. However, this political stance did not distance them from their coreligionists across the Channel, and thereby render them an anachronistic continental sideshow. Rather, after 1688, the religious houses continued to service the English Catholic community in the ways they had done since their inception. They accepted its daughters into their schools and novitiates, provided places of accommodation and worship for travellers, and fostered devotions which sustained the faithful in their homeland. Indeed it might be argued that they provided a vital link between continental and English religion and politics which informed both their own and their kin's identity.

The number of English women who became nuns fell during the eighteenth century.[50] Despite this downturn in recruitment the monasteries continued to provide an alternative to marriage or spinsterhood. The recurrence of the same family names in registers demonstrates that for some households the cloister remained a viable option after 1688, and this was as true for families in England as for those in expatriate neighbourhoods on the continent. The declining recruitment matched trends in other parts of Europe, so was not peculiar to the English Catholic community and certainly should not be read as indicative of distaste for the convents' Jacobitism, which Glickman has argued proved attractive rather than a disincentive.[51] Fewer nuns often reflected the financial situation of families whose straitened circumstances, whether because of recusancy fines or broader economic and political factors, like war, reduced their capacity to dower their daughters, even with the lesser sum required for monastic dowries. Monastic registers hint at this being an issue with considerable delays between clothing and profession ceremonies. In the Paris Augustinian convent, the Preston sisters took the habit in 1720 but did not take their final vows until 1728, presumably because their dowries were not forthcoming.[52] In the 1740s Benedicta Caryll of the Dunkirk Benedictines begged her nephew to pay outstanding money he owed the cloister for dowries, constantly citing the nuns' impecunious condition.[53] In 1728 Abbess Elizabeth Widdrington of the Pontoise Benedictines gently reminded James Francis Edward that for ten years she had received no money for Dame Mary Austin Oxburgh and her sister who was a pensioner in the cloister. In response he admitted his circumstances did not permit him to pay what he owed for the two women, but he sent 500 livres to assist the community.[54] One of the problems

---

[50]   Walker, *Gender and Politics*, p. 20; *Who were the Nuns?* http://wwtn.history.qmul. ac.uk/search/csearch.php.

[51]   Glickman argued that 'the institutions flourished visibly through the Jacobite period': Glickman, *Catholic Community*, p. 75.

[52]   AAW, 'Diurnall of the English Canonesses', vol. 1, fol. 276; *Who were the Nuns?*

[53]   BL, Add. MS 28,229, Family of Caryll Correspondence, vol. 4, 1740–47, fols 14, 72–3, 97, 386, 454.

[54]   RA, Stuart Papers, 120/133 (M), Elizabeth Widdrington to James Francis Edward, 26 September 1728; 121/40 (M), James Francis Edward to Elizabeth Widdrington, 31 October 1728.

emanating from the cloisters' affiliation with the exiled courts was that some were persuaded to accept the daughters of impoverished Jacobites on the basis that they would receive recompense 'when God shall restore them to their kingdoms'.[55] It is possible that there were several women, like the unnamed Oxburgh daughter, who would have been professed had dowry money been forthcoming.

Economic distress led cloisters to pursue income-generating ventures which happily also fulfilled their mission to consolidate recusant faith and identity in their compatriots. Several convents expanded their schools. Through their educative apostolate they were able to instil the precepts of the faith into children and young women who, if they did not take the veil, would return to England to raise the next generation of Catholics. The Augustinians in Paris and Bruges ran the larger and more prosperous establishments, which taught 15 to 30 students; most other monastic schools had no more than a dozen pupils.[56] Convent education facilities benefitted from the Jacobite exile. *The Gentleman's Magazine* of May 1766 estimated there were over 260 English and Irish girls educated in the expatriate cloisters in Flanders.[57] This figure was clearly inflated but the piece reveals how entrenched education across the Channel had become by the late eighteenth century, when even Protestant girls were attending the convent schools. Protestants and Catholics alike understood the power of education in confessionalization, and for equipping the young for a life of service to their church and their country. In correspondence between the Dunkirk Benedictine abbess, Mary Caryll, and her brother at the Jacobite court at St Germain, sister and brother discussed the settlement of nieces and nephews. In 1706 John Caryll insisted that one particularly troublesome youth should attend 'some College where he may be bred a Christian'. His sister concurred, writing, 'my intention being only that our fammilly may propagate Religion, and be servisable to theyr King, as theyr Anti[e] sters have bin'.[58] The correspondent in the *Gentleman's Magazine* confirmed the establishments' religious and political indoctrination, caustically claiming to have seen 'repeated instances of children's opposing the religion and government of their country with rancour and fury, at fourteen years of age'.[59]

Similar economic, spiritual and political imperatives drove convents to expand their boarding facilities for lay guests. The religious houses' limited guest facilities were stretched as kin increasingly sought refuge during times of tension in England. The Popish Plot saw a flood of Catholics arrive in need of accommodation and the cloisters struggled to house them. The Pontoise Benedictines were overwhelmed by the volume of such guests and had to move younger nuns and novices from their cells in order to find them all beds.[60] As the Poor Clares in Rouen commented,

---

[55]   *HMC 15th Report (Stuart MSS)*, vol. 1, p. 107.

[56]   Walker, *Gender and Politics*, p. 93.

[57]   *The Gentleman's Magazine* (May 1766), pp. 226–7.

[58]   BL, Add. MS 28,226, fols 26–7.

[59]   *The Gentleman's Magazine* (May 1766), p. 227.

[60]   'Registers of the English Benedictine Nuns of Pontoise, now at Teignmouth, Devonshire, 1680–1713', in *Miscellanea X*, CRS, 17 (London, 1915), p. 324.

> many persons of quality came to live in this town and most of them instantly
> intreated and begged that if they could not lodg, at least they might dyet here.
> Our house for neere 6 yeares was full of our friends that pensioned here, which
> was a great labour and trouble to the Community … but there was no remedy;
> Rd Mother Abbess could not refuse them.[61]

The sisters were similarly inundated in 1688 when they housed refugees in the confessor's house.[62] In 1715, the annals again reported the 'Fifteen rendering England uncomfortable for some Catholics' they asked to lodge at the convent.[63] Familial bonds aside, the nuns considered it their religious obligation to assist compatriots who were suffering for religious and political separatism. Opening their guest quarters, confessors' lodgings and own cloisters to these refugees was considered a vital aspect of their pastoral work. They might not be able to succour the needs of coreligionists in their homeland, or take up arms to support their deposed monarch, but they could support his cause and the necessities of the refugees from within their own convent walls.

The practical work of education and provision of accommodation aside, the nuns continued to provide their countrymen and women with devotional sustenance too. The convents were commonly centres of worship where the English might access Catholic prayer and sacraments in all their liturgical splendour. Certain houses, like the Paris Augustinians and the Bruges Franciscans, were renowned for their musical prowess and attracted the expatriate English and locals alike to their religious services. When the Jacobite earl of Perth, James Drummond, visited several cloisters in 1694, he conversed with nuns, sometimes over a light meal, and enjoyed their religious services. He kept the feast of Corpus Christi at the Louvain Augustinian cloister, attended the service of compline at the Bruges convent, and also heard the famed English Franciscan nuns there sing. While such visits combined sociability and the curiosity of a sightseeing tourist, the earl was evidently keen to access the full gamut of devotional experiences. When touring the Capuchins' garden at Tirlemont, he described the 'litle chapels in grottos adorned with doleful pictures of our Lord's dolorous passion [which] excited our devotion'.[64] The nuns were acutely aware that their compatriots lacked access to the miraculous shrines and basilicas that continental Catholics freely frequented. So they advised visitors of worthy holy sites, which might be imbued with an English flavour. In 1663, visiting the Ghent Benedictines, Sir Philip Skippon was given a printed account of the miraculous cure in 1660 of the nun, Mary Minshull, whose lameness was healed with oil from the sanctuary lamp in Our Lady of

---

[61] Ann M.C. Forster, 'The Chronicles of the English Poor Clares of Rouen – I', *Recusant History*, 18/1 (1986): p. 96.

[62] Ibid., p. 96.

[63] Forster, 'Poor Clares of Rouen – II', p. 150.

[64] William Jerdan (ed.), *Letters from James Earl of Perth Lord Chancellor of Scotland to his Sister, the Countess of Erroll and Other Members of his Family* (London, 1845), pp. 29, 43–4.

Succour's chapel in Brussels. Two days later he visited the chapel where the miracle occurred. The Dunkirk Benedictines advised him to visit St Omer where he would find the bodies of some English saints.[65]

Other nuns initiated their own forms of devotion. This was most obvious through their spiritual writings. The Carmelite prioress at Lierre, Margaret Mostyn, who was especially devoted to the Virgin Mary, composed her own way of meditating through the mysteries of the rosary. Her hagiography instructed others in her method.[66] In Bruges, Augustinian prioress, Lucy Herbert, composed *Several Excellent Methods of Hearing Mass* (1722) and *Several Methods and Practises of Devotion* (1743); both of which were reprinted throughout the eighteenth and nineteenth centuries. The reprints were testament enough to the influence of such works, but as well as providing spiritual guidance to England's Catholic minority, they compelled some readers to devote their lives completely to God. In 1677 Anne Hanne was professed as Dame Gertrude in the English Benedictine cloister in Paris. Hanne had previously served Alethea Fairfax, who with her mother, Abigail Fairfax, and aunt, Appolonia Yate, provided her monastic dowry, and they were arguably behind her vocation. The pious Lady Abigail had lent Hanne copies of the Cambrai Benedictine nun, Gertrude More's *Confessiones Amantis*, and the house's spiritual director, Augustine Baker's *Sancta Sophia* which confirmed her previous desire to enter a cloister.[67] The influence of these books, written in the Cambrai Benedictine cloister, published abroad and clandestinely sent into England, evidently encouraged devotion in the Fairfax household and ultimately spawned a monastic vocation.

The nexus between the provision of devotional aids and Catholic activism was perhaps best illustrated in the convents' promotion of specifically English hagiographies and devotions. The Augustinian nuns at Bruges enjoyed the countess of Nithsdale's gripping account of her husband's daring escape from the Tower on the eve of execution for his part in the 1715 rebellion, which was engineered by his enterprising wife. The countess, Lady Winefrid Maxwell, was the sister of Prioress Lucy Herbert.[68] The story was related in much the same fashion as the heroic tales of the cloisters' early nuns who had tricked pursuivants searching for priests, harbourers and Catholic devotional objects. The intended cause for persecution might have shifted slightly from disobedience to the Protestant Church

---

[65] Philip Skippon, 'An Account of a Journey Made Thro' Part of the Low-Countries, Germany, Italy and France', in A. and J. Churchill (eds), *A Collection of Voyages and Travels*, 3rd edn (6 vols, London, 1746), vol. 6, pp. 384, 387, 377. For another example of relics see p. 376.

[66] Anne Hardman, *Mother Margaret Mostyn: Discalced Carmelite, 1625–1679* (London, 1937), pp. 119–22.

[67] Joseph Hansom (ed.), 'The English Benedictine Nuns of the Convent of Our Blessed Lady of Good Hope in Paris, now at St Benedict's Priory, Colwich, Staffordshire. Notes and Obituaries', *Miscellanea VII*, CRS, 9 (London, 1911), pp. 372–4; Michael Hodgetts, 'The Yates of Harvington 1631–1696', *Recusant History*, 22/2 (1994): p. 163.

[68] Durrant, *A Link Between Flemish Mystics*, pp. 318–24.

to insurgence against the English state, but the nuns nonetheless portrayed such heroism as suffering for the faith. They cherished the memory of James Radcliffe, styled earl of Derwentwater, who did not escape the executioner's block for the 1715 rising. The earl bequeathed the 'precious guift of his Noble hart, as a testimony of his kindness & esteem' to the Paris Augustinians, although it initially resided in the Pontoise Benedictine house.[69] In 1723 his widowed countess was buried in the church at the Augustinian cloister in Louvain, and their son was buried alongside her in 1731. As a result the convent treasured various Radcliffe memorabilia.[70] The Paris Augustinians celebrated an annual mass of the dead for Derwentwater throughout the eighteenth century. In November 1732 they gained custody of his heart and ceremoniously placed it in a monument in their choir. The annals reflected widespread belief in his sanctity, stating this was done 'rather hopeing his Lordship would intercede to Almighty God for us, then that he wanted our prayres'.[71]

At the centre of this new cult of political martyrdom stood the Stuarts themselves. James II was reinvented as a tragic monarch, wronged by his subjects who rebelled against him as the parliamentarians had fought Charles I. The nuns did not originate this tradition of the suffering king, but they did much to promote it.[72] The relic of James II made by Prioress Ann Tyldesley and installed in the Paris Augustinians' choir, with the prayers and ceremonies surrounding it, provided a clear example of their intention to venerate the deposed monarch. The Dunkirk Benedictines had been given a wax model of the head of James II. Described by Abbess Benedicta Fleetwood as 'our greatest treasure', it was shown to visitors.[73] The cults continued into the next generation. In October 1735 Mary Rose Howard sought 25 pounds from James Francis Edward to complete an altarpiece containing a relic of St Dominic which his wife, Clementina, who had died in January, had given the nuns. When it was completed she predicted many would come to see it 'no less as being sent by so holy a Princess as to pay

---

[69]   AAW, 'Diurnall of the English Canonesses', vol. 1, fol. 234; Adam Hamilton (ed.), *The Chronicle of the English Augustinian Canonesses Regular of the Lateran, at St Monica's in Louvain* (2 vols, London, 1904–6), vol. 2, p. 209.

[70]   Hamilton (ed.), *Chronicle*, vol. 2, p. 209.

[71]   AAW, 'Diurnall of the English Canonesses', vol. 1, fols 326, 327, 354, 358, 364; vol. 2 [fols 48, 50].

[72]   For a discussion of the role played by English Benedictine monks and the French Visitation nuns at Chaillot in initiating and spreading the cult of James II, see Dom Geoffrey Scott, *'Sacredness of Majesty': The English Benedictines and the Cult of King James II*, Royal Stuart Papers, 23 (Huntingdon, 1984). Glickman, *Catholic Community*, pp. 198–203, considers Jacobite culture and its devotional ramifications in male and female cloisters. The participation of English and Irish nuns in this cult is explored in Niall MacKenzie, 'Gender, Jacobitism and Dynastic Sanctity' (University of Cambridge PhD thesis, 2003). See also Neil Guthrie, *The Material Culture of the Jacobites* (Cambridge, 2013), pp. 115–20.

[73]   *A History of the Benedictine Nuns of Dunkirk* (London, 1958), p. 72.

devotion to the Saint'. Clearly touched by the nun's piety, James acquiesced, and he added to the convent's store of potential relics, sending some locks of Clementina's hair in recompense for all the prayers expended upon his family's behalf.[74]

Abbess Margaret Xaveria Arthur of the Ypres Benedictines requested a copy of the late Clementina's life in 1736, which 'we are told is to be writ'.[75] Mary Rose Howard was more importunate, begging James Edgar, James's secretary, for a copy of Clementina's life or her picture because 'I have letters from our Chife famulys in England pressing me to get them any the least thing of our Queens out of there veneration to her Magestys memory'.[76] While assuring both women that there were no moves in Rome towards beatifying Clementina, he sent Howard a picture and more of her hair, and promised a published account of her funeral in the future.[77] In 1734 Edgar had sent Howard a dozen prints of Charles Edward and of Henry Benedict at her request, apologizing for the poor quality, but hopeful 'they will answer the ends you propose by them'. By way of compensation he added two silver medals of much better quality, one of James Francis Edward and Clementina, the other of their two sons.[78] The images of the princes were presumably to be sent to those same devotees in England who later desired relics of Clementina to be put to Jacobite devotional purposes. Spiritually charged objects travelled in both directions. In 1723 Howard had sent James Francis Edward 'a little Cross of my worke' to protect him 'from future harmes', showing how nuns might invest their needlework with supernatural qualities to assist the cause.[79] The translation of Stuart memorabilia into objects of worship was evident in the Ghent Benedictine nuns' conversion of a red Jacobite banner 'with the initials "J.R." worked in gold' into a chalice veil for their sacristy.[80] In 1737, the Paris Augustinians obtained the 'pretious Gift' of a 'noble Carpet of Crimson Velvet embrothered with Gold and Silver', which had hung in James II's and Mary of Modena's chapel at Whitehall for use in their church. It was accepted with reverence, the nuns 'esteeming it a treasure that can never sufficiently be valued'.[81] Thus, as Gabriel Glickman observed, 'in the weekly prayers of the Benedictine

[74] RA, Stuart Papers, 183/65 (M), Mary Rose Howard to James Francis Edward, 13 October 1735; 184/25 (M), 11 November 1735.

[75] Ibid., 192/54 (M), Margaret Xaveria Arthur to James Edgar, 9 December 1736.

[76] Ibid., 192/60 (M), Mary Rose Howard to James Edgar, 11 December 1736.

[77] Ibid., 193/49 (M), James Edgar to Margaret Xaveria Arthur, 9 January 1737; 193/63 (M), same to Mary Rose Howard, 12 January 1737; 204/48 (M), same to same, 18 January 1738.

[78] Ibid., 167/172 (M), James Edgar to Mary Rose Howard, 23 January 1734; Durrant, *A Link Between Flemish Mystics*, p. 327.

[79] RA, Stuart Papers, 71/19 (M), Mary Rose Howard to James Francis Edward, 9 December 1723.

[80] *Annals of the English Benedictines of Ghent*, p. 42.

[81] AAW, 'Diurnall of the English Canonesses', vol. 1 [fol. 359].

monasteries, in the embroiderings of the royal arms put together by the nuns at Louvain, and the exchange of relics, crosses and healing "touchpieces" bearing the Stuart image, the English houses created a ceremonial culture of Jacobite worship'.[82]

This was reflected ceremonially in the masses and memorials for James Francis Edward and his cause. In February 1735 the Paris Augustinians held a service for his recently deceased wife, Clementina, in a church 'adorn'd in the best manner we could' to which 'all the English Catholicks of note that are in Towne were invited'.[83] Three years later they reported singing a high mass for the conversion of England.[84] In 1766 the Rouen Poor Clares recorded the death in Rome of 'our dear King James the third [the Old Pretender], having liv'd all his life banished from his three kingdoms, England, Ireland and Scotland'. They held a service for the repose of his soul on 4 February and sent printed bills to 'all the English, Irish and Scotch, all the persons of quality and to all our French friends and to the convents'. On 1 March the convent hosted a 'most noble and magnificent service for our holy King James the third' attended by English, Irish and Scottish exiles and the Rouen elites.[85] Although the Jacobite cause had withered by the time of James Francis Edward's passing, many cloisters continued to pledge their allegiance and provide a venue where English expatriates might meet to reminisce and mourn lost hopes and dreams.

Accordingly the continental religious houses can be seen as centres of female Catholic Jacobitism which sustained compatriots who refused to accept the political and religious realities post-1688. Although not in tune politically with all their coreligionists, the nuns were an integral link between their aristocratic and gentry families and continental Catholicism, as their schools, religious services, guesthouses and devotional writings reveal. Through these ongoing services they were able to impart something of their belief in the Stuart cause, which for many religious women was not inconsistent with their own experience, nor indeed that of many lay Catholics. More than a century of separation from the Protestant church and state, and over 80 years of exiled monasticism had left their mark on the English cloisters. In the cult of persecution for the faith that the convents had fostered from their first inception, many nuns discovered their political voice, and it found its natural expression in their support for the Stuarts after 1688. As religious émigrés they felt a deep affinity with James II, Mary of Modena and James Francis Edward, who they considered to have been similarly exiled for their Catholicism. Thus, letters were steeped in the language of affliction. Mary Rose Howard assured James Francis Edward in 1724 that 'wee glory to suffer with your

---

[82]   Glickman, *Catholic Community*, pp. 201–2.
[83]   AAW, 'Diurnall of the English Canonesses', vol. 1, fol. 343.
[84]   Ibid., fol. 364.
[85]   Forster, 'Poor Clares of Rouen – II', p. 154.

Magesty & as banished from our country for our religion to all losses we redily conforme and are perfectly easy in'.[86] Nuns like Howard integrated the Stuart exile into their own history of persecution in such a way that Jacobitism was a central strand in their monastic identity. It inevitably had an impact upon how they perceived themselves, their country and their sense of mission, and it arguably informed English Catholic identity on the continent and in the households of their kin in England.

---

[86] RA, Stuart Papers, 74/113 (M), Mary Rose Howard to James Francis Edward, 2 June 1724.

Chapter 6

A Latitudinarian Queen:
Mary II and her Churchmen

Melinda Zook

The sudden death of Mary II in the winter of 1694 resulted in a phenomenal and unprecedented outpouring of grief, not only in the British Isles, as we might expect, but across the Protestant world.[1] In England, 36 medals were cast to commemorate the occasion and more sermons and elegies were published honouring the queen than any previous monarch, including Elizabeth I.[2] Still, while Mary was beloved by many of her contemporaries, she has been nearly forgotten by historians. Naturally, there are some obvious and understandable reasons as to why this has been the case. Mary II's reign was brief – just one month short of five years – while the other half of the dual monarchy, William III, reigned for another six years. It is King William's War and his leadership that have traditionally dominated the narratives of the 1690s. But there are more insidious reasons as to why Mary's legacy has suffered, which cluster around the simple facts that she was a woman; that she was pious; and that she was attracted to the pleasures of domesticity – all things which, at one time or another, the male-dominated, often secular-minded, scholarly elite has been prone to trivialize.[3] She also betrayed her father, James II,

---

[1] This chapter draws upon information published in my book, *Protestantism, Politics, and Women in Britain, 1660–1714* (Basingstoke, 2013), in particular, chapter 4, 'An Incomparable Queen: Mary II, the Protestant International and the Church of England', reproduced with permission of Palgrave Macmillan.

Poems and essays written in Mary's honour after her death were published on the continent and in America. See, for example, Pieter Rabus, *Uitvaart, Van Haar Grootmagtigste, Majesteit Maria, Koninginne van Groot Britanje, Vrankrijk en Yerland* (Rotterdam, 1695); Cotton Mather, *Observanda. The Life and Death of the Late Q. Mary* (Boston, MA, 1695).

[2] At least 67 poems were printed on the death of Mary, compared to approximately 25 each at the deaths of Charles II, William III, and Queen Anne. In addition, 36 funeral sermons were published, almost four times the usual number on the death of an English monarch in this period.

[3] Mary, like William, was interested in architecture, gardening and interior design. She also enjoyed collecting porcelains as well as needlework. For hostile accounts, see Lacey Baldwin Smith, *This Realm of England, 1399–1688*, 8th edn (New York, 2000), p. 339; Mark Kishlansky, *A Monarchy Transformed: Britain, 1603–1714* (London, 1996), pp. 301–2.

in support of her husband and the Revolution, a fact not lost on those scholars with Jacobite sympathies.[4]

By the late twentieth century, however, the historical profession had undergone profound changes in both its membership and in the range of topics under study. In a world where scholars not only take women in the past seriously, but religious devotion as well, interest in life and deeds of Mary II has revived.[5] In the 1980s and 1990s, historians Lois Schwoerer and William Speck argued that Mary's presence within the dual monarchy was crucial to the legitimization of the Revolution. They also pointed out that Mary was both a consort and regnant queen and that during her six regencies, she proved herself an astute and capable leader.[6] More recently, historians studying the Church of England and the moral reformation in the 1690s have also taken an interest in Queen Mary. In 1993, Craig Rose spoke of the 'distinctly latitudinarian tone' of Mary's churchmanship. A few years later, he wrote admiringly of Mary's 'broad Protestant sympathies and a personal piety [which] ... was as deep as it was unaffected'. He also gave Mary, together with Archbishop John Tillotson and William III, credit for filling the bishoprics left vacant by the Nonjurors.[7] In his 1996 book on the moral reformation that followed the Glorious Revolution, Tony Claydon claimed that all ecclesiastical policies in the early 1690s were delegated to Mary and that the queen played a 'pivotal role' in the development of court propaganda.[8] Finally, in 2002, perhaps the strongest affirmation of Mary's importance to the history of religion in the era

---

[4]   The most obvious example is Agnes Strickland; she devoted nearly two volumes of her 12 volume *Lives of the Queens of Scotland and England* to Mary II. Her portrait of Mary is both scholarly and insightful, but unfortunately marred by her frequent lapses into unabashed partisanship. She detested William III and had no sympathy for the Revolution. See Agnes Strickland, *Lives of the Queens of Scotland and England and English Princesses Connected with the Regal Succession of Great Britain* (12 vols, New York, 1851–59), vols 5–6.

[5]   In addition to the scholarship mentioned below see, Melinda Zook, 'History's Mary: The Propagation of Queen Mary II, 1689–1694', in L.O. Fradenburg (ed.), *Women and Sovereignty* (Edinburgh, 1992), pp. 170–91; Molly McClain, 'Love, Friendship, and Power: Queen Mary II's Letters to Frances Apsley', *Journal of British Studies*, 47/3 (2008): pp. 505–27; Melinda Zook, 'The Shocking Death of Mary II: Gender and Political Crisis in Late Stuart England', *British Scholar*, 1/1 (2008): pp. 21–36.

[6]   Lois G. Schwoerer, 'The Queen as Regent and Patron', in Robert P. Maccubbin and Martha Hamilton-Phillips (eds), *The Age of William III & Mary II: Power, Politics, and Patronage, 1688–1702* (Williamsburg, VA, 1989); Lois G. Schwoerer, 'Images of Queen Mary II, 1689–1695', *Renaissance Quarterly*, 42/4 (1989): pp. 717–48; W.A. Speck, 'William – and Mary?', in Lois G. Schwoerer (ed.), *The Revolution of 1688–1689: Changing Perspectives* (Cambridge, 1992), pp. 131–46 ; W.A. Speck, 'Mary II (1662–1694)', *Oxford Dictionary of National Biography*.

[7]   Craig Rose, 'Providence, Protestant Union and Godly Reformation in the 1690s', *Transactions of the Royal Historical Society*, 6th ser., 3 (1993): p. 163; Craig Rose, *England in the 1690s: Revolution, Religion and War* (Oxford, 1999), pp. 41, 157.

[8]   Tony Claydon, *William III and the Godly Revolution* (Cambridge, 1996), p. 71.

of the Revolution was made by Mark Goldie. 'Calvinist William left the church matters to his Anglican wife'. 'She was', in Goldie's estimation, a 'woman with decided views, a Latitudinarian queen'.[9]

This essay builds on this perspective, situating Mary II's importance firmly within the new history of religion and, more particularly, within the history of the Church of England. It contends that Mary's most lasting significance is not found simply in her promotion of the moral reformation, although in that she certainly played a key part. It also finds the designation of Mary as a 'Latitudinarian queen', pure and simple, problematic, as is the term 'latitudinarian' itself. Rather this essay sees Mary as a progenitor of a distinctly new direction within the Church, particularly through the clergy, with which she chose to surround herself and prefer to positions of power and responsibility. Through Queen Mary's guidance, patronage and leadership, the Church of England was set on something of a new trajectory after the Glorious Revolution. Mary II and the clergy whom she promoted to the episcopal bench transformed the Church from one that was sacerdotal, coercive and exclusive to one that was conciliatory, pragmatic and enlightened.

Latitudinarianism has become something of a contested site for scholars.[10] While certainly not a full-fledged ideology, latitudinarianism did characterize an increasingly strong tone or temper within the post-Revolution Church. Queen Mary's churchmanship was often in line with the latitudinarian mood of men like John Tillotson, Simon Patrick, Gilbert Burnet, Edward Fowler and others, especially if we characterize latitudinarianism as an alternative to both the rigid Calvinism of some Dissenters and the coercive dogmatism and exclusivity of the Church of England following the Restoration. On the other hand, the queen was hardly a slave to a movement that was Cambridge-based and carved out of English experience. Rather, Mary's religiosity was moulded out of her positive experiences of the great variety of reformed practice that she encountered in the Netherlands. It was also shaped by the close proximity and constant threat of French Catholicism to the United Provinces. Mary had witnessed the aftermath of Louis XIV's revocation of the Edict of Nantes in 1685. She had seen the streams of Huguenot refugees entering the Low Countries, and she had heard of the horrors, some real and some fabricated, inflicted on those Protestants who remained in France. Thus Mary's religiosity was born of her European experiences but nonetheless had several key features in common with men like John Tillotson and Simon Patrick. To say that the queen and the circle of clergy around her were latitudinarian in their approach to religion and the Church is to say simply that they

---

[9]   Mark Goldie, 'John Locke, Jonas Proast and Religious Toleration, 1688–1692', in John Walsh, Colin Haydon, and Stephen Taylor (eds), *The Church of England, c. 1689–c. 1833: From Toleration to Tractarianism* (1993; Cambridge, 2002), pp. 143–71.

[10]   See, in particular, John Spurr's objections to the imprecise labelling of various prominent churchmen as 'latitudinarian' by scholars in John Spurr, '"Latitudinarianism" and the Restoration Church', *The Historical Journal*, 31/1 (1988): pp. 61–82.

believed in a practical Christianity that demonstrated itself not through ceremonies or sacerdotalism, but rather through everyday Christian living, including charity to other Protestants.

Princess Mary, eldest daughter of James, duke of York, was married to her cousin, Prince William of Orange, stadtholder of the United Provinces in 1677. Their marriage was a piece of statecraft, to be sure, arranged by Mary's uncle, Charles II, in order to gain further control over his difficult nephew. It had the added advantage of being popular with the English people who, concerned over the growing Catholicism at court rejoiced in this most Protestant match. Mary, aged 15, cried at the sight of the pockmarked, diminutive prince of Orange, 12 years her senior and four inches shorter.[11] But she grew to love, passionately it would seem, the man, and more than the man. She came to identify herself with all that the house of Orange signified. In the Netherlands, the Dutch Reformed Church had long envisioned the princes of Orange as the defenders of the reformed religion in Europe.[12] This cause, the defence of the Protestant International, was one which Mary zealously embraced, and it was for this cause that she would later so readily consent to her husband's usurpation of her father's throne.

Mary's nine years in the United Provinces had an exceedingly formative influence on the kind of queen that she would become. The extraordinarily international character of the Netherlands in the 1680s, with its rich confessional diversity and teeming refugee populations, shaped the broad irenic Protestantism of Mary. Although Charles II had made sure for political reasons that the royal princesses, Mary and Anne, were raised in the traditions of the established Church of England, any Anglican presence at The Hague was minimal. Princess Mary's first Anglican chaplain, William Lloyd, took her to services at the English Church at The Hague which was led by Presbyterians. Nor did Prince William do anything to encourage Mary's Anglicanism. Her second chaplain, the more traditional George Hooper, did manage to transform the princess's dining room into an Anglican chapel. But like all of Mary's chaplains from England, Hooper's time at the Orange court was short. The blustery, intemperate behaviour of William usually led to their early departures.[13]

---

[11]   Edward Lake, 'Diary of Dr. Edward Lake, Archdeacon and Prebendary of Exeter', ed. G.P. Elliott, *Camden Miscellany* (London, 1846), vol. 1, p. 5; John Miller, *The Stuarts* (London, 2004), p. 205. The story of Mary's shock at the prospect of marriage to the prince of Orange is recounted in numerous sources, but Miller's description of Mary's initial impression and subsequent relationship with William is among the most intelligent.

[12]   Hans Bots, 'William III and His Fellow Calvinists in the Low Countries', in J. Van Den Berg and P.G. Hoftijzer (eds), *Church, Change and Revolution* (Brill, 1991), pp. 122–5.

[13]   William Lloyd, later bishop of Worcester, was fiercely anti–Catholic but friendly to Dissenters. He was one of the seven bishops imprisoned and prosecuted by James II in 1688, and he was duly rewarded by William and Mary after the Revolution. On his relationship with Mary in Holland see Lake, 'Diary of Dr. Edward Lake', pp. 8, 26; A. Tindal Hart, *William Lloyd, 1627–1717: Bishop, Politician, Author and Prophet* (London,

There are no records to indicate that Mary protested at this situation. Rather, she embraced the opportunity to listen to the sermons of various Protestant preachers throughout the United Provinces. The princess had considerable leisure time and independence. William was often preoccupied by politics or hunting, leaving Mary free to pursue her own interests. She continued to attend the English Church at The Hague, where she was considered a benefactor and where she had a special suite built for herself and her entourage so that they could attend without disturbing the congregation.[14] She also went to hear popular preachers throughout the Netherlands. She visited churches in Amsterdam, Rotterdam, Brielle, Utrecht, Delft and Leiden. She encountered a wide variety of reformed practices in these cities. A seventeenth-century English travel guide to Amsterdam describes the city as having, in addition to many Dutch Reformed churches, a Lutheran church, a French church, an Arminian church, an English church, one Family of Love and three Anabaptist meeting houses which were also used by Socinians and Arians. The city hosted three synagogues and numerous Catholics who worshipped in private residences.[15] This plurality of faiths, living in relative harmony, could not have failed to impress the young princess.

Mary's wide-ranging sermon-going, as well as her position at the Orange court, brought her into contact with many of the Low Countries's leading intellectuals and theologians. She knew many of the academics, ministers and journalists at the forefront of the early Dutch Enlightenment. Among this intellectual milieu was a French-speaking coterie of Protestant ministers that included Pierre Jurieu. In 1683, Mary took her cousin, James, duke of Monmouth, to hear Jurieu in Rotterdam; he had become one of her favourite preachers. Jurieu was an extraordinarily prolific theologian, moral philosopher and historian as well as an ardent supporter of the house of Orange and a millenarian who predicted the overthrow of the anti-Christ, meaning the papacy, in 1689.[16] Jurieu enjoyed the princess's presence at his fiery sermons. He considered her a 'mother and protectoress' of his Walloon Church.[17] But Jurieu was hardly the only leading light with whom Mary was familiar in the 1680s. She was also well acquainted with Friedrich Spanheim, the younger, an orthodox Calvinist professor of divinity at Leiden and 'one of

---

1952), p. 26. On George Hooper and Mary, see 'Appendix. Extract from a Manuscript Account of Dr. Hooper', in Arthur Trevor, *The Life and Times of William the Third, King of England, and Stadtholder of Holland* (2 vols, London, 1835–36), vol. 2, p. 467.

[14]   After the Revolution, Mary procured from the Exchequer an annuity of £30 for this church. See Fredrik Oudschans Dentz, *History of the English Church at The Hague, 1586–1929* (Delft, 1929), p. 22.

[15]   William Brereton, *Travels in Holland, the United Provinces, England, Scotland, and Ireland*, ed. Edward Hawkins (London, 1844), pp. 67–8.

[16]   Pierre Jurieu, *L'accomplissement des prophéties ou la deliverance* (Rotterdam, 1686). On Jurieu's life, see F.R.J. Knetsch, *Pierre Jurieu: Theoloog en Politikus der Refuge* (Kampen, 1967).

[17]   Pierre Jurieu, *A Pastoral Letter Written on the Occasion of the Death of the Late Queen of England* (London, 1695), p. 6.

the most considerable men of the reformed church', according to Pierre Bayle.[18] Additionally, the princess knew Johannes Georg Graevius, the great classicist and chair of history at the University of Utrecht, someone intimately acquainted with Benedictus de Spinoza. She was also on friendly terms with Jacob Perizonius, professor of ancient history at Franeker and Leiden, who was thought to be the greatest scholar in Europe of his generation.[19] When Mary died in 1694, these men, the preachers and professors of the Dutch Enlightenment, published deeply moving funeral sermons in her honour. Time and again, they described Mary's piety as 'enlightened devotion', without superstition or ostentation, and nursed by 'frequent discourses with learned and able divines'.[20]

Mary also spent a good deal of time reading or being read to by her ladies-in-waiting. She erected an impressive library at Het Loo Palace, filled with books in English, French and Dutch on history, architecture, geometry, geography and theology. She read the works of Jurieu and Spanheim. She read English Dissenters, being particularly fond of the Presbyterian writer, William Bates. She read Gilbert Burnet's *History of the Reformation*, William Camden's *Annals of Queen Elizabeth* and Father Paul's *History of the Council of Trent*, which was a favourite among Protestants.[21] The princess was also renowned for her charitable giving, especially for Protestant causes. In 1685 Mary and William made the plight of the Huguenot refugees streaming into Dutch cities following the Revocation of the Edict of Nantes, one of their particular concerns. The princess's largesse, along with her frequently observed devotional practices, made her exceedingly popular in the Netherlands. So much so that on a visit to Amsterdam, the common people stopped her coach 'that they might kiss the wheels' or snatch something of hers as a 'relic'.[22] Thus it was that when the Revolution came in 1688, Princess Mary was

---

[18]   Pierre Bayle, *The Dictionary Historical and Critical of Mr. Pierre Bayle* (5 vols, New York, 1984), vol. 5, p. 194. Bayle's *Dictionary* was first published in 1695.

[19]   Both Graevius and Perizonius honoured the Princess when she died. See *A Funeral Oration of J.G. Grevius, Upon the Death of Mary II* (London, 1695); Jacob Perizonius, *A Funeral Encomium upon the Queen. Most Serene and Potent Princess, Mary II* (London, 1695). Both were translated into English from Latin. On Perizonius's reputation see Joseph M. Levine, *Dr. Woodward's Shield: History, Science, and Satire in Augustan England* (Berkeley, 1977).

[20]   *A Funeral Oration on the Most High, Most Excellent, and Most Potent Princess, Marie Stuart* (London, 1695), pp. 14–15. This was translated from the French and originally printed at The Hague.

[21]   *A Funeral Oration, Pronounc'd upon the Death of the Most Serene and Potent Princess, Mary Stuart* (London, 1695), p. 8; William Payne, *A Sermon upon the Death of the Queen, Preached in the Parish-Church of St. Mary White-Chappel* (London, 1695), p. 24; Gilbert Burnet, *An Essay on the Memory of the Late Queen* (London, 1695), p. 38. Paulo Sarpi's bitter account of the Council of Trent was translated into English in 1620 and influenced generations of Protestants.

[22]   The National Archives, Kew, SP 84/216/134; a slightly altered version is found in W.D. Cooper (ed.), *Savile Correspondence: Letters to and from Henry Savile Esq.* (London, 1858), p. 182.

intellectually sophisticated, enjoyed a degree of personal popularity, in love with her husband and all that he stood for, and above all, trusting in God's providence. She was neither timorous about defying her father, the king of England, nor about defending the true religion. Gilbert Burnet saw Mary immediately before William's expedition and reported that 'she seemed to have a great load on her spirits, but to have no scruple as to the lawfulness of the design'.[23]

William and Mary were crowned king and queen of England on 13 February 1689. Although Mary was considered a regnant queen, all true sovereignty rested in William alone when he was in England. But when the king was abroad, making war on France or tending to his responsibilities in the United Provinces, Mary was invested with executive authority.[24] When William returned, Mary resumed her role as a consort queen. As both a regnant and as a consort queen, Mary II was able to exercise considerable influence, particularly over the Church of England. Mary's ability to guide the Church was made all the more vital after William made several early blunders in his dealings with Anglican churchmen. The prickly sensibilities of the clergy needed to be handled with more care than the indelicate Dutchman was capable of.[25] Mary, a true daughter of the Church of England, easily filled the breach.

What Mary found in England upon her arrival in February shocked her. 'The first thing that surprised me at my coming', she wrote, 'was to see so little devotion in a people so lately in such eminent danger'.[26] She continued to be dismayed by the established Church, its ceremonialism, its treatment of Protestant Dissenters, and the general laxity of the clergy. She immediately set out to change things. Inspired by her experiences in the Netherlands, Mary sought to reform the Church from within and seek to accommodate, if not comprehend, the nonconformists. Her goal was simply to establish a stronger, purer reformed Church that could lead the Protestant world. To do so, she would need like-minded churchmen and thus she surrounded herself with men whose concerns were her concerns: pastoral care, moral reform and charitable giving. In short, Mary and her clergy sought to create a rational, benevolent church.

The months immediately following the Revolution were fundamental to the reshaping of the religious landscape in England, and particularly the Church of

---

[23]   R. Doebner (ed.), *Memoirs of Mary, Queen of England (1689–1693)* (Leipzig, 1886), p. 3; Gilbert Burnet, *Bishop Burnet's History of His Own Time* (hereafter cited as *HOHOT*) (6 vols, Oxford, 1833), vol. 3, p. 311.

[24]   Mary's regencies were 11 June–10 September 1690; 6 January–10 April and 1 May–19 October 1691; 5 March–18 October 1692; 24 March–29 October 1693; and 6 May–9 November 1694.

[25]   William's mistakes are recounted in G.V. Bennett, 'King William III and the Episcopate', in G.V. Bennett and J.D. Walsh (eds), *Essays in Modern English Church History* (London, 1966), pp. 113–55. See also Rose, *England in the 1690s*, pp. 162–5; Thomas Birch, *The Life of the Most Reverend Dr. John Tillotson, Lord Archbishop of Canterbury* (London, 1753), p. 156.

[26]   Doebner, *Memoirs*, p. 11.

England. William and Mary, along with their allies among the Whigs and Low Churchmen, hoped to see the Church accommodate moderate nonconformists through some kind of 'comprehension', a concept floated during the Restoration which had never come to fruition.[27] Many moderate clergymen had long insisted that certain Anglican rites and ceremonies could be suspended, altered, or made optional in an effort to reconcile nonconformists, particularly Presbyterians, to the Church. But the more conservative and jealous elements within the established Church thwarted all designs to comprehend moderate Dissenters, and the failure of comprehension led to the more radical Act of Toleration passed by Parliament in May 1689.[28] Similarly, an ecclesiastical commission charged by the crown with the task of reviewing the Church's liturgy and canons and with the goal of broadening the Church was also derailed. Conservative or High Churchmen, feeling that the passage of the Act of Toleration had already given far too much to nonconformity, would not consent to any reforms and either refused to attend or walked out of the process. Increasingly, the Church bifurcated between the moderates around the court and those High Churchmen bent on preserving the Restoration Church, exclusive and hierarchical. Nonetheless, the court still had tremendous power over the direction of the Church, especially through the power of ecclesiastical appointment. The opportunities given to the new regime to reshape the character of the church hierarchy were vast due to the number of deaths and deprivations following the Revolution. Between 1689 and 1692, the dual monarchy preferred 17 new bishops, translated another three in England, and appointed two more in Wales. Thus out of the 27 English and Welsh sees, 25 were filled by bishops who owed their positions to the dual monarchy by 1692.[29]

William and Mary made several of their most crucial appointments by 1689. Naturally, as newcomers to the turbulent political and religious milieu of London, they depended on those whom they knew and trusted for advice. Among the most knowledgeable was amiable and self-confident Gilbert Burnet. Like so many Scots and English refugees in the 1680s, Burnet had made his way to the Orange court in 1686. He became enchanted by the princess and was soon her close confidant and advisor. James II repeatedly warned William and Mary against entertaining Burnet, whom he considered seditious. But Mary defied her father; she was fond of the highly learned and loquacious Scot. In 1686, her latest chaplain, William Stanley, reported to Whitehall that Burnet was 'perpetually desiring to talk with

---

[27] Tillotson and Stillingfleet, along with several leading Presbyterians tried to bring about such a project in 1668. See Burnet, *HOHOT*, vol. 1, p. 259.

[28] The Act of Toleration (1689) was 'an act for exempting Their Majesties' Protestant subjects dissenting from the Church of England from penalties of certain laws': John Raithby (ed.), *Statutes of the Realm* (11 vols, London, 1810–22), vol. 4, pp. 74–6.

[29] The situation was similar in Ireland. William and Mary appointed 19 of the 23 bishops in Ireland by 1694. F.M. Powicke's *Handbook of British Chronology* (London, 1939), lists the succession of the bishops in England, Wales and Ireland. See Powicke, *Handbook*, pp. 132–272.

the Princess in private and too often gets the liberty'.[30] William may have been less impressed by the garrulous Burnet, but he found his knowledge of the British indispensable and, as Lois Schwoerer and Tony Claydon have both pointed out, Burnet became one of the chief architects of the Revolution.[31]

In the winter of 1688–89 Burnet gave William a list of 10 clergy whom Burnet recommended for promotion to the episcopal bench.[32] Within the next two years, most of those men had been preferred by William and Mary. Burnet himself was consecrated bishop of Salisbury in March 1689. The highly intellectual Edward Stillingfleet became the bishop of Worcester in October 1689 and the latitudinarian Simon Patrick was translated to Chichester at the same time. Mary herself preferred Edward Fowler, a long time protector of nonconformists against persecution, to the see of Gloucester in July 1691. In December 1691, she nominated Thomas Tenison to the bishopric of Lincoln. He too had a reputation for his moderation towards Dissenters. Burnet, Patrick, Fowler, Stillingfleet and Tenison were among the most gifted men in orders.[33] All had much in common with the most significant clergyman in Mary's life, John Tillotson, dean of Canterbury.

By all accounts, John Tillotson was a calm, discreet man, firm in his beliefs, mild and even-tempered in his deportment, and as such he appealed to both William and Mary. They saw in him a man on whom they could place absolute trust and Tillotson's rise in favour and rank was rapid following the Revolution. He was appointed clerk of the king's closet in April 1689. In November 1689 he was made dean of St Paul's, and in May 1690 archbishop of Canterbury. Canterbury was certainly not something that Tillotson had sought. His health was imperfect and he was not without enemies; nor had there been another married archbishop since the time of the Reformation. But William and Mary were adamant; they would have no one else.[34] While Tillotson's three and a half years as archbishop were often fraught with conflict among the clergy, his vision of the Church fit perfectly with the queen's. Together they were able to redirect it away from the exclusive and

---

[30] Burnet, *HOHOT*, vol. 3, pp. 204–7; Bodleian Library, Oxford, Rawlinson MSS, 983 C, William Stanley to Henry Compton, August 1686.

[31] Lois G. Schwoerer, 'Propaganda in the Revolution of 1688–89', *The American Historical Review*, 82/4 (1977): pp. 843–74; Claydon, *William III and the Godly Revolution*, pp. 29–63.

[32] Burnet's list is published in R.W. Blencowe (ed.), *Diary of the Times of Charles the Second by Honourable Henry Sidney* (2 vols, London, 1843), vol. 2, pp. 281–8. Those men listed are: John Tillotson, Simon Patrick, Thomas Tenison, Edward Stillingfleet, John Sharp, William Sherlock, Dr. Ayrshott, William Wake, Edward Fowler and Anthony Horneck.

[33] On these men as a group, see Gordon Rupp, *Religion in England, 1688–1791* (Oxford, 1986), pp. 29–39; W.M. Spellman, *The Latitudinarians and the Church of England, 1660–1700* (Athens, GA, 1993).

[34] On Tillotson's reluctance to accept Canterbury, see *Letters of Lady Rachel Russell: From the Manuscript in the Library at Wooburn Abbey* (London, 1801), pp. 240–42. See also Burnet, *HOHOT*, vol. 2, pp. 74–6.

dogmatic institution that came out of the Restoration settlement, and toward the eighteenth-century latitudinarian Church.

Like so many of Mary's bishops, Tillotson had been a Cambridge man during the heady days of the Civil Wars and Commonwealth. And, like so many of the men who were later styled 'latitudinarians', Tillotson came from nonconformist stock and retained a certain sense of Puritanism throughout his life. On the other hand, he was also one among a group of young clergy who rejected doctrinaire Calvinism. At Cambridge, Tillotson, as well as Patrick, Tenison and Fowler, was influenced by Platonists, men like Benjamin Whichcote and Henry More. In the late 1660s, Tillotson was in London, where his weekly lecture at St Lawrence Jewry was attended by 'a numerous audience brought together from the remotest parts of the metropolis'.[35] Tillotson's sermon style was something altogether new. He rejected the ornate and elaborate metaphysical discourses characteristic of the best early Stuart divines like John Donne, as well as the enthusiastic digressions and cant of the Puritans. Instead, he appealed 'to reason and to commonsense, the careful, comprehensive argument, solid, unhurried, unadorned'.[36] In 1666 he became one of Charles II's chaplains, and in 1672 he was appointed dean of Canterbury. John Spurr makes the point that Tillotson aimed to please; he had friends in all camps, including rationalists like John Locke and Socinians like Thomas Firmin, and this, in the end, made him mightily vulnerable to attack, particularly from High Churchmen.[37] But what seemed to most characterize Tillotson's religiosity was his thorough-going reasonableness; his view that reason and religion were compatible, even essential to one another, and this above all elides to the great popularity of Tillotson's sermons in eighteenth-century England and America.[38]

Tillotson's liberal theology with its emphasis on practical spirituality and ethical behaviour appealed to Mary's desire for a moral reformation. Like William and Mary, Tillotson had no interest in the retrenchment of inessential dogmas, of fighting old battles over rituals, signs or formulaic prayer. In this new age of reason, such 'things indifferent' were not worth squabbling over. Tillotson believed in a rational, ethical Christianity, one that promoted virtue, prudence, charity and

---

[35]   Birch, *Life*, p. 29.

[36]   Charles H.E. Smyth, *The Art of Preaching: A Practical Survey of Preaching in the Church of England, 747–1939* (London, 1940), p. 146; Norman Sykes, 'The Sermons of Archbishop Tillotson', *Theology*, 58/422 (1955): p. 297.

[37]   Spurr, '"Latitudinarianism" and the Restoration Church', p. 73.

[38]   Various collections of Tillotson's sermons were in print throughout the eighteenth century; they were particularly recommended to country clerics to imitate and borrow. See, for example, the advice in *The Spectator*, 447 (2 August 1712). For the influence of Tillotson in America, see Norman Fiering, 'The First American Enlightenment: Tillotson, Leverett, and Philosophical Anglicanism', *The New England Quarterly*, 54/3 (1981): pp. 307–44; Richard Beale Davis, *A Colonial Southern Bookshelf: Reading in the Eighteenth Century* (Athens, GA, 1979), pp. 79–80; Kevin J. Hayes, *A Colonial Woman's Bookshelf* (Knoxville, TN, 1996), p. 50.

enlightened self-interest in everyday living. The persecution of Dissent was an abomination to him. Rather, he wished to broaden the Church and, like the queen, was earnest in his desire for comprehension. Thus with Tillotson and Burnet at her side, the queen sought to lead the Church, promoting moral reform, pastoral care and moderate clergymen, whom, to varying degrees, accepted and supported the Revolution.[39]

The queen, Tillotson and Burnet not only shared a similar vision for the Church and for the Protestant world; they also shared a genuine sympathy, respect and admiration for one another. Tillotson and Burnet had long been friends. Tillotson had read the manuscript of Burnet's *History of the Reformation of the Church of England* in the late 1670s and Burnet later wrote that he 'learned the best part' of what he knew from Tillotson.[40] Tillotson, in turn, relied heavily on Burnet during his years at Canterbury, seeking his advice and help on numerous occasions. He worked on an even more intimate and regular basis with the queen whose wisdom and piety he admired. She was, he wrote, 'a great example to us of a decent and unaffected devotion of a most serious and steady attention, without wandering, without diversion, and without drowsiness'. In a letter to Rachel, Lady Russell, Tillotson described the queen's reaction to his acceptance of the primacy of Canterbury. 'She came out of the closet on Sunday last, commanded me to wait upon her after dinner, which I did'. Once together, the queen began their conversation by speaking to 'a treatise sent to her in manuscript out of Holland' by Frederick Spanheim about a union among Anglicans and English Dissenters. This was a project close to the queen's heart. Tellingly, and rather typically of Mary who was often both sagacious and circumspect in her handling of the clergy, it was only after recommending Spanheim's treatise to Tillotson that she expressed her 'great joy' over his promotion. Later Tillotson wrote again to Lady Russell, 'The queen's extraordinary favour in me to a degree much beyond my expectation is no small support to me'.[41] Over the next four years, until his death in November 1694, Tillotson and the queen worked closely together, organizing a series of national fasts and thanksgivings, initiating moral reforms and charity projects. So often did Tillotson seek the queen's council, that in June 1692, when he composed a list of resolutions, he wrote: 'Not to trouble the Queen anymore with my troubles' and

---

[39] Norman Sykes, *Church and State in England in the XVIIIth Century* (Cambridge, 1934), pp. 256–61; John Walsh and Stephen Taylor, introduction to Walsh, Haydon and Taylor (eds), *Church of England, c. 1689–c. 1833: From Toleration to Tractarianism*, pp. 35–47.

[40] Burnet is referring to both Tillotson and William Lloyd in this quote: Burnet, *HOHOT*, vol. 1, p. 191. Following Tillotson's death, Burnet wrote a passionate defense of his friend and himself in response to George Hickes. 'He was the greatest example I have ever known of a gentleness … he is now above envy, and beyond slander; and his name is and will be long remembered with honour': Gilbert Burnet, *Reflections upon a Pamphlet Entituled [Some Discourses upon Dr. Burnet and Dr. Tillotson, Occasioned by the Late Funeral Sermon of the Former upon the Latter]* (London, 1696), p. 90.

[41] *Letters of Lady Rachel Russell*, pp. 265, 282.

'Not to disturb the Queen on the Lord's day, or, if I speak with her, to speak only on matters of religion'.[42] The relationship between Mary and Gilbert Burnet was equally intimate. Burnet had a weekly audience at Whitehall with the queen; he seems to have been utterly devoted to her. He later wrote, 'I never admired any person so entirely as I did her.... The purity and sublimity of her mind was the perfectest [sic] thing I ever saw; I never felt myself sink so much under anything that happened to me as by her death'.[43]

Together, the queen, Tillotson and Burnet were responsible for two of the greatest Anglican treatises of the era: Burnet's *Discourse of the Pastoral Care* (1692) and his *Exposition of the Thirty Nine Articles*, which was not published until 1699. Burnet's *Discourse* came out of the queen's desire for the bishops to act as role models within their dioceses. Mary wished to root out absenteeism and non-residency and she urged her bishops to be exemplars of piety and charity to all at the local level. Her influence is reflected throughout Burnet's *Discourse*, a handbook on pastoral care and responsibilities, which details the benefits of vigorous pastoral care, catechetical instruction and the enforcement of moral discipline. At the heart of the *Discourse* is the notion that by setting an exemplary model, the clergy of the Established Church might win back the Dissenters, 'for the manners and the labors of the clergy, are real arguments which all people do both understand and feel'. Pious actions were better than dogmatic rules and ritualism.[44] Burnet dedicated his book to the queen, although she would only allow the barest of dedications; 'She says she knows', wrote Tillotson to Burnet, '[that] you can use no moderation in speaking of her'.[45] Shortly, thereafter, Mary and Tillotson asked Burnet to write a justification of the Thirty-Nine Articles (1563) which had been originally devised to clarify the Church's positions in relation to Catholicism and continental Protestantism. Again, Burnet's *Exposition* on the articles clearly represents the moderate churchmanship of the queen. It is at once both a comprehensive apology of Anglican principles and a plea against religious rigidity. Tony Claydon is certainly right to assert that Burnet sought to appeal to both moderate Dissenters and High Churchmen.[46] The fact that both the *Discourse* and the *Exposition* went into multi-editions and were listed time and again on 'recommended reading' lists for Anglicans throughout the long eighteenth century attests to the influence and legacy of this threesome.

Among the initial ecclesiastical matters that fell into the hands of the queen was the knotty problem presented by those clergy that refused to accept the Revolution.

----

[42]   Birch, *Life*, p. 269.

[43]   T.E.S. Clarke, H.C. Foxcroft and C.H. Firth, *A Life of Gilbert Burnet, Bishop of Salisbury* (Cambridge, 1907), p. 286; Gilbert Burnet, *A Supplement to Burnet's History of My Own Time*, ed. H.C. Foxcroft (Oxford, 1902), p. 405.

[44]   Burnet, *Supplement*, p. 507; Gilbert Burnet, *A Discourse of the Pastoral Care* (London, 1692), p. x.

[45]   Tillotson cited in Birch, *Life*, p. 266.

[46]   Claydon, *William III and the Godly Revolution*, p. 175.

Mary was extremely eager to prevent a schism within the Church between the abjuring and nonjuring clergy. She was also unwilling to allow the Nonjurors the slightest chance to play the part of martyrs. For two years, the nonjuring clergy were left unmolested and in possession of their dioceses, giving them plenty of time to rethink their decision, one that meant losing their incomes. But by the summer of 1691, the government's patience had run out. The Nonjurors had to be removed and the new bishops appointed. With the king abroad, the queen oversaw to the removal of the nonjuring clergy and began 'filling the Bishopricks'.[47] It was Mary who ordered Archbishop William Sancroft to vacate Lambeth Palace. The queen also understood the opportunity that had been given her and she strove to 'produce a great change in the church and in the temper of the clergy' through promotion and translation.[48] For the most part, Mary's appointees were Low Church. These were men interested in enlightened, practical solutions to the Church's problems rather than theological dogmatism.

But Mary would also make appointments based on political convenience, particularly in her effort to reconcile those clergy having twinges of conscience over the Revolution. As Burnet would later put it, 'The Queen hoped to overcome the peevishness of the leaders of the [High Church] party by preferring them'.[49] She tried this tactic with the important bishopric of Bath and Wells. In 1691 she nominated William Beveridge to replace the nonjuring Thomas Ken. Mary knew that Ken had 'a great desire to be a martyr' and determined that he should not be gratified.[50] While Beveridge was no friend of the Revolution, his monastic lifestyle and 'Anglo-Catholic' piety resembled that of Ken's, and the queen hoped that Beveridge's replacement of Ken would make for an easy transition for the diocese.[51] Her plan backfired when Beveridge, on the advice of Nonjurors and Jacobites, refused. The queen then turned to Richard Kidder, another moderate and member of Tillotson's circle.[52]

Mary, together with Tillotson, also saw to the promotion of the High Churchman, John Sharp. In this case, they were more successful. Sharp was one of the ten clergymen recommended to William by Burnet in the winter of 1689. Like many of the leading London clergy in the 1680s, Sharp had both distinguished himself in defense of the Church and acquired James II's wrath with his anti-Catholic preaching. In 1690 Sharp was offered his choice of the sees vacated by

---

[47] Doebner, *Memoirs*, p. 37.

[48] Burnet, *HOHOT*, vol. 4, p. 212.

[49] Burnet, *Supplement*, p. 504.

[50] Burnet, *HOHOT*, vol. 4, p. 11, n. 1.

[51] Gareth Bennett refers to Ken's theological outlook as Anglo-Catholic, meaning that Ken had little interest in Reformation theology, preferring instead the study of the Church Fathers and the councils of the early Church. See Gareth Bennett, *To the Church of England* (Worthing, 1988).

[52] E.H. Plumptre, *The Life of Thomas Ken, D.D.* (2 vols, London, 1890), vol. 2, p. 51. See also White Kennett, *Compleat History of England* (3 vols, London, 1706), vol. 3, p. 634.

the Nonjurors. But he refused, not wishing to enjoy what these men, many of them his friends, had lost. William was apparently disgusted by Sharp's sympathies, but Mary much less so. She had been impressed by Sharp when he first preached before her in the spring of 1689.[53] Mary and Tillotson oversaw Sharp's elevation to the bishopric of York in July 1691 upon the death of the former occupant. As Sharp became increasingly aligned with Tory and High Church politics, Burnet would assert that Sharp's promotion had been a mistake. Similarly, the duchess of Marlborough described Sharp as 'a warm and zealous man for the church', but, in fact, Sharp was no militant.[54] He would forbid the clergy in his diocese from 'railing at Dissenters' in their sermons. More importantly from Mary's perspective, he had supported the new regime, earned her admiration at the pulpit, and ultimately proved on numerous occasions that he was far more interested in pastoral care than politics.[55]

Mary's promotion of John Sharp and other High Churchmen such as George Hooper, who she appointed to the deanship of Canterbury in the summer of 1691, is certainly proof that she was not merely interested in Whiggish, Low Church, or latitudinarian-tempered clergy.[56] She was attracted to clergymen of solid intellectual and moral calibre. Mary's keen regard for Edward Stillingfleet, bishop of Worcester, is a case in point. Upon the death of Tillotson in November 1694, Mary was a warm supporter of Stillingfleet's promotion to Canterbury and spoke to the king about him on several occasions.[57] Stillingfleet had been an early and ardent supporter of the queen's reformation movement which, no doubt, endeared him to her. He was also fond of Mary. When Princess Anne sent Stillingfleet to the queen to mediate in a quarrel between the two sisters, he returned from his meeting with Mary enamoured. 'I find him very partial to her', Anne lamented in a letter to Lady Churchill.[58] Stillingfleet was on good terms with Tillotson and his circle and while often labelled a 'latitudinarian', Stillingfleet's theological temper was complex.[59] He had little sympathy for Dissenters whom he regarded as schismatic without good reason.[60] He was also a first-rate theologian who saw the threat that John Locke's epistemology posed to the mysteries of Christianity, such the historic doctrine of the Trinity. In fact, throughout much of the early 1690s, he carried out

---

[53]   Thomas Sharp, *The Life of John Sharp D.D.* (2 vols, London, 1825), vol. 1, pp. 106–11.

[54]   Sarah Churchill and Nathaniel Hooke, *An Account of the Conduct of the Dowager Duchess of Marlborough* (London, 1742), p. 134.

[55]   Burnet, *Supplement*, p. 504; 'John Sharp', *Oxford Dictionary of National Biography*.

[56]   'Appendix. Extract from a Manuscript Account of Dr. Hooper', p. 471.

[57]   Burnet, *HOHOT*, vol. 4, p. 238.

[58]   Churchill and Hooke, *Account of the Conduct*, p. 75.

[59]   In return, Tillotson had a deep and abiding respect for Stillingfleet, dedicating his famous *The Rule of Faith* (London, 1666) to Stillingfleet.

[60]   Edward Stillingfleet, *The Unreasonableness of Separation* (London, 1681).

a heated political debate with the great philosopher.[61] Little wonder the Whigs around William III found Stillingfleet's principles 'too high', and in the end, the king rejected his wife's advice and gave Canterbury to Thomas Tenison instead.[62] The more moderate Tenison did prove a good choice. He carried on the policies of Tillotson and the queen throughout his long tenure and not always under the most auspicious circumstances. Following her accession to the throne, Queen Anne spurned Tenison whose Low Church leanings and Williamite loyalties she detested, preferring Sharp and High Churchmen at her court.[63]

Although Queen Mary did not seek simply to fill the church hierarchy with like-minded men and valued, above all, clerics of learning and piety, the episcopal bench during her short reign came to be dominated by moderates, men whom H.C. Foxcroft called 'Tillotsonian' and whom, more recently, Tony Claydon has labelled 'Burnetine'.[64] These were the men who accepted the Revolution and who shared, for the most part, the queen's concerns: pastoral care, moral reformation, and a reaching out to Dissenters at home as well as the Protestant International in Europe and America. We might call these clergymen, 'Marite'. Many of them preached before the queen, had their sermons published by her order, and wrote deeply felt funeral sermons on the occasion of her sudden death. These churchmen included not only prelates, but numerous members of the lower clergy as well. Anthony Horneck, a German Protestant, who made his career in the Church of England, was given a prebend at Westminster Abbey by the queen in July 1691. Horneck was not only friends with Tillotson, Burnet and Richard Kidder, he was a scholar, a popular preacher and an early supporter of the Reformation of Manners.[65] In 1692, the Dissenter turned High Churchman, Samuel Wesley, the father of the more famous Wesley brothers, dedicated his *The Life of our Blessed Lord and Saviour Jesus Christ* to Mary, famously comparing her to the Virgin Mary. He later credited the queen with his appointment to the rectory of Epworth,

---

[61] In November 1696, Stillingfleet published *A Discourse in Vindication of the Doctrine of the Trinity* which was a response to both Locke's *The Reasonableness of Christianity* (London, 1695) and the application of Lockean epistemology in John Toland's *Christianity not Mysterious* (dated 1696 but published in December 1695). The polemical debate between Locke and Stillingfleet was carried out from 1696 until Stillingfleet's death in March 1699, each writing three tracts.

[62] Burnet, *HOHOT*, vol. 4, p. 244. Tenison was by no means disagreeable to Mary, and she defended him against his detractors shortly before her death. See *Memoirs of the Life and Times of the Most Reverend Father in God, Dr. Thomas Tennison* (London, 1716), p. 20.

[63] Edward Carpenter, *Thomas Tenison, Archbishop of Canterbury, His Life and Times* (London, 1948), pp. 415, 422.

[64] Clarke, Foxcroft and Firth, *Life of Gilbert Burnet*, p. 325; Claydon, *William III and the Godly Revolution*, p. 68.

[65] Richard Kidder, *The Life of the Reverend Anthony Horneck, D.D., Late Preacher at the Savoy* (London, 1698), pp. 21, 45–6.

Lincolnshire.[66] At the time of her death, Mary was also supporting the career of a young Irish minster, John Finglas, who had come to England to study and was, apparently, often in the queen's presence. He found her death devastating, calling her 'the most careful, prudent, and most tender and indulgent Queen, and in all respects my parent!' In his funeral sermon for the queen, Finglas, like so many of the lower clergy, challenges his audience to continue to honour her by supporting her charities and her work with the Church and especially by placing 'a double value' on the king. 'Let this heavy stroke render his life more dear to us'.[67]

These men all remained strong supporters of the Williamite regime throughout the 1690s. While Mary's death in December 1694 was seen as a severe blow to the Church, many of the clergy who honoured her in their eulogies also used the occasion to further justify the Revolution, lambast Jacobites and Nonjurors, and promote Mary's vision for the Church. The queen was 'a true tender nursing mother to the best of Churches', Thomas Bowber told his parishioners at St Swithin in London, but 'her chief care was to support the Protestant interest and religion throughout all Europe'. Edward Fowler, bishop of Gloucester, who had waited on the queen for several years as her chaplain and whose political and religious beliefs were in complete accord with the new regime, declared that Mary was a 'second Elizabeth', whose zeal for the Church had not corrupted her with 'any sour prejudices against other Protestant churches'.[68] Her time in Holland had broadened her scope and endowed her with empathy, understanding and charity towards all, as William Payne put it, 'sober Dissenters'. Payne, a zealous supporter of the Revolution, and a chaplain-in-ordinary to William and Mary, declared in his funeral sermon that 'her religion lay not in affected singularities, in pharisaical showes and pretences ... or in any bigotry and immoderate zeal for little indifferent things of no value or importance in religion; but it lay in solid and substantial, in wise and regular and decent piety and devotion'. Her task had been 'building up and repairing the whole Church of England ... improving its worship, ordering its discipline, amending its defects, in making up its breaches, and bringing all sober Protestants to worship to one communion, which would have been the greatest blow to popery'. Mary's Church stood between Catholicism and Puritanism;

---

[66] Wesley was appointed to Epworth in March 1695 after the queen's death that winter. Mary could have made the appointment before her death or simply suggested it, and William and Tenison saw to it. See Luke Tyerman, *The Life and Times of Rev. Samuel Wesley* (London, 1866), p. 193.

[67] John Finglas, *A Sermon Preached at the Chappel Royal in the Tower, upon Sunday the Sixth Day of January, 1694/5* (London, 1695), pp. 21, 25.

[68] Thomas Bowber, *A Sermon Preached in the Parish-Church of St. Swithin, London, March 10th, 1694/5, upon the Much Lamented Death of Our Most Gracious Queen* (London, 1695), p. 19; Edward Fowler, *A Discourse of the Great Disingenuity and Unreasonableness of Repining at Afflicting Providences ... Published upon the Occasion of the Death of Our Gracious Sovereign Queen Mary* (London, 1695), p. 17.

between, as Payne put it, the 'garish dress of too many ceremonies … [and] the naked and sordid undress of none'.[69]

Of course, the *via media* was always the Anglican way, and yet it was so often lost amid the extremes that marked seventeenth-century religious history, from Archbishop Laud to Hugh Peters, from the persecuting Restoration Church to undermining policies of James II. Mary and her clergy strove for balance and for moderation. And while Mary's reign was short, the churchmen she helped to places of power carried on her vision and that of John Tillotson. Edward Fowler (died 1714), Simon Patrick (died 1707), William Lloyd (died 1717), Richard Kidder (died 1703) and, above all, Gilbert Burnet (died 1715) and Thomas Tenison (died 1715), along with legions of Whiggish lower clergy, led the Church through its 'Age of Danger', and it was this 'latitudinarian' temper within the eighteenth-century Church that would see it safely across the high seas of Enlightenment and evangelicalism.

---

[69]   Payne, *Sermon upon the Death of the Queen*, pp. 16, 23–4.

Chapter 7
Religion and Sociability in the Correspondence of Damaris Masham (1658–1708)

Sarah Hutton

Damaris Masham has acquired a modest fame chiefly for her friendship with the philosopher, John Locke. Latterly she has attracted interest as a woman philosopher in her own right, for her two books, *A Discourse Concerning the Love of God* (1696) and *Occasional Thoughts in Reference to a Vertuous or Christian Life* (1705) – both published anonymously.[1] As these titles indicate, the content of these publications is as much religious as philosophical. She also wrote letters, most famously to Locke and Leibniz.[2] As one might expect from correspondence with philosophers, these deal with philosophical topics, but as in her books, the philosophical matters discussed are cognate to religion – for example the existence of God and the religious foundations of morality. But there is far more to these letters than philosophical exchange, and there is more to her treatment of religion than its philosophical aspect. A sufficient number of the letters have survived for us to form an impression of her personality and interests. We can gauge something of her intellectual life from the books which she mentions. The letters show that she was sociable by nature, someone who valued her friends, and particularly valued the intellectual conversation which they could provide. Since her letters

---

[1]   For Damaris Masham as a philosopher see Jacqueline Broad, *Women Philosophers of the Seventeenth Century* (Cambridge, 2003); Sarah Hutton, 'Damaris Cudworth, Lady Masham: Between Platonism and Enlightenment', *British Journal for the History of Philosophy*, 1/1 (1993): pp. 29–54; Margaret Atherton, 'Women Philosophers in Early Modern England', in Steven M. Nadler (ed.), *A Companion to Early Modern Philosophy* (Oxford, 2005), pp. 404–21. The growing literature is critiqued by James G. Buickerood in his rather intemperate and anti-feminist article, 'What is it with Damaris, Lady Masham?: The Historiography of One Early Modern Woman Philosopher', *Locke Studies*, 5 (2005): pp. 179–214. For a balanced reply see Richard Acworth, 'Cursory Reflections upon an Article Entitled "What is it with Damaris, Lady Masham?"', *Locke Studies*, 6 (2006): pp. 189–97.

[2]   Lady Masham's correspondence with Locke is printed in E.S. De Beer (ed.), *The Correspondence of John Locke* (8 vols, Oxford, 1976–89). All quotations from this edition are made by permission of Oxford University Press. Her correspondence with Leibniz is printed in G.W. Leibniz, *Die Philosophischen Schriften von Gottfried Wilhelm Leibniz*, ed. C.I. Gerhardt (7 vols, Berlin, 1875–90), vol. 3.

are in effect conversations with her correspondents, we encounter her religious opinions in the context of social exchange. Sociability gives a further dimension to her references to religion. On the personal side, it is perhaps, surprising to find that someone who published serious moral philosophy, often made humourous references to religion. On the other hand her letters show that religion evidently had a socially propaedeutic function, which was particularly useful for a woman seeking an entry point into the homosocial world of philosophical debate. In this regard her discussion of religion offers an insight into how she managed to achieve an intellectual life. In this chapter, I start by placing Damaris Masham in the social and religious context of her time, focusing particularly on her position as an educated woman. I reflect on the importance of letters for women philosophers, by way of introduction to a discussion of how religion figures in her correspondence with Locke and Leibniz.

By all accounts, Lady Masham was a highly intelligent woman with a vibrant personality. Locke's friend, Anne Grigg called her 'an intolerably witty Lady'. In an otherwise peevish letter to her, Locke makes appreciative mention of 'The perfection and goodnesse of your inlightened and enlarged minde'.[3] He told Philip van Limborch that she was 'a remarkably gifted woman', adding that 'I know few men capable of discussing with such insight the most abstruse subjects'. Her interest in 'abstruse subjects' was both fostered and hindered by her personal circumstances. She came from an intellectual background: she was the daughter of the Cambridge Platonist, Ralph Cudworth, and Damaris Andrews. She grew up in Restoration Cambridge, where her father was Master of Christ's College and Regius Professor of Hebrew. Her academic family background notwithstanding, she was discouraged from pursuing intellectual interests as a girl ('But as I was Diverted from It when I was Young, first by the Commands of Others'). She was further hindered by poor eyesight ('that Weakness which Hapned in my Sight').[4] Through her marriage to Sir Francis Masham, whom she married at the relatively mature age of 27 in 1685, she acquired the status of titled gentlewoman. The Mashams were landed gentry with estates at the manor of Oates in the parish of High Laver, Essex. This marriage made her stepmother to her husband's eight children. She had one child of her own, Francis Cudworth Masham. As the wife of a country squire, she found herself fully, and not always happily, occupied with domestic and rural affairs. The practical business of running a household and raising a numerous family left her little time or opportunity to pursue her intellectual interests. She confided to Locke that 'The World through long Acquaintance begun almost to Claime All my Thoughts'.[5]

We can get a measure of what country living was like for an educated woman from the account which she gives of the hazards of being a philosophical lady in her *Occasional Thoughts*. This is the book in which she makes a case for the

---

[3]   Locke, *Correspondence*, letter 1322, vol. 4, p. 142.

[4]   Ibid., letter 1040, vol. 3, p. 431.

[5]   Ibid., pp. 431–2.

education of women, on the grounds that they are expected to be the moral tutors of their children, but that they can only do this effectively if they understand what they are doing. Damaris Masham acknowledges the various disincentives to female education, among them the discouraging image of the educated lady, especially of the philosophical lady – and the reference to philosophy here means that this is quite possibly a self-portrait.

> But in the countrey she would probably fare still worse [than in the town]; for there her understanding of the Christian Religion would go nearer to render her suspected of Heresy even by those who thought the best of her: while her little zeal for any Sect or Party would make the Clergy of all sorts give her out for a *Socinian* or a Deist: And should but a very little Philosophy be added to her other Knowledge, even for an Atheist. The Parson of the Parish, for fear of being ask'd hard Questions, would be shy of coming near her, be their Reception ever so inviting; and this could not but carry some ill intimation with it to such as Reverenc'd the Doctor, and who, it is likely, might already be satisy'd from Reports of Nurses and Maids, that their Lady was indeed a Woman of very odd Whimsies.[6]

One can well understand that faced with the kind of prejudice and opprobrium which she here describes, an intelligent countrywoman might be taken to be controversial, whether she wished to be or not, and why she might protest her religious orthodoxy rather loudly in order to avoid accusations of heterodoxy or atheism. Everything we can gather about Damaris Masham indicates that there was ample scope for intimidating the local parson (though there is no evidence that she actually did). She certainly had a reputation for being knowledgeable on religious matters. We have Locke's testimony that she was 'much occupied with study and reflection on theological and philosophical matters'.[7] The titles and content of her two published books bear this out. Even when she was very young ('lorsque j'étois fort jeune'), she was perceptive enough to note discrepancies between her father's religious beliefs and the Anglican creed as set out in the Thirty-Nine Articles.[8] Her reputation for acumen in bible interpretation was such that no less a person than Isaac Newton sought her opinion on his interpretation of

---

[6]   Damaris Masham, *Occasional Thoughts in Reference to a Vertuous or Christian Life* (London, 1705), pp. 199–200.

[7]   'Domina ipsa ita in Theologis philosophisque studiis et contemplationibus versata est ut paucos invenias homines quibuscum majore cum fructu et jucunditate verseris: Limatissimi inprimis est judicii. paucosque novi qui tanta cum perspicuitate de rebus abstrusissimis et a captu non dico faeminarum sed etiam plerorumque literatorum remotis <disserant> et difficultates <solvant>' : Locke, *Correspondence*, letter 1375, vol. 4, p. 237.

[8]   As she reported to Philip van Limborch: see A. des Amorie van der Hoeven, *De Joanne Clerico et Philippo a Limborch: Dissertationes Duae* (Amsterdam, 1843), pp. 137–8 (original, Universiteitsbibliotheek Amsterdam, Amsterdam, UBA.MS.31.c). Characteristically, she quizzed her father about it.

a passage in the Book of Daniel.[9] Yet she herself made no presumptions about her own theological expertise.

If Damaris Masham felt out of place in rural Essex as a thinking woman, there was certainly common ground between her and her husband's family in point of religious and political sympathies. Both the Cudworths and the Mashams were families with a history of parliamentary and puritan affiliations. Sir Francis Masham's father took the side of Parliament in the Civil War.[10] Though not a regicide, he had been a member of the Republican Council of State, and had supported Cromwellian rule subsequently. Damaris Masham's father, Ralph Cudworth, had Parliamentarian connections. He owed his early promotion at the University of Cambridge to Parliamentary purges of Royalist sympathizers. He preached to the House of Commons during the Civil War and subsequently advised Cromwell's government on such matters as the readmission of the Jews and the statutes for the proposed college at Durham. He even considered dedicating a work to Richard Cromwell in 1659.[11] The Mashams became conforming members of the Church of England, who donated altar silverware to their parish church to replace silver plate lost in the Civil War (the Masham silverware is still in the possession of the High Laver church), but they belonged to the moderate middle ground, which might nowadays be called 'broad church'. And they were sympathetic to the cause of religious toleration. After the Revolution Settlement of 1689, the Mashams returned to mainstream politics in the Whig ascendancy. Damaris's father, too, conformed at the Restoration. But others in his family had strong non-conformist sympathies, which were less easily accommodated at the Restoration. Ralph Cudworth retained his college post with some difficulty after 1660: along with his Christ's College colleague, Henry More, he was pilloried as a 'latitudinarian' by dogmatic Restoration Anglicans.[12] His doctrinal orthodoxy was called in question by some: after the delayed publication of his magnum opus, *The True Intellectual System of the Universe* (1678) he was accused of heterodoxy in point of Trinitarianism. Cudworth's strongly eirenic stance on religious differences finds an echo in his daughter's attitude to religious disputes, and would have struck a chord with John Locke's advocacy of religious toleration. Likewise, his Cambridge Platonist accommodation of reason and religion is consistent with both Locke's and Lady Masham's commitment to the compatibility of reason and faith. This

[9]   Locke, *Correspondence*, letter 1405, vol. 4, p. 288.
[10]   Peter Laslett, 'Masham of Otes', *History Today*, 3/8 (1953): pp. 535–43; Mark Goldie, *John Locke and the Mashams at Oates* (Cambridge, 2004).
[11]   On Cudworth and the interregnum, see my 'A Radical Review of the Cambridge Platonists', in Ariel Hessayon and David Finnegan (eds), *Varieties of Seventeenth- and Early Eighteenth-Century English Radicalism in Context* (Farnham, 2011), pp. 161–82.
[12]   Marjorie Nicolson, 'Christ's College and the Latitude Men', *Modern Philology*, 27/1 (1929): pp. 35–53; David Dockrill and J.M. Lee, 'Reflections on an Episode in Cambridge Latitudinarianism: Henry More's Epistle Dedicatory to Gilbert Sheldon of his *Enchiridion Metaphysicum*', *Prudentia*, Supplement (1994): pp. 207–23.

latitudinarian legacy is evident in Damaris Masham's writings. In her *Occasional Thoughts* she positions herself as a member of the Church of England, and that church as a church of the middle way between superstition (Roman Catholicism) and enthusiasm (fundamentalist dogmatism). The *via media* is distinguishable from either extreme by its reasonableness. In *A Discourse Concerning the Love of God*, she emphasizes that Christianity is a *practical* religion, which grounds morality in an *active* life. We 'are sent into the World for … *doing* good' (my italics),[13] she writes, and we are guided by reason to understand both our religious and moral duties. It is clear that her sense of religious sensibility is firmly rooted in *this* world. Our knowledge of God is something we acquire by applying reason to the world around us. We know God through his works and 'by the Existence of the Creatures'.[14] The objections which she makes in *A Discourse* to the occasionalism of John Norris are very much against the unworldly character of his account of how we come to love God. Where Norris had claimed, 'That God, not the creature, is the immediate, efficient Cause of our Sensations', Damaris Masham argued that it is our delight in this world which leads us to a knowledge and love of God. The moral philosophy which she outlines in her books is also a *social* philosophy: 'There is nothing more evident than that Mankind is destin'd for a sociable Life'. And moral action entails social *interaction*: without 'commerce with Men', people will 'grow Wild' rather than improve morally.[15]

I. Letters, Religion and Female Philosophers

Damaris Masham's tiny published output, and the anonymity of her published writings, are not untypical of early modern women, especially philosophers. But her extant correspondence is unrepresentative of women of this period, by virtue of the fact that most of the surviving letters are between a woman and male correspondents to whom she was not related. Friendships between men and women were not unknown in this period—the most well-known example being that between John Evelyn and Margaret Godolphin.[16] Damaris Masham's correspondence is also untypical of women's letters because most of her correspondence was with philosophers. Not only that, but her philosophical correspondents happened to be two of the most famous living philosophers of her time, John Locke and Gottfried Wilhelm Leibniz. Unsurprisingly, therefore, the main focus of attention to her has been philosophical. But I want to leave aside the primarily philosophical aspects of her letters, and to focus on their religious content, such as it is.

---

[13] Damaris Masham, *A Discourse Concerning the Love of God* (London, 1696), p. 126.

[14] Ibid., pp. 62, 65.

[15] Ibid., pp. 123, 126.

[16] Frances Harris, *Transformations of Love. The Friendship of John Evelyn and Margaret Godolphin* (Oxford, 2003).

If the philosophical content of Masham's letters is untypical for early modern women in general, it is not unusual for female philosophers whose letters are largely taken up with philosophical discussion. In fact letters are especially important as evidence for female philosophical activity, as in the case of Anne Conway and Damaris Masham. In many cases letters are the only source we have for their philosophy (the most notable case being Princess Elisabeth of Bohemia, correspondent of Descartes).[17] A striking feature of the correspondences of these philosophical women is the fact that so many of their letters are linked to religion in one way or another. Much of Anne Conway's correspondence with Henry More is devoted to discussing the views of different sectarian leaders, and the mysteries of the Jewish kabbalah.[18] Catharine Trotter Cockburn's interventions in print focus on what seem to be abstruse points of divinity, and she defended Locke's *Essay Concerning Human Understanding* partly on religious grounds.[19] Mary Astell's correspondence with John Norris centres on the relationship between God and his creation.[20] (The only seventeenth-century woman philosopher specifically to eschew discussing religion is Margaret Cavendish.) The predominance of religious topics in the correspondence of philosophical women in part reflects the fact that at this time the boundary between philosophy and theology was porous. Many philosophers oscillate between theology and philosophy. Some of the most secular works of philosophy have religious aims: this is true of Locke's *Essay Concerning Human Understanding*, which he conceived as a ground-clearing exercise to remove confusion in religious debates. However, it is especially true for female philosophers that religion served as a portal to rational reflection. This is particularly the case with those who, like Damaris Masham, accepted the compatibility of reason and faith. But there was unquestionably also a close link between religion and philosophy in the respect that religion provided an opportunity for women to be intellectually active. Damaris Masham acknowledged this when she suggested to Locke, that the chief difference between them was just a matter of the time available to devote to them. 'Religion is the Concernment of All Mankind; Philosophy as distinguish'd from It, onely of Those that have a

[17]   Princess Elisabeth of Bohemia, *The Correspondence between Princess Elisabeth of Bohemia and René Descartes*, ed. and trans. Lisa Shapiro (Chicago, 2007).

[18]   Marjorie Nicolson (ed.), *The Conway Letters: The Correspondence of Anne, Viscountess Conway, Henry More and their Friends, 1642–1684*, rev. Sarah Hutton (Oxford, 1992).

[19]   Catharine Trotter Cockburn, *Philosophical Writings*, ed. Patricia Sheridan (Peterborough, 2006); Patricia Sheridan, 'Reflection, Nature, and Moral Law: The Extent of Catharine Trotter Cockburn's Lockeanism in her Defence of Mr. Locke's Essay', *Hypatia*, 22/3 (2007): pp. 133–51.

[20]   Mary Astell and John Norris, *Letters Concerning the Love of God*, ed. E. Derek Taylor and Melvyn New (Aldershot, 2005); William Kolbrener and Michal Michelson (eds), *Mary Astell: Reason, Gender, Faith* (Aldershot, 2007). On Astell and religion, see Sarah Apetrei, *Women, Feminism and Religion in Early Enlightenment England* (Cambridge, 2010).

freedome from the Affaires of the World'.[21] In so saying, she may have had in mind that she, as a woman, had less time than male scholars to devote to philosophy. For this reason the chance to discuss religious topics could offer a substitute for philosophy to overstressed wives and mothers who did not have sufficient time to indulge in philosophizing.[22] In this respect, they could use religion as a means to discuss philosophy.

II. Damaris Masham and Her Correspondents

Letters were important to Damaris Masham in many ways, not least as a means of maintaining friendships at a distance: 'there is nothing that I love better than good letters', she told Locke in her very first letter to him.[23] Nevertheless she came to regard letters as a poor substitute for the presence of friends. She missed the spontaneity and informality of actual conversation, and thought letter writing only served to underline absence. By 'the Tedious way of letters', she complained to Locke, 'one has never with any Freedome the most Proper and Pleaseing Sattisfactions of Friendship, To Laugh with Them when one is Merry; and to Complaine to them when one is Sad'.[24]

However, without 'the Tedious way of Letters', historians would have not communication with the past. And, for Damaris Masham, especially when she lived in relative isolation at her married home at Oates, correspondence was an emotional and intellectual lifeline. But even before that, letters were a dimension of her social life and her *entrée* into the world of ideas beyond her immediate family. Correspondence, for all its limitations, was a vital means of achieving the 'rational conversation' which, she told Leibniz, 'has the greatest charmes that I know in life'.[25] If Lady Masham's description of the misperceptions of the educated 'lady of quality' had any basis in her own experience, it is no wonder that she set so much store by the epistolary company of Locke and correspondents abroad like Limborch and Leibniz. After Locke's return from exile, his frequent visits to, and eventual residence at, her home brought his intellectual world to her hearthside.[26] This was a world where she could ask 'hard questions', without fear of deterring her interlocutors, and without fear of being thought at best strange, at

---

[21] Locke, *Correspondence*, letter 1040, vol. 3, p. 432.

[22] Her own letters testify to the domestic demands (from 'the management of a dairy' to nursing sick children) which made finding time to read difficult.

[23] Locke, *Correspondence*, letter 473, vol. 2, p. 678.

[24] Ibid., letter 870, vol. 3, p. 49.

[25] Leibniz, *Philosophischen Schriften*, vol. 3, p. 361.

[26] On the 'salon at Oates', see Luisa Simonutti, 'Circles of *Virtuosi* and "Charity under Different Opinions": The Crucible of Locke's Last Writings', in Sarah Hutton and Paul Schuurman (eds), *Studies on Locke: Sources, Contemporaries and Legacy* (Dordrecht, 2008), pp. 159–76.

worst heretical, or even that 'too much Learning might in Time make her Mad'.[27] On the contrary, her correspondents expressed admiration for her intellectual talents—Limborch praised not just her virtues but her rare gifts of mind.[28] Leibniz described her as an 'esprit si élevé'.[29] Instead of dismissing her as a 'Woman of very odd Wimsies', he thought her views worthy of referral to the queen of Prussia. And Locke encouraged her to publish.

The earliest record of Damaris's epistolary life begins in January 1682 when she began to correspond with John Locke, with whom she probably became acquainted through their mutual friend, Edward Clarke. They continued to exchange letters until 1690 when he took up residence at her home at Oates. Some 45 of their letters are extant, most of them by Damaris. Initially, their friendship seems to have been intense: among their earliest letters is a group of pastoral love poems, conducted under the noms de plume, Philoclea and Philander. They continued to correspond on a variety of subjects during Locke's exile in Holland. Throughout this time Damaris employed the name 'Philoclea' as her signature, also styling herself Locke's 'governess', sometimes 'old governess'.

Lady Masham's correspondence with Leibniz comprises 11 letters written between 1704 and 1705.[30] Leibniz wrote in French, she in English. The letters to Leibniz are chiefly concerned with philosophical matters—ostensibly clarifications of Leibniz's theory of pre-established harmony. But the topics discussed have a religious aspect since pre-established harmony is a philosophical explanation of the workings of divine providence and of God's relationship to the world. In the last letters, she steers the discussion in the direction of her father's philosophy, in particular Bayle's critique of his 'Hypothesis of the plastick nature', originally set out in his *True Intellectual System of the Universe* (1678) and later published in French in the *Bibliothèque Choisie* edited by Jean Le Clerc. Her defence of her father has a religious aspect, since what is at issue is his account of the relationship of God to the world, as explained through his hypothesis of 'Plastic Nature'.[31]

If we try to use her letters to place Lady Masham on the spectrum of confessional allegiances in late seventeenth-century England, there is not a great deal to go

[27]   Masham, *Occasional Thoughts*, p. 200.

[28]   Universiteitsbibliotheek Amsterdam, UBA, MS D. III.16, 53, Limborch to Lady Masham, 24 March 1705.

[29]   Leibniz, *Philosophischen Schriften*, vol. 3, p. 352.

[30]   On Leibniz's correspondence with Lady Masham, see Robert C. Sleigh, 'Reflections on the Masham-Leibniz Correspondence', in Christia Mercer and Eileen O'Neill (eds), *Early Modern Philosophy: Mind, Matter, and Metaphysics* (Oxford, 2005), pp. 119–27; Pauline Phemister, '"All the Time and Everywhere Everything's the Same as Here": The Principle of Uniformity in the Correspondence between Leibniz and Lady Masham', in Paul Lodge (ed.), *Leibniz and his Correspondents* (Cambridge, 2004), pp. 193–213; Pauline Phemister and Justin Smith, 'Leibniz and the Cambridge Platonists: The Debate over Plastic Natures', in Pauline Phemister and Stuart Brown (eds), *Leibniz and the English-Speaking World* (Dordrecht, 2007), pp. 95–110.

[31]   Leibniz, *Die Philosophischen Schriften*, vol. 3, pp. 370–72.

on. Her letters do not give much away about her religious commitments or her personal spirituality since she makes no personal declarations of faith. However, we can gather she is a Protestant and a member of the Church of England. Although she scarcely makes any biblical references (apart for a general reference to the Epistles of Paul) and she names few living clerical contemporaries, she was certainly knowledgeable about religious beliefs and the Bible. And she was aware of the variety of competing religious denominations. However, she repeatedly declined to set herself up as an authority on divinity or get involved in theological disputes. She told Le Clerc that she regarded religious controversy as useless and counterproductive.[32] To Locke she expressed her view that it was better to focus on the purpose of religion than trying to sort out points of doctrine and the problems 'that the Witts of Men have Intangled them with'.[33] Her reading included religious material to be sure – George Bull on the Trinity, Edward Stillingfleet, George Burnet, Philip van Limborch's *Holy Office*. However, such serious theological reading matter, much of it theologically mainstream, was more than matched by her secular reading which included Voiture, Cervantes, Sidney's *Arcadia*, the poets Abraham Cowley and Katherine Phillips and of course philosophical texts—especially the Cambridge Platonists, Henry More and John Smith, but also Descartes and Marcus Aurelius.

The secular and intellectual content of her letters mark Damaris Masham as a woman of the 'enlightenment'. It is also consistent with the fact that in her letters to Locke and Leibniz, a good deal of her interest in religious themes is philosophical. This in turn is consistent with her accommodation of reason and religion and the latitudinarian views expressed in her writings. A good example of both her rational approach to religion and her philosophical interest in religious matters is her defence of the Cambridge Platonist, John Smith, against Locke's charge that he was a religious enthusiast. In a group of early letters to Locke written in 1682, Damaris Masham tried to persuade Locke that, although we may not reach perfection through 'the Powers of meere Unassisted Reason', we may, nonetheless, 'by constantly adhereing to the Dictates of it [reason]', 'at length come to be acted by a Higher Principle' – but this is what Locke calls 'Enthusiasm', though supported by 'several places in St Paul (which seemed not difficult before)'.[34] Some 20 years later, writing to Jean Le Clerc she contrasts her position with those (un-named) who believe that religion to be incompatible

---

[32]   Universiteitsbibliotheek Amsterdam, Remonstrants MSS J. 57a, Damaris Masham to Le Clerc, 21 June 1705.

[33]   Locke, *Correspondence*, letter 1040, vol. 3, p. 432. Although Masham did not get personally involved in theological disputes, she did not eschew religious controversy altogether. I deal with Masham and religious controversy in 'Debating the Faith: Damaris Masham (1658–1708) and Religious Controversy', in Anne Dunan Page and Clothilde Prunier (eds), *Debating the Faith: Religion and Letter Writing in Great Britain, 1550–1800* (Dordrecht, 2013), pp. 159–76.

[34]   Locke, *Correspondence*, letter 684, vol. 2, p. 485; letter 687, p. 488; letter 696, p. 500.

with philosophy and reason, by quoting a line from the preface to the *Éloge* of Locke which he printed in *Bibliothèque choisi*: 'Pieté n'est pas compatible avec La finesse du raisonnement & l'étude de la Philosophie'.[35] She had high regard for Locke's *Reasonableness of Christianity*, singling it out for mention to Leibniz as one of the books which Locke had donated to the Bodleian Library, Oxford, and offering to send Leibniz a copy.[36]

III. Laughing with the Labadists

Damaris Masham's letters to Locke are the most intimate or 'familiar' letters in her extant correspondence. They contain very few references to religion outside a philosophical context, apart from those letters where, perhaps surprisingly, her references to religion are humourous. This is refreshing, given her serious background as the daughter of the first Englishman to claim to have written a philosophy of religion. In these letters Damaris Masham makes play of confessional differences, playfully figuring personal news in terms of confessional allegiances. So, for example, between 1684 and 1687, while Locke was in Holland, she questioned him about the Labadists (followers of the mystical Protestant convert, Jean de Labadie, who had set up his exiled community in Friesland). Locke had sent her a book about the Labadists (not identified). Damaris Masham's references to Labadism were tongue-in-cheek. They occur in the context of thoughts about marriage, and mention of conversion to Labadism evidently signifies marriage: 'Yet may I Hope to be a Labadist too', she writes—in other words, marry. Not only that, but, she imagines herself marrying a Labadist.

> I shall have an extreame Desire to Marry a Labadist, and be one my self for that very Reason. For if the Notion I have of them is right, and there be any Happiness to be found in Marriage it must Certainly be amongst them, who I suppose Consider nothing in it but to Please them selves … I … am almost in Love with some unknowne Brother alreadie.[37]

In an earlier letter (1682), she jokes about remaining unmarried in terms of becoming a nun:

> I should grow extraordinarie Devout and Religious … Here is a Friend of yours who doubts not in a little time but that she shall see her selfe an Abbess With whom I question not but you have sufficient Interest to Procure that I may be one of Her Nuns.[38]

---

[35]   Universiteitsbibliotheek Amsterdam, Remonstrants MSS J. 57a, Damaris Masham to Le Clerc, 21 June 1705.

[36]   Leibniz, *Philosophischen Schriften*, vol. 3, p. 366.

[37]   Locke, *Correspondence*, letter 787, vol. 2, p. 639.

[38]   Ibid., letter 805, vol. 2, p. 678.

The identity of this 'Abbess' is not obvious to us now, but the opinion of Locke's editor, De Beer, is that she was Locke's cousin Anne Grigg, a woman with high-church sympathies who nevertheless was linked to Latitudinarian circles. Five years later (by which time she was married), Damaris Masham represented Locke's lady admirers as Catholics (nuns) and teases Locke as a non-Catholic 'Reprobate', remarking, 'so far I fear from that necessarie Duty of Al good Christians, Fasting twice in a Weeke, as scarse to do it on Good Frydays'. The jocular references here are perhaps political rather than matrimonial, possibly alluding to James II's open Catholicism. She says she might contact one 'Urgunda' in order

> to know whether it is to Contribute towards the Nunnerie, or No that your Lady Abess is such Distress to Write to You, who I Fancie [the lady Abess] receives no Small Humiliation by the turne of Affairs that she can Condiscend to Correspond with such a Reprobate as You are; who are so far I fear from that necessarie Duty of Al good Christians, Fasting twice in a Weeke, as scarse to do it on Good Frydays, And I begin now to beleeve that a Deane who Eates Flesh in Lent and Can preach on a Tuesday, may be in Her Account something a better Churchman of the Twoo then Mr Ferguson.[39]

Damaris Masham also mentions accusations of being 'Jesuitical' made against her by the same 'Urgunda' (whom De Beer identifies as Stillingfleet's wife, who was related to Damaris Masham's husband) – she mentions, her 'unjust Accusation of me for some Jesuitical Principles'.[40] What exactly she means is unclear – presumably a reference to her practising some kind of deception. But the irreverent references to Catholicism are patent.

This playful use of religious allusions is taken further in one of the poems which she encloses in a letter to Locke of 13 March 1686. She suggests to Locke that the author is unknown to her. But the use of religious terminology is very much in keeping with her letters. Whether she was the author or not, she obviously thought it had entertainment value. In the poem a lover 'Like a Dyeing Penitent' resents his sins, reproaching a 'Deare Sister' for being 'The very'st Reprobate I yet ere Knew', telling her that 'Unbelief's a Deadly Sin', and urging her to heed her reason, to think about her 'Future Dome' lest she 'Dye Excommunicate'. In amongst this pseudo-pious banter we find a serious definition of 'True Religion' as the medium between extremes – though posed negatively as True Religion being vulnerable to extremes – 'by each Extreame oe'r throwne', and a defence of reason 'Because that some Abuse it/It follows not Others may'n't Use it', eventually signing off

> Nor is't for Mee to Talk, and Rant
> Like Any Old Experienc'd Saint,
> That Am But yet a Pentitent.[41]

---

[39]   Ibid., letter 950, vol. 3, p. 238.
[40]   Ibid.
[41]   Ibid., enclosed with letter 847, vol. 3, pp. 795–800.

These examples are not, of course, revealing about Damaris Masham's personal spirituality. Rather they are a jocular take on her social circle and personal relationships. They may also possibly be a humourous barometer of the religious politics of the day. Their significance was no doubt more obvious to their recipients. As we try to make sense of them it is worth recalling Locke's own cautions about readers over the shoulder of private letters.

> The Nature of Epistolary Writings, in general, disposes the Writer to pass by the mentioning of many Things, as well known to him to whom his Letter is address'd, which are necessary to be laid open to a Stranger, to make him comprehend what is said: And it not seldom falls out, that a well penn'd Letter, which is very easy and intelligible to the Receiver, is very obscure to a Stranger, who hardly knows what to make of it.[42]

IV. Letters to Leibniz

Joking aside, Damaris Masham had religious and moral issues at her finger tips—and some of the best evidence of this is the way in which she invoked religion to facilitate her entry into the Republic of Letters. This is particularly evident in her correspondence with Leibniz. This correspondence is an important collection of philosophical letters, in which the discussion ranges over a variety of topics relating to Leibniz's philosophy—in particular, his theory of pre-established harmony, freewill, and the question of whether God can superadd the power of thought to matter. And that is where the critical discussion has focused. But it is worth attending to Damaris Masham's strategy for commanding attention and eliciting a positive response. In her letters to Leibniz, she can be seen to be using an appeal to religious common ground as a means of initiating debate, and of ensuring that she is taken seriously. In this way religious references serve as a kind of calling card to open the way to more serious discussion. This is not to say that her invocation of religion was not serious. On the contrary, it leads directly to the philosophical issues which she sought to discuss.

The correspondence was initiated by Leibniz when he heard that Lady Masham intended to present a copy of her father's *True Intellectual System* to him. Her motives for doing so may have had something to do with her dispute with Pierre Bayle mentioned above.[43] Leibniz's motive in writing to her may well have been his hope of entering into dialogue with Locke.[44] In their approaches to one

---

[42] John Locke, 'An Essay for the Understanding of St. Paul's Epistles, by Consulting St. Paul Himself', in Victor Nuovo (ed.), *John Locke: Writings on Religion* (Oxford, 2002), p. 51

[43] On which see Rosalie Colie, *Light and Enlightenment: A Study of the Cambridge Platonists and the Dutch Arminians* (Cambridge, 1957).

[44] Leibniz told Thomas Burnet, 'Je considere la correspondence que j'ay avec Mylady Masham, comme si je l'avois avec Mons. Locke luy même en partie, car puisqu'il estoit chez

another Leibniz smoothed his way with flattering remarks about the 'penetration des Dames Angloises' (citing Anne Conway as an example) and commending Damaris Masham as 'une Dame dont le discernement est si delicat'.[45] In reply, Damaris Masham deceptively figures herself as undeserving of his compliments. She describes herself 'an ignorant woman', liable to make mistakes, only to brush aside his flattery as, 'the Language of Civilitie to Ladys'. But she goes on to make a series of penetrating criticisms of his philosophy.[46] Her claim to attention from Leibniz is made not on the basis of her connections (for having Locke as 'the best friend in the world', or for her being the daughter of England's most famous Christian philosopher). Rather, she invokes religion. More specifically, she appeals to theism as the common ground between them, presenting herself as 'a Mind Possess'd ... with Due Admiration of the works of God', to whom 'Nothing is more Gratefull than by farther discoveries therein of his Divine Perfections, to be sensibly engag'd to Adore that Being which Reason Pronounces ought to be the supreme object of our Affections'.[47] She commends Leibniz's philosophy as 'tending to inlarge our eminence of its Author, but particularly also as tending to inlarge our Idea of the Divine Perfections and the beautie of his Works'.[48] Leibniz, she says, 'gave a very Becomeing Idea of the Wisedome of God in his works'. Her flattery of Leibniz focuses on his pious design. His hypothesis is, she says 'a very transcendent conception of the Divine Artifice', and is the mark of 'one possess'd with the highest admiration of the thoughts of his maker'.[49] But it is precisely on religious grounds that she requests clarifications about Leibniz's philosophy, and permits herself the penetrating criticisms which she makes of his system.

Her request did indeed elicit from Leibniz a positive response, in the form of a long letter summarizing his system. (He then wrote to his patroness, Queen Sophie Charlotte of Prussia, entreating her to something similar.) Two months later, on 3 June (though it probably did not reach him for at least another month), Lady Masham replied. She was not persuaded that Leibniz had done anything more than produce a beautiful hypothesis. Leibniz wrote again, defending his hypothesis of pre-established harmony, as being more worthy of the dignity of God than occasionalism, which required continuous interventions by God, every one of them a miracle. But Lady Masham pointed out that this still amounted to no more than a hypothesis. For a theory to be conclusive, it requires more than simply a demonstration that it was consonant with a particular conception of

---

elle à Oates, lorsque cette dame m'ecrivoit et me repondoit sur mon hypothese philosophique et marguoit même que Mons. Lock voyoit nos lettres': Leibniz, *Philosophischen Schriften*, pp. 297–8.

   [45]   Ibid., p. 352.

   [46]   Phemister, '"All the Time and Everywhere"'; Phemister and Smith, 'Leibniz and the Cambridge Platonists'.

   [47]   Leibniz, *Philosophischen Schriften*, vol. 4, p. 348.

   [48]   Ibid.

   [49]   Ibid., p. 358.

God. In the ensuing letters, Leibniz had to defend his theory, while she raised further objections. The precise details need not concern us here. My present point is that Masham persisted in her objections, but in the most gracious possible way, commending his conception of God's handiwork even as she cast doubt on his argument— she still cannot see, she says, how 'Organisme' (organization) is essential to matter or what he means by saying that organism is only essential to 'matter arranged by sovereign wisdome'.

> What you would build upon this, forms a very transcendant conception of the divine Artifice; and such as I think could onely occur to the thoughts of one possess'd with the highest admiration of the wisdom of his maker: but, if you infer the truth of this notion onely from its being the most agreable one that you can frame to that attribute of God, this singley seemes to me not to be concludeing. Since we can in my opinion onely infer from thence that whatsoever God dos must be according to infinite Wisdome: but we are not able with our short and narrow views to determine the operations of an Infinitely wise being must be.[50]

Before signing off this letter she made just one more objection to pre-established harmony – that it is incompatible with free will. In other words, implicitly, pre-established harmony is *not* the best possible hypothesis. But she did not actually state that. The deaths of both Locke and the queen of Prussia interrupted the correspondence. When it resumed, the ground shifted somewhat, and the focus of their discussion became Cudworth's doctrine of Plastic Nature. But the correspondence came to an end shortly afterwards. The last letter is an incomplete one by Leibniz, which was, possibly, never sent. With the death of Locke and the termination of her correspondence with Leibniz, the letter trail comes to an end. The reasons for the termination of the correspondence are unknown. But while it lasted, Lady Masham's skilful use of the conventions of female politeness had successfully taken a religious subject, such as might be deemed appropriate for a female correspondent, and extended into a philosophical debate.

Damaris Masham's correspondences with Locke and Leibniz exemplify 'rational conversation' in action. In both conversations, their philosophical engagement turned on religious topics. To participate in such conversations was to be part of the Republic of Letters of which both Leibniz and Locke were eminent members. The differences of tone adopted by Lady Masham reflect the difference between conversing with a friend and with a stranger. This perhaps accounts for some of the differences in Lady Masham's treatment of religion – the humour of her letters to 'Philander' (Locke) and the formality of her address to the 'eminent' philosopher of Hanover. The letters are models of enlightenment sociability, where we can see the claims of friendship and civility serving as a portal to intellectual engagement. In this way Damaris Masham was able get an entry into the republic of philosophical letters, and ask 'hard questions' about religion without being suspected of being a Socinian, a Deist or, worse, an atheist.

---

50   Ibid., pp. 358–9.

Chapter 8

Slander, Conversation and the Making of the Christian Public Sphere in Mary Astell's *A Serious Proposal to the Ladies* and *The Christian Religion as Profess'd by a Daughter of the Church of England*

William Kolbrener

Publicizing the private (that is, what had once been the exclusive sphere of a private realm) is, as Michael McKeon argues in his *Secret History of Domesticity*, one of the primary means through which the configurations of the public sphere emerge. In what becomes a paradigmatic instance of the constitution of a virtual public space, McKeon cites Joseph Addison's *The Spectator*: 'It was said of *Socrates*, that he brought Philosophy down from Heaven, to inhabit among Men; and I shall be ambitious to have it said of me, that I have brought Philosophy out of Closets and Libraries ... to dwell in Clubs and Assemblies, at Tea-Tables, and in Coffee-Houses'.[1] For Addison, such places presuppose universality and are made possible, in Habermas's terms, by 'the principle of reason and the possibility of reciprocal and unforced egalitarian communication'.[2] The public sphere – defined as rational and informed by egalitarian principles – allows Addison, in imitation of his ancient antecedent Socrates, to bring philosophy out of the closeted private sphere into 'Clubs and Assemblies'.[3]

---

[1]   Michael McKeon, *The Secret History of Domesticity: Public, Private, and the Division of Knowledge* (Baltimore, 2005), pp. 79–80; Joseph Addison, *The Spectator* (5 vols, Oxford, 1965), vol. 1, p. 44.

[2]   Jürgen Habermas, *The Structural Transformation of the Public Sphere*, trans. and ed. Thomas Burger and Frederick Lawrence (Cambridge, MA, 1989), p. 18. For a critique of this notion as it actualized itself – or failed to do so, see Brian Cowan, *The Social Life of Coffee*: *The Emergence of the British Coffeehouse* (New Haven, 2005), pp. 255–6. See also Craig Calhoun (ed.), *Habermas and the Public Sphere* (Cambridge, MA, 1992).

[3]   The sense of conceptualized space, corresponding to actual places, writes Michael McKeon, is essential to this conception of public sphere 'where the circulation and exchange of virtual entities – information, polemic, commodities – establishes an imagined collectivity that is all the more compelling for not being limited by actuality': Michael McKeon, 'Parsing Habermas's "Bourgeois Public Sphere"', *Criticism*, 46/2 (2004): p. 276.

In the more traditional culture which precedes it, in McKeon's historiography, 'religious experience is tacit in the sense that it suffuses all of life through the media of sacred time and spaces, habitual and ritual behavior, common practices, and unrationalized convictions'. But in the new realm of the coffee house, philosophy, coming out of the closet, becomes the privileged discourse, while religion, as McKeon writes, becomes 'separated out from the rest of experience as the specialized realm of worship, doctrine and conscious belief'.[4] Indeed, in the framework of the spaces which make up the emergent public sphere, religion is increasingly consigned to a realm of private and more passive devotion, precisely because its principles and suppositions impede the ideal of egalitarian communication imagined in the public sphere. The consigning of the religious impulse to that private realm is one of the signal moments of the public sphere's emergence and triumph.

Corresponding to the institutional secularization established in the public sphere, was a highly circumscribed 'private realm of religion', writes C. John Sommerville. Sommerville notes the Addisonian advice 'that every family should set aside an hour each morning for tea and bread and butter and reading of the day's *Spectator*' as a modern and rational 'substitute' for 'morning devotions'. In what Sommerville calls an era of the narrowing and 'privatization of piety', both Anglicans and their dissenting opponents turned away from languages of reason associated with the public sphere, and instead relied upon scripture as 'the only safe authority for religious authors'. As the virtual place of the coffee house gained authority, the discourses of religion were marginalized into the private realm of domesticity, citing, in Sommerville's reading, only scriptural sources for their increasingly problematic self-justification.[5] While the public sphere was more and more the province of fact and evidence, marginalized religious discourses turned, in the story that Sommerville tells, to an increasingly discredited realm of scripture.[6]

I turn to the works of Mary Astell to complicate accounts of representations of the public sphere, and more particularly the role of theology in such representations. As Sharon Achinstein has written, though 'the separation of private and public achieved through liberal political theory and practice was to consign religion to the private sphere', the 'triumph of the feminist Astell is that she disrupts a history of the consignment of women to the domestic and the separation of public from private'.[7] Astell's work, from her early *A Serious Proposal to the Ladies* of 1694

---

⁴   McKeon, *Secret History*, pp. 33, 39.

⁵   C. John Sommerville, *The Secularization of Early Modern England: From Religious Culture to Religious Faith* (Oxford, 1992), pp. 183, 185; Addison, *The Spectator*, vol. 1, pp. 44–5.

⁶   See Barbara J. Shapiro, *A Culture of Fact: England, 1550–1720* (Ithaca, NY, 2000).

⁷   Sharon Achinstein, 'Mary Astell, Religion and Feminism: Texts in Motion', in William Kolbrener and Michal Michelson (eds), *Mary Astell: Reason, Gender, Faith* (Aldershot, 2007), pp. 18–19. See also Patricia Springborg, 'Mary Astell (1666–1731), Critic of Locke', *American Political Science Review*, 89/3 (1995): p. 621.

to *The Christian Religion as Profess'd by a Daughter of the Church of England*, published over a decade later in 1705, represents a refusal of the narratives of the emergence of the 'latitudinarian' public sphere present in the works of her contemporaries, as well as in contemporary historiography. For Astell, a representative of the politically and theologically conservative High Church, did not turn away from the rationalist registers of the public realm, but rather invoked them in the process of attempting, not only as Achinstein writes, to disrupt them, but also to *transform* them. To be sure, as McKeon writes, Astell herself, like many women of the period, was herself consigned (or perhaps resigned) to the realm of domesticity, and thus 'deprived … of direct access to the public realm'. Notwithstanding what might be seen as Astell's willed martyred resignation to the realm of domesticity, what McKeon calls 'public privation' and the 'cautious elation of integrity' it entails, Astell does nonetheless imagine a vision – however utopian – of the public sphere, that 'discursive realm' in McKeon's terms, 'of imagined collectivity where people "come together"'.[8]

Yet while the public sphere as conventionally configured is presupposed upon an egalitarian communication made possible through the exclusions of theology, in Astell's work it is only theology which makes such communication – 'conversation' in a lexicon which she shares with her contemporaries – possible. True, by the end of her career – her last major work was published in 1709 although she lived on until 1731 – the notion of a public realm of conversation, informed by feminine and rational principles, seemed all the more distant, but it does exist as a set of possibilities, even if only as a fading ideal. The coffee house was one construct of an ideal public sphere. Astell's own construct – certainly more marginal – helps to provide a thicker description of 'latitudinarian' discourse, particularly conflicting and contested conceptions of reason and the public sphere.

Astell presents a perplexing if not problematic case: for her work confounds contemporary historiographical categories. She manifests a dual and seemingly contradictory commitment to the languages which invoke the authenticity and authority of traditional theological and political authorities, as well as the emergent registers of enlightenment. Canonized as a proto-feminist primarily because of her *A Serious Proposal to the Ladies* and *Some Reflections upon Marriage* (first published in 1700 and expanded in 1706), Astell is also associated with the High Church and the absolutist ideals embraced by Jacobites, those loyal to their Royal Martyr, Charles I, executed on the scaffold in front of Whitehall in 1649 and, more immediately, to the exiled James II and his offspring. Starting in the 1690s, the arguments of Astell and High Church contemporaries were dismissed for their rejection of reasoned 'moderation' (the construct of the emergent Whig orthodoxy), as well as their supposedly fanatical adherence to atavistic theological and political conceptions of authority.[9] Contemporary critics have often followed the

---

8   McKeon, *Secret History*, pp. 148–9; McKeon, 'Parsing Habermas's', p. 276.

9   For Astell's critique of this construct see her *Moderation Truly Stated* (London, 1704).

same tendency as the High Church's opponents: Astell's political and theological arguments, with those of her High Church and Jacobite contemporaries, have been dismissed as unsophisticated polemic, departing from 'common sense', thus a strange and unfortunate contradiction to her progressive conceptions of feminine agency and liberty.[10]

Yet Astell's works do not merely advocate a nostalgic turning-back to a pre-enlightened age: in fact, Astell's arguments show themselves to be framed in, indeed made possible by, the very languages of her polemical adversaries.[11] There was no escaping Enlightenment and a secularizing public sphere; and as much as Astell may have protested its ascendance, she also employed its arguments and tactics. Astell did not turn away (nor did her High Church contemporaries) as Sommerville's argument suggests, from the claims and registers of the promise held out by the interpretive space of the public sphere; rather she engaged with them and attempted to transform them for her own purposes. Determined in her principles, yet flexible in her strategy, Astell absorbed and then appropriated the languages of enlightenment which she so vehemently opposed in order to make her arguments for her version of the Christian public sphere – however idealized and utopian – for an Enlightenment age.

In this sense, Astell's work entails what Quentin Skinner – following J.L. Austin – describes as a 'move', as she transforms Whig conceptions of the public sphere for her own High Church agenda.[12] Astell's work registers her awareness of the utopian public sphere based upon moderate rationality; both her *A Serious Proposal to the Ladies* and her *Christian Religion as Profess'd by a Daughter of the Church of England*, in different ways, provide a High Church correlate, if not a corrective, to the emergent liberal ideal. Astell was actively involved in the establishment of a charity school for girls in Chelsea: itself part of a broader Anglican educational movement for the refinement of manners. But such efforts were also accompanied by the more theoretical articulations of her prose works. The conception of the public sphere and the emphasis on conversation throughout her works provides an *imaginary* correlate to the public

---

[10]   For an account of Astell's reception, see the introduction to Kolbrener and Michelson (eds), *Mary Astell: Reason, Gender, Faith*, pp. 1–9. For the continued failure to address High Church registers in their own terms, see William Kolbrener, '*The Charge of Socianism*: Charles Leslie's High Church Defense of "True Religion"', *Journal of the Historical Society*, 3/1 (2003): pp. 3–6.

[11]   On Astell's appropriations of enlightenment registers, see William Kolbrener, '"Forc'd into an Interest': High Church Politics and Feminine Agency in the Works of Mary Astell', *1650–1850: Ideas, Aesthetics, and Inquiries in the Early Modern Era*, 10 (2004): pp. 3–31.

[12]   Quentin Skinner, 'Motives, Intentions and the Interpretation of Texts', in James Tully (ed.), *Meaning and Context: Quentin Skinner and His Critics* (Princeton, 1988), p. 77.

sphere of emergent liberal discourses which would reach its most complete conceptualization in *The Spectator*.[13]

While Addison and Richard Steele were turning towards the coffee house, founding an imaginative space built upon principles of rational politeness, manners and taste, Astell saw that realm as irremediably corrupt, characterized by flattery, slander and deceit. What was construed in the latitudinarian imagination as a space for disinterested conversation, in Habermas's terms, 'rational critical public debate', was for Astell, a realm contaminated by party and partisanship. As Brian Cowan has written, in some sense confirming Astell's perceptions, the space marked out by the coffee house was not designed to create a 'bourgeois public sphere', but rather to make 'Britain safe for an elitist Whig oligarchy'.[14] That is, the coffee house represented a sphere of political interest, not an abstract philosophical universality. Where the public sphere as figured in Addison and Steele promised reciprocity, Astell saw only inequality and partisanship, and saw her own vision – however embattled – as a possible corrective.

The fate of Astell's notion of the public sphere articulated in her later *The Christian Religion as Profess'd by a Daughter of the Church of England* can only be fully understood in relation to her earlier writings, particularly the first part of *A Serious Proposal to the Ladies*, of the mid-1690s. In the *Serious Proposal to the Ladies*, Astell had forwarded a notion of feminine friendship – idealized as 'a Type and Antepast of Heav'n' – as an alternative and potential antidote to the debased realm of masculine courtship. In her works that followed, some of which focus on the history and politics of the revolution of the 1640s and its aftermath, the flattery and deception of courtship becomes a cultural principle – associated with a public domain almost always gendered as masculine. In Astell's nostalgic version of historiography, modernity began decisively at the moment when Charles I was murdered on the scaffold in front of Whitehall. For Astell, from the 1640s onwards, a new culture based upon a particularly vulgar form of masculinity – associated with latitudinarians, dissenters and moderates – came to define the modern. It was this realm of the modern which by 1705 and her writing of *Christian Religion*, Astell would abandon altogether.

If the polite culture of 1690s England had deteriorated into flattery, artifice and slander, Astell saw what she called disinterested conversation leading not to the enlightenment heralded by her political adversaries, but rather to a public sphere based upon fully Christian principles. In *Christian Religion*, the representations of 'Crafty and Designing Men' led to the pursuit of what she termed later in the text

---

[13]   For more on Astell's educational efforts in the framework of the Anglican attempt to refine manners and the Society for Promoting Christian Knowledge (SPCK), see Hannah Smith, 'Mary Astell, *A Serious Proposal to the Ladies* (1694), and the Anglican Reformation of Manners in Late-Seventeenth-Century England', in Kolbrener and Michelson (eds), *Mary Astell: Reason, Gender, Faith*, pp. 31–47. On the 'metaphorical' nature of the public sphere, see McKeon, 'Parsing Habermas's', pp. 275–6.

[14]   Cowan, *Social Life of Coffee*, p. 256.

as 'Temporal Interest or Party' and the impoverishment of a thoroughly masculine public sphere.[15] Feminine friendship and the conversation it promises, outlined in a *Serious Proposal to the Ladies*, provide the elaboration of an alternative to the corruption of that sphere. Even in that later, far more resigned and cynical work, conversation holds out the possibility of a 'Reason', uncontaminated by the corrupt realms of manners and taste and man's 'Artifices'. Astell does not abandon, as Sommerville argues, the registers of reason, though her rationality is firmly based upon theology, and in *Christian Religion* its full realization is postponed seemingly indefinitely to an uncorrupted and messianic future (*CR*, 187–8).

Astell's most devastating account of masculine artifice is her *Some Reflections upon Marriage*. In this tract devoted not only to marriage but to the sociology of courtship, artifice and the attendant flattery and design are the predominant province of men. Courtship is founded upon the masculine abuses of 'Wit' – women are 'dazled' with the 'Glitter and Pomp' and 'false Appearance' of masculine artifices.[16] 'Pretences', 'Plot', 'Policy' and 'Design' are methods of this deceit (*SR*, 62–4). Sexual politics are defined in terms of a lack of authenticity; the masculine artifice of courtship dictates feminine behaviour.[17] Thus men and women enact the rites of courtship: to Astell's eyes, rituals of codependency always initiated by the masculine sex. Addison in *The Spectator* had associated such artifice with the 'fantastical Disposition' of the feminine, *not* the masculine. Writing in March 1711, Addison describes women as drawn to the 'superficial Parts of Life'. Women 'never cast away a Thought on those Ornaments of the Mind, that make Persons Illustrious in themselves, and Useful to others'. Their conversation, Addison remarks, 'very much cherishes this Natural Weakness of being taken with Outside and Appearance'. In 'Pursuit' of 'glittering Trifles', women 'are more attentive to the superficial Parts of Life, than the solid and substantial Blessings of it'.[18] As a further attack on the 'superficial' character of women, Addison writes in December 1711 that only a woman could discourse hours 'upon nothing'; and only a woman could provide an 'extempore Dissertation upon the Edging of a Petticoat … in all the Figures of Rhetorick'. And so he quips that Socrates must have been instructed in the 'Art' of Eloquence by a woman, suggesting that 'the Universities would do well to consider whether they should not fill their Rhetorick Chairs with She Professors'.[19] For Astell, by contrast, the cultural principles of

---

[15]   Mary Astell, *The Christian Religion as Profess'd by a Daughter of the Church of England* (London, 1705), pp. 162, 181 (hereafter cited as *CR*).

[16]   Mary Astell, *Reflections upon Marriage*, 3rd edn (London, 1706), pp. 51, 53–4 (hereafter cited as *SR*).

[17]   William Kolbrener, 'Gendering the Modern: Mary Astell's Feminist Historiography', *The Eighteenth Century: Theory and Interpretation*, 44/1 (2003): pp. 10–11.

[18]   Addison, *The Spectator*, vol. 1, pp. 67, 69; Kolbrener, 'Gendering the Modern', p. 7.

[19]   Addison, *The Spectator*, vol. 2, p. 458. Addison sought a 'physiological' explanation to the feminine 'arts of Dissembling', speculating, on the advice of 'an excellent Anatomist' whether there may be in a 'Woman's Tongue … certain Juices which render it so wonderfully

falsehood and artifice – the superficiality of meaningless and misleading rhetoric – are masculine. That is, Astell looked beyond the sphere of courtship to the public sphere as constructed by moderates and dissenters as based upon a similar inauthenticity, founded at the moment of the regicide, and the sundering of the bonds of cultural authenticity and unity held together in the image of Charles I.

For Jacobites and avatars of the High Church, Charles I represented the fantasy of a cultural *integritas*, in Peter Laslett's terms, a 'world that had been lost'. In 1693, Thomas Long would hail the *Eikon Basilike* – the book ostensibly written by Charles before his death (and now attributed to Bishop John Gauden) – as showing the identification between appearance and reality: 'as Words were, such were his Deeds'. The king's 'Heart and Mind was seen in his Actions, and his Actions expressed in lively, charming, pious, and powerful Words'. Charles, and especially his image in the *Eikon Basilike*, embodied the principles of 'Reason' and 'Religion', and he represented the coming together of 'Heart and Mind', 'Actions' and 'Words'.[20] After his death, for Astell and her High Church contemporaries, the nation had fallen into the irremediably corrupt realm of politics.

It was Astell's innovation, however, to gender this account and to associate the decadence of modern politics with the masculine. The 'Domestic Flatterers' associated with the deceitful masculine world of courtship in *Some Reflections upon Marriage* are, in Astell's political musings *An Impartial Enquiry into the Causes of Rebellion and Civil War* (1704), akin to those 'Flatterers of Mens Follies ... to gain them to their Party'. The 'Artifice us'd by Factious Men', is 'artfully instill'd into the Minds of the People by Cunning Men and their Instruments'.[21] In *Some Reflections upon Marriage*, Astell believes it impossible to 'reckon up the divers Stratagems Men use to catch their Prey, their different ways of insinuating' (*SR*, 70). In the *Impartial Enquiry into the Causes of Rebellion and Civil War*, Astell argues that no 'Stratagems are omitted', noting shortly afterwards in the text that 'Men ... infect the Peoples Minds with evil Principles and Representations', and with 'secret Hints and Insinuations' (*IE*, 7–8). Astell lists the stratagems of those '*Men of Craft*' similar to those of the 'Lover' represented in the earlier work on courtship: 'They Bribe, they Threaten, they Solicit, they Fawn, they Dissemble, they Lye, they break through all the Duties of Society, violate all the Laws of GOD and of Man' (*IE*, 5, 7).[22] Both courtship and the public sphere, for Astell, are characterized and compromised by the arts of political seduction.

---

voluble or flippant', leading to seem like 'a Race-Horse, which runs the faster the lesser Weight it carries': Addison, *The Spectator*, vol. 2, p. 460.

[20] Thomas Long, *Dr. Walker's True, Modest and Faithful Account of the Author of Eikon Basilike Strictly Examined* (London, 1693), p. 56. On the function of the *Eikon Basilike* in the conflict about authentic England, see William Kolbrener, '"Commonwealth Fictions" and "Inspiration Fraud": Milton and the *Eikon Basilike* after 1689', *Milton Studies*, 37 (1999): pp. 166–97.

[21] Mary Astell, *An Impartial Enquiry into the Causes of Rebellion and Civil War in this Kingdom* (London, 1704), p. 7 (hereafter cited as *IE*).

[22] See Kolbrener, 'Gendering the Modern', p. 16.

Astell's *Christian Religion*, though primarily a record of her theological perspectives, also provides a formulation of a utopian Christian public sphere. *Christian Religion* relies on the critical energies of *Some Reflections upon Marriage*, but her alternative conception of the emergent liberal public sphere has its origins in her earlier meditations on friendship in *A Serious Proposal to the Ladies*. In *A Serious Proposal*, Astell entertains the possibility of an embodiment of her ideals in feminine friendship and learning. By *Christian Religion*, Astell may elaborate the contours of a public-spirited idealism. But her increasing resignation about the nature of masculine corruption, articulated with such force in *Some Reflections upon Marriage*, has her, in the latter tract, turning inwards, and articulating languages of withdrawal and martyrdom.

In *A Serious Proposal to the Ladies*, Astell construed feminine friendship – figured in her proposal as a religious retreat for women – as the refuge from the corruption of masculine deceit, and the reduction of relationships to political seduction.[23] Here also, conversation, nurtured first in the realm of feminine withdrawal, is primary. So Astell enjoins her women readers to 'quit the Chat of insignificant people for an ingenious Conversation' (*SP*, 19). What Astell calls 'Disinterress'd Friendship' will not be served by the 'idle tales' in which women are habitually immersed, but only through those 'instructive discourses' through which women can 'communicate' 'useful *knowledge*' (*SP*, 19–20). When women are assimilated into masculine contexts, they do 'mischief to one another, by an uncharitable and vain Conversation'. As a way of escaping this fate, Astell advocates 'Retirement' where women can, combining the language of feminine grace and Baconian utility, adorn 'their minds with useful Knowledge' (*SP*, 24).

In the idealization of *A Serious Proposal to the Ladies*, Astell imagines a retirement that allows for the 'perpetual Display of the Beauties of Religion in an exemplary Conversation' (*SP*, 28–9). Though Astell in this earlier work imports a visual register, it is still retirement that is salvific, helping to push off 'temptation' and 'redeems our time'. This is not the retirement of an individual, but of a feminine community. For the conversation between women leads to redemption, made possible by a return to the ethical: 'Great are the Benefits', Astell writes, 'of holy *Conversation* which will be here enjoy'd'. As 'Vice is, so Vertue may be catching'. Astell emphasizes the importance of 'a Religious Retirement and holy Conversation', which will minimize the possibility of 'false Representations and Impostures', what characterizes the masculine world of artifice (*SP*, 30, 33–4). For instead of the 'froth and impertinence' with which, she writes, 'Feminine Conversations so much abound' in a world defined by the masculine, the retirement of women should allow for 'tongues employ'd in making Proselytes to heaven, in running down Vice, in establishing Vertue and proclaiming their Makers Glory' (*SP*, 38). The friendships nurtured in this closed environment themselves become

---

[23]   Mary Astell, *A Serious Proposal to the Ladies Parts I & II*, ed. Patricia Springborg (Toronto, 2002), p. 21 (hereafter cited as *SP*).

an 'emblem' of what Astell calls 'this blessed place' – Heaven – and creating a 'blessed World ... shining with so many stars of Virtue' (*SP*, 37–8).

So great are the powers of such feminine conversation that their rhetorical powers not only reinforce feminine friendship, but allow, in Astell's imagination, for the feminine transformation of the masculine. In the idealism of the mid-1690s, the wife, described by Astell as 'good and prudent', will work 'wonderfully' even on 'an ill man'. 'He must be a Brute indeed', Astell continues, 'who cou'd hold out against all those innocent Arts, those gentle persuasives and obliging methods she wou'd use to reclaim him' (*SP*, 42). Though Astell may reject 'Plays and Romances' and other 'trifling Arts', the joining of an emphasis on truth and reason, and a feminine prudential rhetoric frames the 'innocent Arts' that Astell imagines in 1694 'can hardly fail of prevailing' (*SP*, 23, 42).[24] So confident is Astell in the powers of 'an ingenious Conversation' that she imagines the virtues of feminine retirement will translate even into the male-dominated domestic sphere. Such conversation, Astell writes, 'will make his life comfortable, and he who can be so well entertain'd at home, needs not run into Temptations in search of Diversions abroad' (*SP*, 42). Whatever virtues have been learned in the provinces of Astell's feminine withdrawal are translated into a realm of domesticity itself susceptible of reformation.

In *Christian Religion*, Astell articulates the possibility of a rational and reciprocal discourse, based upon the model of the interaction between women forwarded in the *Serious Proposal to the Ladies*. But in *Christian Religion*, the idealism about the powers of conversation to shape a public realm of communication is more powerful than in the earlier tract, the cynicism and resignation at the failure of such an ideal even greater still. True, '*Conversation*', Astell writes, is not only useful and entertaining, but it also has a higher end: 'the end of Speech is to communicate our Thoughts for mutual advantage' (*CR*, 355–6). But the linguistic ideal of reciprocity and mutuality is for Astell evasive in a culture now fully defined by flattery and misrepresentation: for 'alas', she despairs, 'among all the Talk that is in the World, where shall we find the Conversation?' (*CR*, 356). Astell laments the lack of the very communication said to characterize the culture of her opponents. Religion, she writes sardonically, is 'a Business to be Transacted in our Closets only' (*CR*, 356). With Astell's ideals for feminine education pursued in retirement dashed, the private realm of the individual remains the only place for the pursuit of religion, for her figured in theological but also rational terms.

Addison may have taken philosophy out of the 'closet'; such a move, Astell herself realizes, has led to the closeting of religion. The choice not to allow religion in the world to 'spoil' the 'conversation' has led to its impoverishment – a mere 'Business' – or indeed its very impossibility (*CR*, 356). In her appropriation, however, High Church religion and Enlightenment Reason are coterminous. The

---

[24]   For more on conversation in Renaissance rhetorical theory, see Jane Donawerth, 'Conversation and the Boundaries of Public Discourse in Rhetorical Theory by Renaissance Women', *Rhetorica: A Journal of the History of Rhetoric*, 16/2 (1998): pp. 181–99.

mannered behaviour of her contemporaries, by contrast, is associated not only with the arts, tastes and manners celebrated by *The Spectator*, but with a corrupt conception of artifice. The older binary worldview of the culture of Milton's *Paradise Lost* – which might be seen as present – in Astell's work, associates the Satanic artifice and design of Milton's epic with masculine latitudinarians.[25] While dissenters and even latitudinarians had flattened the political world into equivalent parties – so Daniel Defoe asks, 'where is the Difference between Church Loyalty and Whiggish Loyalty, Round-head or Cavalier, Churchman or Dissenter, Whig or Tory?' – Astell relies on an older dualistic sensibility.[26] In Astell's work, the inheritors of regicide, of which Milton obviously was a leading proponent, were associated with the artifice of Satan in Milton's epic. And for Astell, like many of her Jacobite and High Church contemporaries, the cause of Truth and Vertue is tied in with the providence of God, and *his* 'Designs' spoiled by the 'plausible harangues and pretences of Crafty and Designing Men' (*CR*, 162). While Astell argues for 'Common Interest', this pursuit is rendered impossible by those who, in their respect for those who '*wears the gay Cloathing*', have led men to 'become *Partial* … that is, False Reasoners' (*CR*, 244). For Astell, the satanic partiality of slanderous discourse is the greatest betrayal of the promise held out by her conception of the Christian public sphere. In the realm of *Christian Religion*, only the stoic individual pursues virtue – in solitude.

Astell goes on to lament that were all 'the Vices of the Tongue' curtailed, 'all Prophane and Unseemly, Censorious and Detracting, Slanderous and False, Ill-natur'd and Scurrilous, Boasting and Vain, Rude and Flattering, Pragmatical and Impertinent Talk, there will not much remain … to keep up the common way of Conversation' (*CR*, 357). For Astell, it is 'Tale-bearing and Tattles' (*CR*, 218) which serve 'Temporal Interest' and 'Party', the masculine arts associated in the earlier tract with courtship, symptomatic now of a general descent into corruption (*CR*, 181). The prevalence of the '*Arts* and *Designs*' of 'Factious Men' (*IE*, 5, 7) comes to corrupt what had been in the *Serious Proposal to the Ladies* the inviolate realm of feminine friendship. Not only have ladies become vulnerable to the 'Tools of Crafty and Designing Demagogues' (*CR*, 17–19), they now themselves 'drudge, in the mean Trade of Faction and Sedition' (*CR*, 324), become 'grand Politicians, and every whit as Intriguing as any Patriot of the Good-old-cause' (*CR*, 178–9). Associating women with the 'Good-old-cause', the puritan opposition to Charles I – John Pym's 'Sham Pretences' and Oliver Cromwell's 'Scandalous Stories' which

---

[25]   For Satanic plotting in *Paradise Lost*, see II 193, V 240, VI 901. On questions of Satanic imitation, see Edward Tayler, *Milton's Poetry: Its Development in Time* (Pittsburgh, 1979), pp. 96–7, as well as William Kolbrener, *Milton's Warring Angels* (Cambridge, 1996), pp. 148–9, 152–3. On the uses of Milton by Astell and her High Church and Jacobite contemporaries, see William Kolbrener, 'The Jacobite Milton: Strategies of Historiography and Literary Appropriation', *Clio: A Journal of Literature, History, and the Philosophy of History*, 32/2 (2003): pp. 153–76.

[26]   Daniel Defoe, *A New Test of the Church of England's Loyalty* (London, 1703), p. 410.

had led to the demise of Stuart *integritas* (*IE*, 47) – shows, for Astell, how even the sacred realm of feminine conversation had been compromised by the languages of slander and party. In the earlier tracts, Astell had hoped that women would resist masculine artifice, though in *Christian Religion* they are themselves wearing the 'equipage of Modern Politicians', and been infected by 'Tale-bearing' (*CR*, 179, 218). Where the language of *A Serious Proposal to the Ladies* had suggested the possibility of an ideal place for women – 'a blessed World … shining with so many stars of Vertue' – now even the languages of the feminine had become infected by masculine languages of artifice (*SP*, 38).

For Astell, the ideal speech situation imagined in the public sphere does not come about through what McKeon following Habermas calls a universality 'adjudicating between an indefinite number of inherently legitimate interests'.[27] By contrast, its *fall* into interest makes conversation for mutual benefit impossible. The 'concealing or misrepresenting' of a neighbour's 'Honourable Actions' not only lessens his 'Merit and Reputation' but also robs 'GOD of the Glory that is due to His Grace' (*CR*, 182–3). To 'hurt or vex' one's neighbours, Astell avers, 'is not only Inhuman, but even Devilish' (*CR*, 202). Further, it not only takes away from an individual reputation, but also from 'Vertue' and the divine (*CR*, 182–3). For such false representation aligns the envious with an art and artifice compromised in Astell's lexicon by their relation to the fallen realm of both courtship and politics. Divine glory is revealed through those who 'heartily espouse and vigorously promote every good Work', 'the Duties of Christians … are Equal and Reciprocal and ought to be mutually Receiv'd and Paid' (*CR*, 188, 223). Astell here employs the terms – reciprocity and equality – that her contemporaries (as well as ours) associate with the liberal public sphere. But such reciprocal equality is not realized in relation to the enlightened public sphere, but rather in relation to Astell's Christian correlate. The imagined realm of feminine withdrawal for Astell was the last protest against the encroachment and ascendance of such artifice. For the 'Tale-bearing' and 'Ill report' of the latitudinarian public sphere, symptoms of interest not reciprocity, finally renders impossible Astell's conception of mutually correcting conversation. The culture of slander and envious deceit brings 'Scandal and Dishonour upon Wisdom, Vertue, and Religion' (*CR*, 218–19). Not only, for Astell, have 'our *Evil Communications* … contributed more than any thing to the general *Corruption of our Manners*' (*CR*, 358), but the slanderous mis-representation which it breeds, the insistent pursuit of 'poor little Artifices', provide a disruption of God's providential designs (*CR*, 187). God's glory, for Astell, cannot be revealed in a place where the 'Devilish' designs of men are not only prevalent, but rampant. Satanic stories of individual interest dominate a landscape which should be governed by the one universal and Providential narrative of the divine. But, for Astell, private interests, distilled in the slanderous discourse of her contemporaries, overshadow the divine glory which requires Christian conversation to reveal itself fully.

---

[27] McKeon, 'Parsing Habermas's', p. 275.

So even as Astell continues to idealize conversation, in the end, *Christian Religion* abandons the public sphere of masculine artifice and falsehood for the private feminine world of martyrdom. Here, unlike in Sommerville's account, enlightenment emphases on reason and Christian martyrdom overlap. Indeed, for Astell, the public realm of action is wholly compromised: for one, as she argues, those who pursue 'Wanton Ambition' are 'applauded as a Hero'; while those who 'pursue' their 'designs' by 'the most Tricking and Disingenous Methods' are considered 'Meritorious' (*CR*, 268–9). While, in fact, from Astell's perspective, such actions only come to undermine the revelation of divine glory. For Astell, not only the public sphere, but any form of action itself is compromised. Men may speculate, but only upon 'what will get them a Name in the World'. Genuine speculation, the 'Contemplation of Immaterial Beings and Abstracted Truths, which are the Noblest Objects of the Mind' are, by those very same men rejected as merely 'Visionary'. In a concession to a public sphere defined by scandal, slander and party, Astell acknowledges that 'Womens Lives are not Active', and it is 'Mens Business' that is 'without Doors' (*CR*, 295–6). Women, by contrast, 'who *ought to be Retir'd*, are for this Reason design'd by Providence for Speculation' (*CR*, 296; emphasis added). Astell's feminine self negates itself both in relationship to the exigencies of Christianity and Enlightenment: for Astell, one cannot be either reasonable or a Christian in the public sphere. Even as Astell articulates a conception of conversation which figures the possibility of sociality and a public sphere of reason, she withdraws from that world, proclaiming 'better to live in Desarts among Wild Beasts, open and declar'd Enemies, than in Cities among pretended and deceitful Friends' (*CR*, 150–51). Since there are no longer protected places for feminine withdrawal, she chooses isolation, even 'the Glorious Crown of Martyrdom' as the possibility of a culture based upon conversation recedes into the future (*CR*, 269). So Astell advocates a life of 'Holy Religion' which teaches us to 'deny our Selves, and to despise the World' (*CR*, 301). For despite the promises that conversation holds, there is no one 'who speaks his Thoughts' (*CR*, 356). Rather language is degraded in only giving 'Scandal to the World', in teasing neighbours on 'disputable Points', and in pursuing 'Party' (*CR*, 225).

Notwithstanding the residual idealism about the powers of conversation, and a public sphere modified by the feminine pursuit of reason, Astell resigns herself to a constricted place. 'Our Worldly Affairs', she writes, 'go in a little room'. Though the closet of her worldly affairs is small, it allows for the pursuit of a different kind of business. Not the business of a degraded field of economic and political pursuit, but 'our Real Business, our *Merchandize*, our *Race*, our *Warfare*, the *Pearl of great price*, which all considerate Persons strive to purchase' (*CR*, 301–2). Astell, in this paradoxical way, perhaps somewhat anxiously appropriating the language of commerce, claims to be '*Publick-Spirited*', but very much in private, in her 'little room', pursuing the wisdom and virtue of the 'Masterly Genius' (*CR*, 187).

In the end, Astell is wary of the conceptions of subjectivity upon which the liberal public sphere is based, as she associates the liberal subject not with an incipient rationality but a satanic tendency towards artifice and misrepresentation.

For Astell, the 'scandal' of slander is to blemish the public space with creaturely artifice and design such that the true agency of the divine is obscured. In this sense, Astell's emphasis upon paradoxical notions of subjectivity and what she calls 'self-sufficiency' presuppose obedience, patience and even martyrdom. In the end, Astell takes refuge in the self and a conception of the integrated subject:

> Nothing so Lovely nor consequently so Reputable, as a Life that's all of a Piece; the same even Thread running thro' it from the beginning to the end. When our Words correspond with our Thoughts, and our Actions with both, and all these with each other; so that we are entirely consistent with our selves, and with the Precepts of the Gospel which never interfer. (*CR*, 316)

Astell resists the 'mean Trade of Faction and Sedition' (*CR*, 324), for a unity of thought and deed sundered by the cataclysmic fall into party and corruption – not only among men as in *A Serious Proposal to the Ladies*, but, in *Christian Religion*, among women as well. The tragic paradox for Astell is that only a subjectivity based upon Christian principles will produce a truly reasonable 'Conversation', centred on the 'best and most sublime … Subject' (*CR*, 356), one which would magnanimously assert 'the Cause of God and Religion' (*CR*, 231) in 'the midst of a crooked and perverse Generation' (*CR*, 37). But such a subjectivity, for Astell, is by its very nature (notwithstanding her obvious disappointment in the fact) private.

For figures like Addison and Steele, disinterested conversation led to enlightenment ideals of neutrality and reason. In such ideals, Astell only saw pretence, design and artifice – self-interest and seduction masquerading as 'moderation'. She unveiled the ostensibly neutral pose taken by her adversaries, and in some sense she provides a model for a contemporary critique of universalisms, themselves founded upon interests. For Astell herself, equal and reciprocal conversation meant the possibility of a society informed not by the 'Arts and Contrivances' of men (*CR*, 165), but rather those of 'Truth' and Christian 'Virtue', which would allow for the revelation and the realization of that one true Design. But that true design comes into being not through the 'Arm of Flesh' the 'Worldly Arts and Contrivances' which Astell saw as irredeemably 'Wicked', but only through the increasingly distant-seeming 'Promises and Protection of the Almighty' (*CR*, 165).

Chapter 9
Susanna Centlivre, 'Our *Church*'s Safety' and 'Whig Feminism'

Hannah Smith

In early 1710, England was convulsed by the case of Dr Henry Sacheverell. The doctor had been impeached for a high profile sermon in which he attacked Protestant Dissent and asserted that the Revolution of 1688–89 did not challenge the principle of non-resistance. His trial – a Whig initiative against an already notorious Tory cleric – represented the culmination of the ferocious debates over the alleged threat that Dissent posed to the Church of England, and the nature of royal power, which marked Queen Anne's reign. Against a backdrop of popular rioting in his favour, Sacheverell was found guilty by a small majority, and given a lenient sentence of punishment. Later that autumn, the Tories won a landslide election victory, demonstrating beyond doubt the power of the cry that 'the Church was in danger' under the Whigs.[1]

One aspect of Sacheverell's trial, which contemporaries noted, was the strikingly high degree of female interest that it attracted. Observers described how assiduously women attended the trial, how heatedly they debated the doctor's cause, and how many of them were his fervent supporters.[2] The trial provided them with further evidence of how deeply 'the rage of party' had infiltrated every aspect of English life. It underscored how feminized English politics had seemingly become during the reign of a queen regnant – Anne – with her female favourites, Sarah Churchill, duchess of Marlborough, and Abigail Masham.[3] And it brought home how popular the High Church, Tory and Jacobite causes were amongst women of all ranks. 'Strange! how the Women love a *High Flyer*', commented one

---

[1]   Geoffrey Holmes, *The Trial of Doctor Sacheverell* (London, 1973).

[2]   Donald F. Bond (ed.), *The Tatler* (3 vols, Oxford, 1987), vol. 2, pp. 310, 379; *A Compleat History of the Whole Proceedings of the Parliament of Great Britain Against Dr. Henry Sacheverell* (London, 1710), p. 84; James J. Cartwright (ed.), *The Wentworth Papers, 1705–1739* (London, 1883), p. 112; Geoffrey Holmes and W.A. Speck (eds), *The Divided Society: Parties and Politics in England 1694–1716* (London, 1967), pp. 82–7; Eirwen E.C. Nicholson, 'Sacheverell's Harlots: Non-Resistance on Paper and in Practice', *Parliamentary History*, 31/1 (2012): pp. 69–79.

[3]   On female political involvement in this era see Elaine Chalus, 'Ladies are Often Very Good Scaffoldings': Women and Politics in the Age of Anne', *Parliamentary History*, 28/1 (2009): pp. 150–65; Frances Harris, *A Passion for Government: The Life of Sarah, Duchess of Marlborough* (Oxford, 1991).

pamphleteer.[4] Daniel Defoe was less surprised, arguing that women were naturally more despotic than men. Although he carefully exempted his sovereign from this charge, he claimed that

> Tyranny in Government, and Non-Resistance in Subjects, are Doctrines more Natural, more taking, and more suitable to the Women, than the Men ... they are most apt to Tyrannize themselves; and ... Feel less of the Mischiefs of Tyranny when it falls, than the Men – I am not making Comparisons, nor speaking of Family Tyranny; I do not know, but some Female Government there, might do us good; but I speak of the Propensities of Nature, and the Temper of the Sexes.[5]

Since Sacheverell's trial, women 'turn Privy-Counsellors, and settle the State', and Defoe laid the blame on the clergy's sway over women:

> this new Invasion of the Politicians Province, is an eminent Demonstration of the Sympathetick Influence of the Clergy upon the Sex, and the near Affinity between the Gown, and the Petticoat ... as soon as you pinch the Parson, he holds out his Hands to the Ladies for their Assistance – and they appear as one Woman in his Defence.[6]

Alarm over the extent of female enthusiasm for High Church politics remained acute in the years after Sacheverell's trial. Although the political scene once again changed after the succession of George I in 1714, and the Whig parliamentary victory a year later, Whigs of all hues were preoccupied with how to maintain this ascendancy, traumatized as they were by the political mistake that Sacheverell's prosecution represented, and the strength of the High Church cause. Tellingly, Joseph Addison specifically devoted several issues of *The Freeholder* – designed to bolster support for the Hanoverian dynasty at the time of the Jacobite Rebellion of 1715 – to 'the ladies' to persuade them of the merits of the Glorious Revolution and Protestant Succession. Like Defoe before him, Addison was disturbed by the power of clerical influence. 'The Master Engine, to overturn the Minds of the Female World, is the *Danger of the Church*', he wrote in April 1716. 'I believe there are many devout and honourable Women who are deluded in this Point by the Artifice of designing Men'.[7] Whigs continued to be concerned about female Jacobitism – and female Jacobite feminists – into the late 1740s and the aftermath of the '45 Rebellion.[8]

---

[4]   *The Officers Address to the Ladies* (London, [1710]), p. 2.

[5]   *A Review of the State of the British Nation*, vol. 7, 9 May 1710, p. 71.

[6]   Ibid., pp. 69, 71.

[7]   Joseph Addison, *The Freeholder*, ed. James Leheny (Oxford, 1979), pp. 24–7, 185.

[8]   Paul Langford, *Public Life and the Propertied Englishman, 1689–1798* (Oxford, 1994), p. 120; Paula McDowell, *The Women of Grub Street: Press, Politics, and Gender in the London Literary Marketplace, 1678–1730* (Oxford, 1998); Jill Campbell, *Natural Masques: Gender and Identity in Fielding's Plays and Novels* (Stanford, 1995), pp. 137–59.

The apparent affinity between women and Tory, Jacobite and High Church causes has been highlighted by modern scholars too, who have pointed to the Tory or Jacobite politics of women writers like Mary Astell, Judith Drake, Jane Barker and Anne Finch, countess of Winchelsea.[9] Moreover, it has been posited that the feminist politics they articulated were intrinsic to their Tory or Jacobite commitments; their critiques of the Revolutionary settlement's attack on patriarchy alerting them to the paradoxes it embodied when it came to gender relations. While such a reading has been supported by developments within the political and social sciences which insist on the essentially patriarchal nature of contract theory, and liberalism more broadly, its conclusions have been problematized by recent studies which have drawn attention to the specific theological and spiritual contexts in which 'Tory feminists' wrote, and the theologically and philosophically convulsive atmosphere of the post-Revolutionary period which inspired them.[10]

The rediscovery of a Whig literary canon and greater scholarly interest in Whig or pro-Revolutionary women writers has also complicated this picture, as work on Damaris Masham, Elizabeth Singer (later Rowe), Catharine Trotter, Mary Davys, Jane Brereton and Susanna Centlivre has indicated.[11] Female Whig writers proved firm, sometimes fierce supporters of the Revolution, and the political and religious developments that accompanied it, and their contributions helped to shape the era's political-literary forms.[12] Importantly, like their Tory counterparts, female

---

[9]   Ruth Perry, *The Celebrated Mary Astell: An Early English Feminist* (Chicago, 1986); Carol Barash, *English Women's Poetry, 1649–1714: Politics, Community, and Linguistic Authority* (Oxford, 1996); Kathryn R. King, *Jane Barker, Exile: A Literary Career 1675–1725* (Oxford, 2000); Rachel Weil, *Political Passions: Gender, the Family and Political Argument in England, 1680–1714* (Manchester, 1999); Hannah Smith, 'English "Feminist" Writings and Judith Drake's *An Essay in Defence of the Female Sex* (1696)', *The Historical Journal*, 44/3 (2001): pp. 727–47.

[10]   For an analysis of the debate over the origins of 'Tory feminism' see Mark Goldie, 'Mary Astell and John Locke', in William Kolbrener and Michal Michelson (eds), *Mary Astell: Reason, Gender, Faith* (Aldershot, 2007), pp. 65–6. For theological contexts, see Goldie, 'Mary Astell and John Locke', esp. pp. 81–5; Sarah Apetrei, '"Call No Man Master upon Earth": Mary Astell's Tory Feminism and an Unknown Correspondence', *Eighteenth-Century Studies*, 41/4 (2008): pp. 507–23; Sarah Apetrei, *Women, Feminism and Religion in Early Enlightenment England* (Cambridge, 2010).

[11]   Sarah Prescott, 'Elizabeth Singer Rowe: Gender, Dissent, and Whig Poetics', in David Womersley, Paddy Bullard and Abigail Williams (eds), *Cultures of Whiggism: New Essays on English Literature and Culture in the Long Eighteenth Century* (Newark, 2005), pp. 173–99; Anne Kelley, *Catharine Trotter: An Early Modern Writer in the Vanguard of Feminism* (Aldershot, 2002); Sarah Prescott, 'The Cambrian Muse: Welsh Identity and Hanoverian Loyalty in the Poems of Jane Brereton (1685–1740)', *Eighteenth-Century Studies*, 38/4 (2005): pp. 587–603. For Masham, see Sarah Hutton's chapter in this volume. For the Whig literary canon see Abigail Williams, *Poetry and the Creation of a Whig Literary Culture, 1681–1714* (Oxford, 2005).

[12]   Prescott, 'Elizabeth Singer Rowe', pp. 180–87; Alice Wakely, 'Mary Davys and the Politics of Epistolary Form', in Womersley, Bullard and Williams (eds), *Cultures of Whiggism*, pp. 257–67.

Whig writers also took inspiration from debates over absolute power and passive obedience, and philosophy and religion, to review the position of women within English society. As Kathryn R. King has remarked, 'there is no consistent link to be found between conservative political principles and female public mindedness or between a Tory frame of reference and feminist assertion'.[13]

The most prolific, and certainly the most politically combative, of these female Whig writers was Susanna Centlivre. Centlivre was an actress, playwright and author of a number of occasional poems and articles between circa 1700 and her death in December 1723. The earliest of these were published under the surname of her second husband, Carroll, prior to her marriage in April 1707 to her third husband, Joseph Centlivre.[14] Centlivre has long been recognized as a firmly partisan Whig dramatist of the 1700s and 1710s, whose many plays also exhibited an interest in gender politics.[15] Centlivre's religious concerns, however, in particular her intense anti-Catholicism, dislike of priestly authority and anxiety over the High Church threat to the post-Revolutionary Church of England and Protestant Succession, have not received as much attention. Like many Whigs, Centlivre's political thinking was dominated by a strong confessional and anti-clerical impetus, possibly linked to her family's reputed experiences under the Stuarts; her father was alleged to have been 'a Dissenter, and a zealous Parliamentarian' who was 'very much persecuted at the Restoration'.[16]

Little is known about Centlivre prior to 1700. According to Giles Jacob, who published her biography in 1719, four years before her death, her father was a Mr Freeman from the fenland town of Holbeach in Lincolnshire and her first husband was an (unnamed) nephew of the administrator and financier, Sir Stephen Fox. When she married Joseph Centlivre, a Yeoman of the Mouth to Queen Anne (and later George I), she described herself in the marriage license as a widow, 'Susannah Caroll als Rawkins', leading John Wilson Bowyer to speculate that

---

[13]   Kathryn R. King, 'Political Verse and Satire: Monarchy, Party and Female Political Agency', in Sarah Prescott and David E. Shuttleton (eds), *Women and Poetry, 1660–1750* (Basingstoke, 2003), p. 220.

[14]   For Centlivre's life and publications see John Wilson Bowyer, *The Celebrated Mrs Centlivre* (Durham, NC, 1952); F.P. Lock, *Susanna Centlivre* (Boston, 1979).

[15]   See Douglas R. Butler, 'Plot and Politics in Susanna Centlivre's "A Bold Stroke for a Wife"', in Mary Anne Schofield and Cecilia Macheski (eds), *Curtain Calls: British and American Women and the Theater, 1660–1820* (Athens, Ohio, 1991), pp. 357–70; Laura J. Rosenthal, *Playwrights and Plagiarists in Early Modern England: Gender, Authorship, Literary Property* (Ithaca, 1996), pp. 204–42; Brean S. Hammond, 'Is There a Whig Canon? The Case of Susanna Centlivre', *Women's Writing*, 7/3 (2000): pp. 373–90; Gilli Bush-Bailey, *Treading the Bawds: Actresses and Playwrights on the Late-Stuart Stage* (Manchester, 2006), pp. 190–99; Hilda L. Smith, Mihoko Suzuki and Susan Wiseman (eds), *Women's Political Writings, 1610–1725* (4 vols, London, 2007), vol. 4, p. 163.

[16]   Giles Jacob, *The Poetical Register: Or, the Lives and Characters of the English Dramatick Poets* (London, 1719–20), p. 32.

Rawkins may have been the name of her first husband.[17] That her first husband was called Rawkins is given plausibility by the record of a marriage between one Richard Rawkins, bachelor, to one Susanna Freeman, spinster, on 12 October 1692 at St James, Duke's Place, London.[18] While Fox does not appear to have had a nephew called Rawkins, he had cousins of that name.[19] Furthermore, Fox's son, Charles, had married Elizabeth Carr Trollope in 1679, a Lincolnshire heiress with property holdings in Whaplode, adjacent to Holbeach. It may have been from Whaplode rather than Holbeach itself that Centlivre's family had originated, for a Susanna Freeman was baptized in Whaplode in November 1669.[20] Speculatively, it might have been through Elizabeth Fox's agency that Centlivre first came to London to seek employment where she met Rawkins.[21]

The first half of this chapter delineates Centlivre's fears about popery and Nonjurism and explores her efforts to convince her audiences that it was High Churchmen and women, rather than the Whigs, who posed the real threat to the established Church. The second half of the chapter considers Whig responses to the issue of female politicization. The image of the violently partisan High Churchwoman, consolidated by Sacheverell's trial, continued to have an impact on Whig gender politics as the 1710s progressed, and the views of male Whig commentators, such as Addison, were informed by what they considered to be the problem of female High Church activism. Centlivre's fierce anti-Catholicism and hatred of Nonjurors provoked a similar reaction from her, and she depicted the militant High Churchwoman in an especially unattractive light as a sexually transgressive termagant in her play *The Gotham Election* (1715). Yet while *The Gotham Election* has misogynistic strains, Centlivre also suggested in it that a commitment to Revolutionary principles had implications for how men exercised their patriarchal authority.

---

[17] Jacob, *Poetical Register*, pp. 31–2; Bowyer, *Centlivre*, pp. 13, 92–3.

[18] London Metropolitan Archives, London, P69/JS1/A/002/MS07894/002, Marriage Register of St James, Duke's Place. St James, Duke's Place was a location for clandestine marriages, since they could be performed there without banns or marriage license, which suggests that the Rawkins-Freeman match was performed in haste or secrecy. Susanna Freeman appears to have been given in marriage by one George Powell, possibly the actor and playwright of that name. I wish to thank Andrew Lott of London Metropolitan Archives for information about St James, Duke's Place.

[19] Christopher Clay, *Public Finance and Private Wealth: The Career of Sir Stephen Fox, 1627–1716* (Oxford, 1978), pp. 2–3, 144. Fox owed his education in the 1630s to his great-uncle, Richard Rawkins, and Fox acted as a patron to one John Rawkins in the late seventeenth century.

[20] Clay, *Public Finance*, pp. 267–9; Lock, *Susanna Centlivre*, p. 17.

[21] Elizabeth Fox may well have recruited her household from her home county; in her later years, her female companion was a Lincolnshire woman who, interestingly in the context of Centlivre's history, later married into the Fox family as Sir Stephen Fox's second wife. See Clay, *Public Finance*, pp. 318–19.

I

Centlivre's engagement with the politics of religion focussed on refuting the idea
that the Church was in danger in the hands of the Whigs. Like many pro-Georgian
writers, she endorsed the view that the Church of England had been rescued from
the Popish Pretender by the arrival of the Protestant George I. 'Our pure *Religion*,
long the Mark of *Rome*, / Repriev'd by You Escapes her final Doom', she wrote
to George I on his accession, and she ascribed the Hanoverian succession to
divine intercession.[22] Likewise, Centlivre's poem of 1716, 'writ on King George's
Birth-Day … and sent to the Ringers while the Bells were ringing at Holbeach in
Lincolnshire', focused on George I's role as 'he that sav'd your Church'.[23] Equally
forthright was her poem of the same year attacking the Tories of St Martin-in-the-
Fields who had rung their bells on St George's Day (the anniversary of Queen
Anne's coronation and thus a festal day for Jacobites). 'No more the Danger
of the Church / Shall leave Religion in the Lurch, / To serve a Popish Cause'.[24]
Centlivre viewed George I's grandchildren as fulfilling a similar function to their
grandfather. Writing in 1715, she described them as 'for our *Church*'s Safety
given, / The Darling Hostages 'twixt *her* and *Heaven*'.[25]

While Centlivre was keen to emphasize that the Church was secure under
George I's protection, she remained fiercely concerned about those she considered
its enemies. As might be expected, Catholic priests and laity come under her
attack, most noticeably in her farce *A Wife Well Manag'd* (1715) which featured a
Catholic priest who attempts to seduce a married woman. Centlivre enthusiastically
championed her associate Nicholas Rowe's Protestant melodrama, *The Tragedy of
the Lady Jane Gray* (1715) (which Rowe had dedicated to the princess of Wales)
because of its anti-Catholic impetus. Possibly taking a swipe at the Nonjuring
clergyman, Jeremy Collier, who had so vociferously condemned the stage for
immorality, Centlivre argued that Rowe had 'set the Cruelties of Rome in so true
a Light, that a great Part of our Clergy may blush to see the Stage become a better
Advocate for Protestantism than the Pulpit'.[26]

---

[22]   Susanna Centlivre, *A Poem. Humbly Presented to His Most Sacred Majesty George,
King of Great Britain, France, and Ireland upon his Accession to the Throne* (London,
1715), pp. 6, 8.

[23]   *A Collection of State Songs, Poems, Etc that Have Been Publish'd Since the
Rebellion* (London, 1716), p. 12.

[24]   Ibid., p. 53. A similar sentiment is voiced in the poem by 'S.C.' (probably Centlivre),
in celebration of the anniversary of George I's coronation day and the defeat of the Atterbury
Plot, printed in the *Weekly Journal or British Gazeteer*, 20 October 1722.

[25]   Susanna Centlivre *An Epistle to Mrs Wallup, Now in the Train of Her Royal
Highness, the Princess of Wales* (London, 1715), p. 7. She repeated this belief in 'An
Invocation to *Juno Lucina* for the Safe Delivery of Her Royal Highness the *Princess of
Wales*', *The Protestant Packet*, 21 January 1716.

[26]   Susanna Centlivre, preface to *The Gotham Election: A Farce* (London, 1715).

However, for Centlivre the Church's most immediate enemies were those who pretended to be its most assiduous friends, the High Church clergy and Nonjurors. As she declared in her poem to the Holbeach bellringers:

High-Church Zeal
Is like the Jaw-Daws noisy Peal,
When perch'd up high on Steeple,
Who never to the Church did good,
But only soil and dawb the Wood,
And shi_t down on the People.[27]

The High Church faction were crypto-Catholic traitors attempting to bring in 'Mass and Wooden Shoes / With Transubstantiation'.[28]

Centlivre particularly articulated her fears of an ongoing popish plot in the preface to *The Gotham Election* (1715) which, along with *A Wife Well Manag'd*, had been barred from the stage.[29] Noting that *A Wife Well Manag'd* had been banned because 'it was said there would be Offence taken at the exposing a *Popish Priest*', Centlivre exclaimed, 'Good God! ...', 'Are those worthy Gentlemen (the Emissaries of our most avow'd and irreconcileable Enemy) to be treated with so much Tenderness?' She went on to add, 'It is with the utmost Indignation, that I see those wholesome Laws neglected, which ought to be put in Execution against such profess'd Enemies of our Church and State'.[30]

The Gotham Election reiterated these ideas. Although Centlivre claimed that she had written the farce about a parliamentary election in the proverbial town of fools in order to satirize both Whigs and Tories – thus fulfilling the classic role of comedy – the play is dedicated to the younger James Craggs, a rising Whig politician, and the villains of the piece are the crypto-Catholic Jacobite Mayor of Gotham and High Church Jacobite Lady Worthy.[31] Gotham's parson, Blow-Coal, does not appear on stage but he, too, is described as a Jacobite intriguer who furthers the Pretender's cause by distributing money from the exiled court within the town 'with a strict Charge to have Regard to the Church; the Noise of the Church, you know, does much'.[32] Centlivre voiced her concern about the malign influence that politicized clergymen might exercise in a scene between the Whig

---

[27]   *Collection of State Songs*, p. 13. The poem was also published in *The Flying Post*, 21 June 1716, which appears to print the most accurate version of this verse's last line (cited here).

[28]   Ibid., p. 13. Wooden shoes were popularly associated with poverty, particularly as experienced in absolutist monarchies such as France.

[29]   Jane Milling, '"A Gotham Election": Women and Performance Politics', *Restoration and Eighteenth-Century Theatre Research*, 21/2 (2006): pp. 83–5.

[30]   Centlivre, dedication and preface to *Gotham Election*.

[31]   Centlivre, dedication in *Gotham Election*, pp. 26, 28. See also Milling, 'Gotham Election', pp. 74–89; Lock, *Susanna Centlivre*, p. 100.

[32]   Centlivre, *Gotham Election*, p. 47.

Sir Roger Trusty and Alderman Credulous. Credulous explains that he is going to vote for the crypto-Jacobite candidate, Mr Tickup, on the advice of Blow-Coal. 'The Parson of the Parish, you know ought to be regarded, Sir *Roger*, and he told me that Mr. *Tickup* was a good Churchman, and pray'd me to vote for him, and to get all my Friends to do the same, if I would promote the Interest of the Church'. Trusty enlightens him, replying 'Ay, the Interest of the Church of *Rome*, not that of *England*'. 'It is much to be wish'd for the Honour of our Religion, and the Safety of our State, that those learned Men were more industrious in the Cure of Souls, and less busie in Politicks'.[33] Tellingly, it is Gotham's plain-speaking Quaker, Scruple, who also sees through Tickup's designs. The Church, Centlivre implied, was better preserved by Dissenters than High Churchmen.[34]

Centlivre remained concerned about meddling priests into the early 1720s. It has been suggested that she was the 'S.C' who submitted abstracts from the weekly anti-clerical, pro-Hanoverian journal *The Independent Whig*, written by John Trenchard and Thomas Gordon, to be reprinted in *The Weekly Journal or British Gazeteer* between September and December 1720. Certainly, 'S.C' shared the same preoccupations as well as the same initials as Centlivre. She or he abstracted sections from *The Independent Whig* that attacked Catholicism and 'the High-Church *Jacobite* Clergy', praised George I's policy of religious toleration, and highlighted the link between reason and knowledge, and religion and liberty.[35] If 'S.C' was indeed Centlivre then it is significant that 'S.C' selected an extract concerned with what 'S.C' termed as 'the High Church Religion; and the Hypocrisie of its Priests being expos'd by the famous *Moliere*'.[36] This described the French clergy's angry reaction to Molière's *Le Tartuffe* which led to it being banned from the public stage, a situation somewhat akin to Centlivre's *Wife Well Manag'd* and *The Gotham Election*.

Centlivre's last play, *The Artifice*, first performed in October 1722 but probably written over the course of the two or three previous years, also briefly deals with

---

[33]   Ibid., pp. 58–9.

[34]   Ibid., pp. 65–8. Centlivre's attitude towards the Quakers was more ambiguous than this characterization suggests. Three years later, in *A Bold Stroke for a Wife*, Centlivre follows theatrical convention to satirize her two Quaker characters, Mr and Mrs Prim, as lewd hypocrites.

[35]   Paul Bunyan Anderson, 'Innocence and Artifice: Or, Mrs. Centlivre and "The Female Tatler"', *Philological Quarterly*, 16 (1937): p. 375, n. 32; Bowyer, *Centlivre*, pp. 231–2. That 'S.C' was female is suggested by S.C's phrase that since the original author's style was 'pure, sharp, and masculine, I shall not eleviate [deviate] from it'. However *The Weekly Journal*'s editor believed that 'S.C' was male: *The Weekly Journal*, 10 September 1720. For the preoccupations of *The Independent Whig* see Marie P. McMahon, *The Radical Whigs, John Trenchard and Thomas Gordon: Libertarian Loyalists to the New House of Hanover* (Lanham, 1990), pp. 80, 146–7, 153–5; Justin Champion, '"Anglia Libera": Commonwealth Politics in the Early Years of George I', in Womersley, Bullard and Williams (eds), *Cultures of Whiggism*, p. 92.

[36]   *The Weekly Journal*, 15 October 1720.

these issues. Part of the play's drama arises from the circumstances of Sir John Freeman, whose Nonjuring father disinherited him because, as Sir John explains to his friend Ensign Fainwell, 'one Day, in my Cups, I chanced to stumble into a Non-juring-Meeting, with half a Dozen honest Officers at my Back, drove out the Congregation' and tied up the minister.[37] The ensign implicitly justifies such an action a few lines later, remarking that 'whilst there is one Mischief-making Priest in the World, Soldiers will never want Bread', a probable reference to Francis Atterbury, the High Church bishop of Rochester, who had been arrested in August 1722 for his involvement in Jacobite conspiracies.[38] Centlivre emphasized the Atterbury connection by dedicating the printed edition of the play to Ensign Erasmus Earle – an army officer from a Tory background who had testified concerning the Jacobite conspirator, Christopher Layer, in connection with the Atterbury Plot.[39]

Although *The Artifice*'s main action was only loosely linked to Nonjurism – unlike Colley Cibber's very popular comedy *The Non-Juror* (1717) which directly assailed Nonjurors – it was attacked for its politics. The highly critical *Advice from Parnassus* desired to know 'if Mrs *Centlivre* cou'd imagine it a piece of good Manners, good Breeding, or Fortitude, to make her Hero break into a place of Divine Worship, attack an unarm'd Clergyman'. It concluded that Sir John Freeman's principles 'keep equal Pace with genuine Whiggism, to disregard the Laws of God and Man'.[40] Such an attack did not go unnoticed. An advertisement in *The Daily Journal* for 7 November 1722 signed 'Susan Centlivre' detected that the *Advice*'s author 'must be some Non-Juring Parson; having set himself up for Dramatick Critick, roundly asserts in the Arrogant-stile of his Brother Collier'.[41] But this was then followed two weeks later by a letter in the *St James's Journal*, this time probably from Centlivre, who disowned the advertisement which she believed 'some of my good Friends, the *Jacobites*, had inserted'. Centlivre was unable to track down a copy of the *Advice* but presented her play as a type of martyr to the Protestant cause, and hinted that some courtesy should have been shown to her because of her sex. It was 'rather a Glory to be abus'd than commended by a turbulent Set of People, who ... vented their ill-manner'd Rage upon a Woman: and since they were not able to stab our Laws, and Liberties, they endeavoured to murder a poor Play'.[42]

---

[37]   Susanna Centlivre, *The Artifice* (London, 1723), p. 5; Lock, *Susanna Centlivre*, p. 116.

[38]   Centlivre, *Artifice*, p. 5.

[39]   R.W. Ketton-Cremer, *A Norfolk Gallery* (London, 1948), pp. 138–40; Norfolk Record Office, Norwich, NRS 26,356, John Breval to Augustine Earle, 24 January 1723.

[40]   *Advice from Parnassus* (London, 1722), pp. 32, 35; Bowyer, *Centlivre*, pp. 240–41. The *Advice from Parnassus* was puffed as a monthly pamphlet in the *Freeholder's Journal*, 17 October 1722.

[41]   *The Daily Journal*, 7 November 1722; Bowyer, *Centlivre*, pp. 240–41.

[42]   *St James's Journal*, 22 November 1722; Bowyer, *Centlivre*, p. 241.

II

Centlivre's political and religious stance won her admirers amongst some Whigs. When *The Patriot* journal devoted its 15 January 1715 issue to discussing patriotism and the family, it singled out Centlivre's 'Good Sense and Noble Passion for the Protestant Succession', which 'make her an Honour to her Sex, and a Credit to Our Country … She is Mistress of a True *British* Principle'.[43] The Whig writer, Nicholas Amhurst, praised Centlivre as a Madonna of the Whigs:

> Whilst Party Mad, the *British* Fair,
> On Bigot *Jemmy* [the Pretender] set their Hearts,
> Despise the peaceful House-Wife's Care,
> And practice their Seditious Arts.
>
> Whilst they with Lyes revile the Throne,
> And with Church-Fears their Minds Perplex,
> Their Follies singly you attone,
> And singly you redeem the Sex.[44]

Although Centlivre was, as a woman, ineligible for the types of posts that were available to her male Whig counterparts, her enthusiastic support for the Hanoverian dynasty was not unappreciated by George I and George and Caroline, prince and princess of Wales, who ordered command performances of her plays.[45]

Nevertheless, Centlivre's political activities stirred concern on account of her sex, even amongst those of similar political sympathies. In June 1716, a contributor to George Ridpath's Whiggish *The Flying Post* relayed how he had dined with a friend in London 'whose Wife Entertained me with such Politicks all Dinner Time'. The writer went on to remark that:

> I was in Hopes to have found Women more moderate in London, from what I had lately seen by one come down to Lincolnshire, viz. Mrs. Centlivre, who was Born at Holbeach in that County, and Order'd down thither by the Physicians for her Health. On the 28th of May, which was the Anniversary of King George's Birth, She invited all the Widows, that take Collections of the Parish, to the Tavern, to Supper, where she caus'd them to drink King George's Health, on their Knees … The Musick playing in the Room, and the Bells ringing by her Orders all Supper Time … the whole Town was in an Uproar.[46]

---

[43] *The Patriot*, no. 23, 15 January 1715.

[44] Nicholas Amhurst, 'To Mrs. Centlivre. Upon Her Desiring Him to Read and Correct a Poem', in *A New Miscellany of Original Poems, Translations and Imitations* (London, 1720), p. 334.

[45] Bowyer, *Centlivre*, p. 154.

[46] *The Flying Post*, 21–23 June 1716; Bowyer, *Centlivre*, p. 170.

The report concluded by printing Centlivre's verses to the Holbeach bellringers. That the *Flying Post*'s correspondent was somewhat disquieted by Centlivre's loyalist activities in Holbeach is understandable. According to this account, Centlivre had set herself at the head of a group of women – albeit widowed rather than married women – whose interest in affairs of state should have been minimal, and required that they pledge loyalty to the regime using a socio-political ritual normally associated with men.

The *Flying Post*'s article can be seen as illustrative of the ambiguous reaction of Whig writers towards female political engagement. Addison's *The Freeholder* particularly underscored this ambivalence. Addison disapproved of female political activity, which he considered to be unfeminine, unattractive and beyond the bounds of the sex, and was rendered even more dubious by what he saw as the inability of women to follow political reasoning.[47] Nevertheless, Addison devoted a number of *The Freeholder*'s pages to explaining to his female readers the merits of the Revolution and Hanoverian Succession and urged them to champion it. By doing so, he implicitly acknowledged that women, too, were citizens.[48] This shift in approach, he made clear, was owing to the exceptional gravity of the times and the political problem of Tory and Jacobite women. It had 'become necessary to treat our Women as Members of the Body Politick; since it is visible that great Numbers of them have of late eloped from their Allegiance, and that they do not believe themselves obliged to draw with us, as Yoke-Fellows in the Constitution'.[49] Female support and advocacy for the Hanoverian regime was crucial to its safety, Addison argued, because of the influence that women wielded over their menfolk, a belief that was widely shared.[50] Indeed, six years earlier, the anti-Sacheverellite *The Officers Address to the Ladies* had even asked its female readers to persuade the clergy that alarm over the Church was 'thro' mistake and error'.[51]

Since women needed to be persuaded of the Revolution's advantages, Addison made efforts to point to how their interests were intertwined with its fate. 'They cannot but take Notice what uncomfortable Lives those of their own Sex lead, where Passive Obedience is professed and practised in its utmost Perfection', he maintained.[52] By comparison, in England, women have 'all the Privileges of *English*-born Subjects, without the Burdens' – an argument that was still proving popular with those opposed to female suffrage in the late nineteenth century.[53]

---

[47]   Addison, *Freeholder*, pp. 146–7, 182–3.

[48]   An approach also adopted by Ambrose Philips's journal, *The Freethinker* (1718–19). See Champion, '"Anglia Libera"', p. 89.

[49]   Addison, *Freeholder*, p. 182.

[50]   Ibid., p. 52. See also p. 146. For Centlivre's belief in the persuasive powers of women see Susanna Centlivre, *An Epistle to the King of Sweden from a Lady of Great-Britain* (London, 1717), p. 6.

[51]   *Officers Address to the Ladies*, p. 4.

[52]   Addison, *Freeholder*, p. 52.

[53]   Ibid., p. 54.

Addison also gave a gendered slant to his emphasis that the Church was safe under the Hanoverians by spotlighting the most prominent female member of the dynasty, Caroline, princess of Wales's, 'sincere Piety' and 'constant … Attendance on the daily Offices of our Church'.[54]

Centlivre did not share these reservations about the fundamental appropriateness of female political activity and, more generally, the intellectual abilities of women. It is true that she occasionally alluded to female inferiority. Centlivre noted, in the dedication of her play *The Perplex'd Lovers* (January 1712) to the Whig MP Sir Henry Furnese, that 'we Women are incapable of serving our Country in the Discharge of weighty Affairs'. Yet she added that 'we would not be thought so insipid a Part of it, as not to admire those that are'.[55] She continued in this vein in the play's preface where she defended her support of John Churchill, duke of Marlborough, despite his very recent dismissal from office, 'as I am an English Woman'.[56]

Centlivre also expressed these sentiments via the romantic plotlines of her plays. Centlivre's heroines are usually politically aware young women, committed to the Revolution and Protestant Succession. They actively demonstrate this by turning down wealthy, aristocratic suitors in favour of men who are engaged in the Revolution's defence, often impoverished army officers, risking their lives in the fight against popery, arbitrary government and Louis XIV.[57] The heroine of *The Gotham Election*, Lucy, is politically engaged – 'plaguey Low in her Principles' as her Jacobite father, the mayor of Gotham, puts it – to the extent that she will not accept a proposal of marriage made to her by Sir Roger Trusty's pro-Whig agent, Mr Friendly, unless he brings proofs of his dedication to the Revolution.[58] Yet crucially, while Centlivre's heroines are committed Whigs, they do not engage directly in the cut and thrust of politics, a task they leave to their future husbands. Although Lucy makes it a condition of her marriage with Friendly that he will spend 'every Shilling' of her portion 'in Defence of Liberty and Property against *Perkin* and the Pope', she does not undertake to do so herself.[59] Centlivre's heroines look beyond the realm of domesticity and intellectually and emotionally engage in the party politics of their era, but they retain a respect for traditional gender roles. In this sense, they are the kin of the Whig 'Female-Patriots' praised by Addison, who 'show themselves good Stateswomen as well as good Housewives'.[60]

Centlivre was particularly concerned with delineating the parameters of acceptability when she came to discussing Tory and Jacobite women. In 1710

[54]   Ibid., p. 128.
[55]   Susanna Centlivre, dedication in *The Perplex'd Lovers* (London, 1712).
[56]   Ibid., preface.
[57]   Hannah Smith, 'Politics, Patriotism, and Gender: The Standing Army Debate on the English Stage, circa 1689–1720', *Journal of British Studies*, 50/1 (2011): pp. 65, 69.
[58]   Centlivre, *Gotham Election*, pp. 49, 69–70.
[59]   Ibid., pp. 69–70.
[60]   Addison, *Freeholder*, p. 103.

Defoe had been willing to bet that the 'Virago', the 'Termagant', and 'Whores' were 'for *Sacheverell*', while in 1716 Addison believed that 'every one of them who is a Shrew in domestick Life, is now become a Scold in Politicks'.[61] In *The Gotham Election*, Centlivre similarly depicts the Jacobite Lady Worthy as a disorderly woman, and the antithesis of Lucy. As a character, Lady Worthy bears a strong resemblance to the Jacobite intriguer, Lady Addleplot, in Thomas D'Urfey's play *Love for Money* (1691), which had been played as a comic drag role; possibly the distinctly unfeminine Lady Worthy would have been similarly cast had *The Gotham Election* made it on to the stage. Lady Worthy swears, brawls and subverts patriarchal authority throughout the play in her attempts to further the Jacobite cause. She is desperate to ensure that her husband, Sir John Worthy, loses the election after he refuses to be tough on Dissent. 'I hate a Whig', she declares, 'a Parcel of canting Rogues; they have always Moderation in their Mouths, – rank Resistance in their Hearts, – and hate Obedience even to their Lawful Wives'.[62] Indeed, Lady Worthy uses part of her marriage portion to bribe those Gotham wives who 'wear the Britches' into bullying their husbands to vote for her candidate.[63]

Centlivre's responses to female political activity were complicated by what Whigs, including herself, considered to be the problem of Tory and Jacobite women. Centlivre had to justify female support for Whiggism and condemn similarly partisan-inspired conduct on the part of female Tories and Jacobites. Maintaining that the political engagement of Tory and Jacobite women was reprehensible solely on partisan grounds lacked broader persuasive appeal. Hence Centlivre's interest in defining acceptable and unacceptable political behaviour for women as a way of reconciling the inconsistency of her approach. It is true that Centlivre's own political activities were sometimes more in the contentious spirit of her *Gotham Election* villainess, Lady Worthy, than those of her Whig heroines (Centlivre's unabashed Whiggism allegedly nearly cost her husband his post in the royal kitchens at the end of Anne's reign).[64] Nevertheless, despite the disparity between what she practised and what she prescribed, the thrice married Centlivre appears to have been ideologically committed to the existing gender order.[65] This leads on to a related dilemma for Centlivre, and her audiences and

---

[61]   *Review of the State of the British Nation*, 11 May 1710; Addison, *Freeholder*, p. 136; Nicholson, 'Sacheverell's Harlots', pp. 71–3, 76–8.

[62]   Centlivre, *Gotham Election*, pp. 28, 32; Milling, 'Gotham Election', pp. 81–2.

[63]   Centlivre, *Gotham Election*, pp. 28–9, 33–7. For the influence of wives over husbands in parliamentary elections see Elaine Chalus, 'Women, Electoral Privilege and Practice in the Eighteenth Century', in Kathryn Gleadle and Sarah Richardson (eds), *Women in British Politics, 1760–1860: The Power of the Petticoat* (Basingstoke, 2000), pp. 24–31.

[64]   Bowyer, *Centlivre*, p. 153.

[65]   For Centlivre's depiction of herself as a good wife, and her husband's reaction to her literary activities, see Susanna Centlivre, *A Woman's Case: In An Epistle to Charles Joye, Esq; Deputy-Governor of the South-Sea* (London, 1720), pp. 7–9; Susan Staves, 'Investments, Votes, and "Bribes": Women as Shareholders in the Chartered National

readers. If Centlivre was asking women to support a political doctrine based upon the premise that it was legitimate to resist tyranny, did she endorse the idea that women could justifiably rebel against other forms of tyranny, such as those found within the 'little commonwealth' of the family?

III

Although at least one mid-eighteenth-century feminist found inspiration in Centlivre's work, Centlivre's gender politics have proved more problematic for modern scholars who have highlighted the discrepancies and shifts in her feminism.[66] Several of her plays contain what might be termed 'pro-woman' content. *The Wonder: A Woman Keeps a Secret* (first performed in April 1714 and dedicated to the electoral prince of Hanover, the later George II) revolves around the heroine, Violante who, at considerable personal cost, keeps a secret for a female friend who is trying to escape a forced marriage. The play concludes with the hero remarking that 'Man has no Advantage but the Name' and *The Wonder*'s epilogue, provided by the Whig writer Ambrose Philips and spoken by the actress Hester Santlow, pursued this theme.[67]

> Custom with all our Modern Laws combin'd,
> Has given such Power despotick to Mankind,
> … were the Women all of my Opinion,
> We'd soon shake off this false usurp'd Dominion;
> We'd make the Tyrants own, that we cou'd prove,
> As fit for other Business as for Love.[68]

Many of Centlivre's plays involve an attack on patriarchal tyranny, with capricious, misguided or immoral fathers being opposed by their often Whiggish daughters or wards.[69] However, Centlivre is careful to present this as a revolt against the abuses

---

Companies', in Hilda L. Smith (ed.), *Women Writers and the Early Modern British Political Tradition* (Cambridge, 1998), pp. 265–8.

[66]   *The Works of the Celebrated Mrs. Centlivre* (3 vols, London, 1761), vol. 1, pp. viii–xi; Jacqueline Pearson, *The Prostituted Muse: Images of Women and Women Dramatists, 1642–1737* (Hemel Hempstead, 1988), pp. 223–4, 228; Margarete Rubik, *Early Women Dramatists, 1550–1800* (Basingstoke, 1998), pp. 93–111; Lisa A. Freeman, *Character's Theater: Genre and Identity on the Eighteenth-Century English Stage* (Philadelphia, 2002), pp. 73–5, 152–60; Misty G. Anderson, *Female Playwrights and Eighteenth-Century Comedy: Negotiating Marriage on the London Stage* (Basingstoke, 2002), pp. 109–38.

[67]   Susanna Centlivre, *The Wonder: A Woman Keeps a Secret* (London, 1714), p. 79.

[68]   Ibid., p. 80.

[69]   In particular, *The Beau's Duel* (1702), *The Basset-Table* (1706), *The Man's Bewitch'd* (1709), *The Wonder* (1714) and *A Bold Stroke for a Wife* (1718). See also Pearson, *Prostituted Muse*, p. 223.

of patriarchy rather than patriarchy itself, ensuring that her heroines rebel with the assistance of their future husbands.

In *The Gotham Election*, Gotham's mayor is a crypto-Catholic Jacobite and a bad father, who intends to send his daughter, Lucy, to a French convent so that he can appropriate her dowry to buy a peerage for his equally Jacobite son.[70] This propels Lucy's revolt, who views forcible conversion to Catholicism as a fate worse than death for 'a true British Soul'.[71] Defying her father, she arranges a marriage between herself and the Whig, Mr Friendly, who promises that he will be 'both a Father and a Husband' to her.[72] Centlivre guides the audience's response to this conclusion by inserting a discussion between Sir Roger Trusty and Aldermen Credulous a few scenes earlier. 'We Fathers know what's good for our Children, better than they do themselves', declares the Alderman, 'they have nought to do but to submit to our Pleasures; Passive Obedience is as absolutely necessary in our Wives and Children, as in Subjects to the Monarch; is not your Opinion the same, Sir *Roger*?' Trusty, however, sets straight his social inferior, 'Yes, whilst Husbands, Fathers and Monarchs exact nothing from us, contrary to our Religion and Laws'.[73]

Centlivre is reworking Whig resistance and contract theory in a domestic context. Indeed, Lucy's flight from patriarchal tyranny can be read as an allegory of the Revolution of 1688–89, with Lucy (England) inviting Friendly (William of Orange) to rescue her from her tyrannous Catholic father (James II), who wishes to deliver her into the power of Catholic Europe. But Centlivre does not engage with the provocative question posited by Mary Astell a decade earlier, that '*if Absolute Sovereignty be not necessary in a State, how comes it to be so in a Family?*' and 'If all Men are born free, *how is it that all Women are born Slaves*'.[74] Astell was not the only Tory to point to the vulnerability of Revolution principles when it came to gender relations. In 1717, a correspondent to the Tory-Jacobite *Weekly Journal or Saturday's Post*, edited by Nathaniel Mist, remarked on the hypocrisy of Whigs. 'Those Wretches in their own Houses are always absolute, tho' they'll not allow the Father of the People'. The putatively female writer then declared that whilst her Tory husband 'sets the Example of Non-Resistance and Passive Obedience to his Prince, I'll practise it to him, and that without the least Reluctancy; even tho' he should turn Tyrant; but should he turn Whig, I'll elope from him, and vindicate it by one of their own Arguments'.[75]

If this scenario was alarming, worse was to follow. Whig theorizing, it was insinuated, could be extrapolated to justify female sexual license. As the *Officers*

[70]   Centlivre, *Gotham Election*, pp. 48–9.
[71]   Ibid., p. 69.
[72]   Ibid., p. 72.
[73]   Ibid., p. 56.
[74]   Mary Astell, preface to *Reflections upon Marriage*, 3rd edn (London, 1706).
[75]   *Weekly Journal or Saturday's Post*, 14 December 1717. For a Whig reply see *The Weekly Journal or British Gazeteer*, 21 December 1717.

Address to the Ladies had jokingly argued in 1710 when mocking female enthusiasm for Sacheverell, 'Pray to what else can this Doctrine of *Passive Obedience and Non-Resistance* tend, but to settle the severity of an old *Tasteless* Father, over his *Blooming* Daughter; the Tyranny of an *impotent* Husband over a *craving* Wife?'[76] The idea that the Revolution could be construed as the female libertine's charter was picked up by the *Advice from Parnassus* in its critique of Centlivre's *The Artifice*. The *Advice* complained that 'the whole Scope of the Play is to encourage Adultery; to ridicule the Clergy; and to set Women, above the arbitrary Powers of their Husbands, to exert their natural Rights for the Preservation of their Lusts'.[77]

Centlivre was angered that *The Artifice* had been represented as a play that 'no modest Woman could see'.[78] But her concerns were not only over the commercial impact that such a judgement might have. She was also fighting for her reputation as a respectable married woman. An actress dependent on public approbation for her writing, Centlivre was particularly vulnerable to charges of sexual impropriety, and her personal and professional circumstances can be seen as contributing to a broader support of patriarchal authority found in her writings.

Nevertheless, Centlivre adds a subtle caveat to her endorsement of the existing gender hierarchy, hinting that a commitment to Revolution principles places obligations on Whig men in their interactions with women. Centlivre suggests as much when she repeatedly merges the political and personal in *The Gotham Election*. Lucy rejects the conventional romantic language of Friendly's marriage proposal and instead demands that he brings her 'unquestionable Proofs' that he has 'always been a Lover of your Country, – a true Asserter of her Laws and Priviledges'. Friendly responds, 'If I do not this, may I meet the Fate which every Traytor to his Land deserves, my charming Heroine!'[79] Centlivre underlines the point in a scene immediately after their marriage. When Friendly promises to make Lucy happy, she answers, 'I cannot be unhappy, if your Conduct answers your Character; a moderate Man, from a true innate Principle of Virtue, scorns to betray even his Enemies, much less his Country or his Faith'.[80] Centlivre sums up her suggestion in the final lines of the play, with Lucy's announcement that 'This is my Maxim in a married Life, / Who hates his Country, ne'er can love his Wife'.[81]

The thinking of Centlivre, and other Whig writers, on gender politics was coloured by the experience of Sacheverell's trial which appeared to reveal the popularity of the High Church cause amongst women, and the wider political

---

[76]   *Officers Address to the Ladies*, p. 3.

[77]   *Advice from Parnassus*, p. 33.

[78]   *St James's Journal*, 22 November 1722.

[79]   Centlivre, *Gotham Election*, pp. 69–70; Milling, 'Gotham Election', p. 82. Centlivre makes a connection between personal and political treachery in *The Artifice*, where Sir John Freeman's Jacobite brother, Ned, reneges on marrying his betrothed: Centlivre, *The Artifice*, pp. 7–8.

[80]   Centlivre, *Gotham Election*, p. 71.

[81]   Ibid., p. 72.

ramifications this might have. As Addison reflected in 1716, 'Female Zeal, though proceeding from so good a Principle, has been infinitely detrimental to Society, and to Religion itself'.[82] Fears of this sort remained alive over the next two centuries. The anti-clerical preoccupations of some English Radicals in the late nineteenth and early twentieth centuries lead them to oppose female suffrage on the grounds that women were more susceptible to 'religious bigotry', and so the female vote would increase the power of the clergy.[83] The Revolution of 1688–89 not only created an intellectual environment that enabled gender hierarchies to be scrutinized, even challenged. The intensification of party conflict, which scarcely left any aspect of English life untouched, also shaped the era's gender politics.

---

[82] Addison, *Freeholder*, p. 185.

[83] Martin Pugh, *The March of the Women: A Revisionist Analysis of the Campaign for Women's Suffrage, 1866–1914* (Oxford, 2000), pp. 124–5.

Chapter 10
The Life and Works
of Catherine Talbot (1721–70):
'A Public Concern'

Emma Major

Catherine Talbot was not famous in her lifetime. Yet, for the writer and literary hostess Elizabeth Montagu, the life of the obscure spinster Catherine Talbot was 'a public concern' because of her virtuous exemplarity. As she told their mutual friend the classicist Elizabeth Carter, 'I was very happy when I last saw Miss Talbot to find her health so established; I look upon her life as a public concern, for she is ever ready to relieve distress and protect merit, and she gives a sweet example to the world of the amiableness of virtue'.[1]

Talbot was an educated, well-informed, well-connected and articulate member of the Church of England. Born into a clergyman's family, her father Edward died when she was young. A sickly infant, Talbot was nursed by her mother Mary's friend Catherine Benson, who had taken in the widow and child. When Benson married Thomas Secker, in a ceremony officiated by the infant Talbot's grandfather, William Talbot (then bishop of Durham), the newly married couple insisted that Mary and Catherine Talbot should live with them, and in 1725 'the two Families ... became One'.[2] Catherine was loved by the Seckers as their own, and she soon became an active member of a family of avid readers. Secker's 'enlightened mind soon discovered the extent of her early genius, and was delighted to assist in its improvement'.[3] Her intelligence and precocity were valued by her family, and she was praised and encouraged to a degree which she later found embarrassing: Rhoda Zuk notes that Talbot later had a dread of appearing ridiculous for her learning and literary talents.[4] Her journals and letters

---

[1]   Elizabeth Montagu to Elizabeth Carter, n.d., *The Letters of Mrs Elizabeth Montagu, with Some of the Letters of her Correspondents*, ed. Matthew Montagu (4 vols, London, 1809), vol. 4, p. 221.

[2]   Beilby Porteus, 'Life of Archbishop Secker', in Thomas Secker, *Sermons on Several Subjects* (4 vols, London, 1770), vol. 1, p. x.

[3]   Matthew Pennington, 'Some Account of the Life of Mrs Catharine Talbot', in Montagu Pennington (ed.), *The Works of the Late Miss Catharine Talbot* (London, 1819), pp. ix–x.

[4]   Rhoda Zuk, 'Talbot, Catherine (1721–1770)', *Oxford Dictionary of National Biography*, http://www.oxforddnb.com/view/article/26921, accessed 22 August 2011.

show her reading omnivorously from theological, philosophical and classical works in addition to poetry and novels from both sides of the Channel. Discussion of reading was central to her close relationships all her life.

Talbot's talents meant that she gradually adopted an increasing number of practical roles in the Secker household. She became Secker's amanuensis and almoner, acted as companion and carer for his sick wife until her death in 1748, and eventually ran his household: his dependence on her is reflected in his unusual choice of her as his executrix.[5] Talbot struggled to balance the competing needs of family, household, private devotion and self-improvement. Endeavouring to fulfil the 'distinctively Anglican' conflation of the Martha and Mary roles, Talbot attempted to combine the practical with the reflective in a manner which would not attract criticism for the devotional enthusiasm her contemporaries associated with Roman Catholic nuns or Methodist recluses.[6] In this chapter, I will explore the nature and practice of Talbot's exemplary sociability before discussing her work with Secker and assessing the different ways in which her life might be seen as a 'public concern'. Talbot is a fascinating instance of a woman whose life, letters and publications were recognized by her contemporaries as exemplifying the teachings of her Church. Yet as will become evident, Talbot's life and work, like those of many of her predecessors, challenge eighteenth-century and modern-day assumptions about the gendered division of labour within the Church of England.

The 'public' to which Montagu referred in her letter is one which, as I have argued elsewhere, is a richly layered realm that intersects with the Habermasian print public and the Church of England.[7] Montagu saw herself as presiding over social and literary endeavours that affirmed her country's status as the most civilized and Christian of nations.[8] Montagu and her circle came to be referred to as the Bluestockings, but the term 'bluestocking' can occlude the very important social and denominational differences between the literary women included within that term.[9] Montagu's own rather regal exemplarity was different from that which she

---

[5]   The will clearly states Catherine Talbot as executrix and Daniel Burton as executor (see Lambeth Palace Library, London, Miscellaneous Papers MS 2,165, fol. 32). Subsequent mistaken claims that her mother was the executrix may be due to Porteus using the courtesy title 'Mrs' when referring to Talbot in his *Life of Secker*, p. lxxiii. Unfortunately even the current *Oxford Dictionary of National Biography* entry is mistaken on Talbot and names John Burton instead of Daniel Burton as the other executor: Jeremy Gregory, 'Secker, Thomas (1693–1768)', *Oxford Dictionary of National Biography*, http://www.oxforddnb.com/view/article/24998, accessed 20 August 2011.

[6]   Sylvia Bowerbank, *Speaking for Nature: Women and Ecologies of Early Modern England* (Baltimore, 2004), pp. 85, 98. On mid-century anxieties about women and religious enthusiasm, see Emma Major, *Madam Britannia: Women, Church, and Nation 1712–1812* (Oxford, 2011), pp. 125–65.

[7]   Major, *Madam Britannia*, pp. 1–47, passim.

[8]   Ibid., pp. 69–80, 166–215.

[9]   Much excellent work has followed Sylvia Harcstark Myers's *The Bluestocking Circle: Women, Friendship and the Life of the Mind in Eighteenth-Century England*

ascribed to Talbot, who inhabited more ecclesiastical circles and, like their mutual friend Carter, made only occasional forays into the fashionable and political public world in which Montagu revelled. Montagu's claim for Talbot is important for this collection of essays, for it points to a public beyond that of fashion, politics or, in Habermasian terms, an idealized province of reason. Jürgen Habermas's theory of the print public which emerged in the eighteenth century is very persuasive, but needs to be reconsidered in relation to religion in the period, and in relation to women, specifically women of faith.[10] For the public to which Montagu alludes is one which draws constitutive power from religion, and despite its frequent dismissal in the past by the academy, religion 'is neither merely private ... nor purely irrational'.[11] Talbot, who knew many leading churchmen, and was a good friend of that most reasonable and practical of Anglican apologists, Joseph Butler, was aware of the importance of differentiating the faith of the mid-century Church of England from the Methodism which was attracting charges of religious enthusiasm.[12] Her keen awareness of her duties as a Churchwoman is evident not only in her publications, but in her life and letters, and in the ways in which her contemporaries spoke of her. In the next section, I will explore the nature and some of the uses of Talbot's exemplarity before thinking about ways in which her friendships and Church work might be understood to render this very private woman's life a 'public concern'.

(Oxford, 1990), not least the very useful six volumes edited by Gary Kelly et al, *Bluestocking Feminism: Writings of the Bluestocking Circle, 1738–1785* (London, 1999). See also Harriet Guest, *Small Change: Women, Learning, Patriotism* (Chicago, 2000); Elizabeth Eger, *Bluestockings: Women of Reason from Enlightenment to Romanticism* (Basingstoke, 2011). On the term 'bluestocking', see Major, *Madam Britannia*, pp. 80–84.

[10] Jürgen Habermas, *The Structural Transformation of the Public Sphere: An Inquiry into a Category of Bourgeois Society*, trans. Thomas Burger and Frederick Lawrence (Cambridge, 1992). On Habermas's response to his omission of women, see Craig Calhoun (ed.), *Habermas and the Public Sphere* (Cambridge, MA, 1992). On Habermas and religion, see Jürgen Habermas, *Religion and Rationality: Essays on Reason, God, and Modernity*, ed. and introd. Eduardo Mendieta (Cambridge, 2002); Jürgen Habermas and Joseph Ratzinger (Pope Benedict XVI), *Dialectics of Secularization: On Reason and Religion* (San Francisco, 2006).

[11] Eduardo Mendieta and Jonathan VanAntwerpen (eds), *The Power of Religion in the Public Sphere: Judith Butler, Jürgen Habermas, Charles Taylor, Cornel West* (New York, 2011), p. 1.

[12] On the mid-century Church of England, see K.D.M. Snell, *Parish and Belonging: Community, Identity and Welfare in England and Wales 1700–1950* (Cambridge, 2006); Jane Garnett and Colin Matthew (eds), *Revival and Religion since 1700: Essays for John Walsh* (London, 1993); Geoffrey Best, *Temporal Pillars: Queen Anne's Bounty, the Ecclesiastical Commissioners and the Church of England* (Cambridge, 1964), pp. 1–164. On women, Methodism, and the mid-century Church of England, see Major, *Madam Britannia*, pp. 125–66.

I. Talbot's Exemplary Life

Talbot herself might have been crippled by self-reproach at times, and her letters and journals suggest she found the practice of Christian virtues difficult, but those around her admired her as an exemplary Anglican. In October 1769, on Talbot's fatal illness, Montagu wrote to Carter:

> I think, of all Persons I ever knew, she was the most pure, holy, & righteous. To the strictness, regularity, & abstraction, of an almost Monastick [*sic*] retirement, she added all the meritorious acts of a busy life, imitating the great pattern set by him who went about doing good only. I know not such another instance of a perfectly good life.[13]

Montagu's comments about Talbot perform several functions beyond simple praise: her appreciation of Talbot's goodness affirms Montagu's own virtue in recognizing such a Christian example, while her acclaim of Talbot also binds Montagu closer to Carter. As usual, Montagu has an apt quotation to hand, and her reference to Acts 10:38, which describes how Jesus 'went about doing good', would have been appreciated by the devout Carter, who was deeply grieved by Talbot's decline and thought similarly highly of her. Carter observed,

> Never surely was there a more perfect pattern of evangelical goodness, decorated by all the ornaments of a highly improved understanding, and recommended by a sweetness of temper, and an elegant and politeness of manners, of a peculiar and more engaging kind than in any other character I ever knew. Little alas! infinitely too little have I yet profited by the blessing of such an example.[14]

Carter uses 'evangelical' here not in a party sense, but as a member of a Church which is both evangelical and catholic, a body which leads by following Christ's teachings. It is significant, I think, that she should repeat the phrase 'the blessing of such an example' in her brief advertisement to Talbot's posthumously published *Reflections on the Seven Days of the Week* (1770): 'such an example' offers a 'perfect pattern' for others to follow, and as Carter had written to Talbot in 1751, 'the world … stands so much in need of such examples as your's'.[15] Carter's praise was echoed in the same words when in 1799 the minister Weeden Butler praised Talbot's *Reflections* as offering readers 'the pleasing opportunity of profiting by her *thoughts*, which will ever perpetuate the blessings deduced from her *living*

---

[13] Huntington Library, San Marino, MO 3,361, Montagu to Carter, 31 October 1769.

[14] Montagu Pennington (ed.), *A Series of Letters Between Mrs Elizabeth Carter and Miss Catherine Talbot, From the Year 1741 to 1770. To which are Added, Letters from Mrs Elizabeth Carter to Mrs Vesey, Between the Years 1763 and 1787*, 3rd edn (3 vols, London, 1819), vol. 1, p. xxxi.

[15] Ibid., vol. 2, p. 13, Carter to Talbot, 4 March 1751.

example.[16] Praise for Talbot after her death can be read within the exemplary lives traditions which existed in the Catholic form of saints' lives and the popular Protestant interest in godly lives.[17] Both forms, however, were rooted in the funeral eulogy; one of the notable aspects of Talbot's life is the way in which she was popularly spoken of as an example during her life, and her self-conscious attempts to forge good Christian practice within the realm of polite sociability.

Accounts of Talbot's life, and the posthumous publication of her conduct and devotional literature, meant that Talbot's example and teachings extended beyond her own lifetime and entered the realm of print. In 1770 Carter argued that she was justified in publishing Talbot's *Reflections* (and the *Essays* in 1772) because rescuing these works from Talbot's 'considering drawer' would allow more people to 'enjoy the Blessing of her Example'.[18] Carter's nephew, the cleric Montagu Pennington, added a biography of Talbot to his new edition of Talbot's *Works* in 1809 because 'it seems to be fulfilling a duty to society, to shew that the virtues of her character were not inferior to the excellencies of her writings; .... and that the strict attention to the duties of the Gospel which she so strongly recommended to others, was not less enforced and adorned by her own example'.[19] Here, the praise of good women, and the promulgation of their lives and words, is 'a duty to society', and Pennington sees it as a powerful means of conveying the truth and power of his faith. Recognition of the virtue of such women had long been a means of witness: 'Who, that had any sence of Religion, could forbeare to vallue her exceedingly?' John Evelyn asked in his *Life* of the devout Margaret Godolphin (1652–78).[20] Godolphin, like Talbot, was regarded by her peers as a truly pious Churchwoman, and Evelyn wrote his biography of her in the hope that, though it would take 'the penn of an Angells wing to describe the life of a Saint', even an indifferent account of Godolphin's life 'must raise an Emulation in those that read or hear of it to Imitate her vertues'.[21] The Church of England had a well-established tradition of exemplary women who promoted the Church through their lives and writings. Women such as Anne Bacon and Anne Vaughan Lock had been offered as exemplars to Queen Elizabeth I, who in turn was suggested as a type of model of queenly Protestantism for Mary II and Queen Anne.[22]

[16] Weeden Butler, *Memoirs of Mark Hildesley, D.D. Lord Bishop of Sodor and Mann* (London, 1799), p. 591. Emphasis in original.

[17] See Ralph Houlbrooke, *Death, Religion and the Family in England, 1480–1750* (Oxford, 1998), pp. 295–330; Christine Peters, *Patterns of Piety: Women, Gender and Religion in Late Medieval and Reformation England* (Cambridge, 2003), pp. 195–245.

[18] Carter, 'Advertisement', in Catherine Talbot, *Reflections on the Seven Days of the Week* (London, 1770), p. [i]. For Talbot's 'considering drawer' of potential publications, see Pennington (ed.), *Series of Letters*, vol. 2, p. 145, Talbot to Carter, 12 November 1753.

[19] Pennington, *Works of Talbot*, p. vi.

[20] John Evelyn, *The Life of Mrs Godolphin* (London, 1848), p. 34.

[21] Ibid., p. 4.

[22] Susan M. Felch, 'The Exemplary Anne Vaughan Lock', in Johanna Harris and Elizabeth Scott-Baumann (eds), *The Intellectual Culture of Puritan Women, 1558–1680*

Talbot's *Reflections*, *Essays* and *Works* were reissued in various forms until 1861. In 1809 Pennington asserted that *Reflections* had sold over 25,000 copies, claiming that 'few books of more moral and religious instruction have had a greater sale, and gone through more editions'.[23] The popularity of *Reflections* and *Essays* lay perhaps in the simplicity and practicality of Talbot's guidance on how to bring Christianity and politeness together in everyday life. In 1808, further instruction was offered in the form of Talbot's letters to Carter, which were also published by Pennington, with an epigraph from Psalm 55 – 'We took sweet counsel together, and walked in the house of God as friends' – inviting readers to learn from the exemplary friendship in the women's letters. As Montagu's letters about Talbot to Carter show, female friendship was an important means by which exemplary lives were appreciated, circulated and appropriated: Talbot's virtuous life is echoed by the practice of good friendship in exchanging appreciation of her virtue. The British Library copy of Talbot's *Works* has an inscription which suggests that Talbot continued to facilitate friendships long after her death: the front flyleaf bears the legend 'Elizabeth Deake, the gift of her most sincerely and affectionately attached friend, *Jane Bowdler*. Novbr 19th, 1834'.[24] Such a legacy would have been approved by Talbot and Carter, who firmly believed with the influential Yorkshire abbot and author Aelred of Rievaulx (1110–67), that 'Friendship bears fruit in our present life and in the next'.[25] Christianity is, after all, a religion founded on the concept of fellowship: in John 15:13–15, Jesus tells the disciples, 'Greater love hath no man than this, that a man lay down his life for his friends' (AV) and uses the term 'friend' to honour his followers. Carter's translation of Epicurus doubtless influenced the friends' understanding of the meaning and purpose of friendship, but it is Christian interpretations of classical traditions that are the most important context for considering their relationship.[26]

(Basingstoke, 2011), pp. 23–5; Major, *Madam Britannia*, pp. 1–54. On Lock, see also Patrick Collinson's entry for Anne Locke [*sic*] in the *Oxford Dictionary of National Biography*.

[23]   Pennington, 'Some Account', p. xix. On the popularity of Talbot's works, see also Norma Clarke, 'Bluestocking Fictions: Devotional Writings, Didactic Literature and the Imperative of Female Improvement', in Sarah Knott and Barbara Taylor (eds), *Women, Gender and Enlightenment* (Basingstoke, 2005), p. 460.

[24]   The 'attached friend' may be a descendant of the same Bowdler family that boasted several women who were recognized by contemporaries as exemplary Christians: Elizabeth (d. 1797), Jane (1743–84), and Henrietta Maria Bowdler (1750–1830), but I have been unable to confirm this speculation.

[25]   Aelred of Rievaulx, *Spiritual Friendship*, trans. L.C. Braceland and ed. and introd. M.L. Dutton (Collegeville, MN, 2010), p. 72.

[26]   On classical theories of friendship, see Penelope Anderson, *Friendship's Shadows: Women's Friendship and the Politics of Betrayal in England, 1640–1705* (Edinburgh, 2012), pp. 1–18. Anderson's omission of the importance of religion misses a crucial aspect of understanding the self in relation to others. On religious friendship, see Frances Harris, *Transformations of Love: The Friendship of John Evelyn and Margaret Godolphin* (Oxford, 2003), pp. 148–86. For a brief overview of religious friendship, see Elisabeth Moltmann-

II. Conversation: 'Nothing will contribute more to make our public Instructions effectual'[27]

Conversation was the point at which devotion was transformed into active example, but the balance between that private piety and the performance of the more sociable Christian virtues was one which Talbot found difficult. Bringing piety to fashionable society by conversing in a manner which brought Christianity, politeness and pleasantry together in the correct proportions was felt to be a trying task by Talbot, who reproached herself for finding the formulaic superficiality of polite conversation tedious. Many of her published works take a conversational form – internal dialogues, dialogues between characters – and the popularity of the essay form itself during the eighteenth century can be linked to the period's fondness for literary conversation. These conversations, however, are not those such as Talbot would have had with Carter or Secker, but are an attempt to translate learning and faith into action for a polite audience who could not meet her in intellectual or theological debate. They can be usefully read in the pedagogic tradition of philosophical dialogues which began with Plato, and which, in Talbot's case, are also inflected by the catechetical work she did in the parish. Karen O'Brien comments that Talbot's published works lack the intellectual energy of her correspondence.[28] The disparity reflects the extent to which she found it necessary to translate her broad theological reading into clear, simple precepts for the polite society she wished to persuade into more Christian social practice.

'Conversation has ever justly been accounted a powerful Instrument of Good or Evil; it has ever had a mighty Influence on the Conduct of Human Life; and the Vice and Vertue of the World, has ever in great measure been owing to it' argued Richard Lucas, a Westminster prebendary whose 1708 sermons were popular throughout the eighteenth century and whose writings Talbot considered 'excellent'.[29] Lucas took as his text Proverbs 13:20: 'He that walketh with wise Men shall be wise: but a Companion of Fools shall be destroyed', a text of which Secker was also fond, and one which again emphasizes the Christian dimension of friendship and the importance of company to the promotion of virtue. Several of the theologians and devotional writers Talbot admired also wrote on conversation. One, John Norris, the friend of Mary Astell, published popular sermons on conversation. According to Norris, 'Conversation is the very Air and Breath, I had almost said the *Lungs*,

---

Wendel, *Rediscovering Friendship*, trans. John Bowden (London, 2000), pp. 10–16. On women's friendship, see Joan Chittister, *The Friendship of Women: The Hidden Tradition of the Bible* (New York, 2006).

[27] Thomas Secker, *Eight Charges Delivered to the Clergy of the Dioceses of Oxford and Canterbury* (London, [1769]), p. 27.

[28] Karen O'Brien, *Women and Enlightenment in Eighteenth-Century Britain* (Cambridge, 2009), pp. 64–5.

[29] Richard Lucas, *The Influence of Conversation, with the Regulation Thereof; Being a Sermon Preach'd at St Clement Dane to a Religious Society* (London, 1708), p. 2; British Library, London (BL), Add. MS 46,690, Catherine Talbot, 'Journal'.

of Religion, without which it will be in danger of being stifled and choak'd up, but with which it will glow and flame out, and burn bright'.[30] Both clerics see it as the best means of improving society and promoting virtue, especially when combined with 'a good Life, which ... is itself, whether in the Pulpit or out of it, the best Eloquence'.[31] They warn against giving in to the fears of hypocrisy and of being out of fashion which prevent Christians from mentioning their faith in common talk, and provide instructions on how to converse at appropriate times and in proper ways – though Lucas, whose sermon was still in print in various forms at the end of the century, does acknowledge that some might object that 'It will be very difficult at all times to find Matter and Occasion for good Discourse'.[32]

The role assigned to conversation by Norris and Lucas is inflected by the language of politeness in *Essays* and *Reflections*. In *Reflections*, Talbot writes:

> Have I leisure and genius? I must give a Portion of my Time to the elegant Improvements of Life: To the study of those Sciences that are an Ornament to human Nature: To such Things as may make me amiable, and engaging to all whom I converse with, that by any Means I may win them over to Religion and Goodness. For if I am always shut up in my Closet ... I shall ... be ... useless in the World.[33]

Conversation is here the point at which sociability and evangelicalism meet, and in making it the vehicle of piety, Talbot is drawing on a notion central to the discourse of politeness. Samuel Johnson observed in *The Rambler* that in contrast to card playing, 'It is scarcely possible to pass an hour in honest conversation, without being able when we rise from it, to please ourselves with having given or received some advantages'.[34] The actual practice of such 'honest conversation' could prove dishearteningly difficult, however, and the fashionable world often showed itself reluctant to be improved. Carter lamented to Talbot that 'To be sure the fine folks of this world are as sagacious in finding out the formidable genius

---

[30]   John Norris, 'Of Religious Discourse in Common Conversation', *Practical Discourses upon Several Divine Subjects* (4 vols, London, 1707), vol. 4, p. 21. This sermon was also published separately in 1702 and went through 10 editions. This is probably the edition referred to by Talbot when she says 'Norris's Works my Pocket Companion & a pleasing one': BL, Add. MS 46,688, fol. 26, Talbot, 'Journal', Saturday 10 November 1753. The English Short Title Catalogue has no record of a *Works*.

[31]   Norris, 'Of Religious Discourse', *Practical Discourses*, vol. 4, p. 44. Lucas makes the same point more pithily: 'there are two Things in Wise Men which never fail to work upon their Friends and Acquaintance: First, Good Discourse; Secondly, Good Examples': Richard Lucas, *The Influence of Conversation, with the Regulation Thereof* (London, 1723), p. 8.

[32]   Lucas, *Influence of Conversation*, p. 28.

[33]   Talbot, *Reflections*, pp. 7–8. Talbot's *Reflections* were written in the mid-1750s; see Myers, *Bluestocking Circle*, p. 216.

[34]   Samuel Johnson, 'The Rambler' No. 80, *The Yale Edition of the Works of Samuel Johnson*, ed. W.J. Bate and Albrecht B. Strauss (New Haven, 1958–), vol. 4, p. 59.

of instruction however beautifully disguised, and run away from it with as much horror as good people do from a cloven foot'. She had spent an evening, the letter continues, trying to persuade 'a wit and a fine lady' that there was virtue to be found in dull people, but had been 'unsuccessful in my preachings'.[35]

Conversation, then, could be neither as satisfying or as easy a means of mutual improvement as Johnson or Talbot's *Reflections* imply. Carter often joked about the difficulty of combining fashionable sociability with meaningful discussion, but for Talbot, so often in society, this failure was frustrating as well as sometimes amusing. She writes with unusual bitterness:

> It is not being in *merry*, but in *formal* company that I find fault with, and more than half my life passes in mere empty form. Some of the persons whom you do not know, that I see much the oftenest, are persons of no risibility, of eternal contradiction, and to whom it would be as vain to attempt to do any good, as to expect to learn anything from them. Now is *this the duty* of conversation that one owes to human creatures? In *this case* a puppet or a parrot might perform it quite as well, for 'tis merely uttering sounds.[36]

Talbot's references to puppets and parrots echo Damaris Masham's dry questioning, in 1705, of what good it does to neglect women's education and then confine them to the company of their children, 'when to play with them as a more entertaining sort of Monkeys or Parroquets, is all the pleasing Conversation that they are capable of having with them'.[37] Talbot here finds polite society at odds with humanity: the rituals of politeness have become mere empty trickery, vacuous in repetition. Weary of the 'mere empty form' involved in parroting platitudes, she longs for 'true, for friendly, for improving, or even diverting conversation'; and, in an essay on society in *Essays on Various Subjects*, a protesting voice interjects, 'But conversation is so empty, and so useless'.[38] Surviving praise of Talbot shows it was not always so, and glimpses of her influence are afforded in references in letters of the period. William Freind, writing to Secker in 1755, tells him that Mrs Freind 'insists upon my saying that she has followed a hint of Miss Talbots with respect to Civility, & has found good Effect from it'.[39]

For Talbot as for Secker, the 'Civility' alluded to in this letter is primarily important in theological rather than polite terms, and conversational practices were a particular concern in the Secker household. Secker urged his congregation, 'If then you have any concern, either for the honour of that church to which you belong, for the welfare of your country, or the salvation of your souls, *let your*

---

[35] Pennington (ed.), *Series of Letters*, vol. 2, p. 164, Carter to Talbot, 18 March 1754.

[36] Ibid., pp. 248–9, Talbot to Carter, 29 July 1757.

[37] Damaris Masham, *Occasional Thoughts in Reference to a Vertuous or Christian Life* (London, 1705), p. 213.

[38] Catherine Talbot, *Essays on Various Subjects* (2 vols, London, 1772), vol. 1, p. 186.

[39] Thomas Secker, *The Correspondence of Thomas Secker, Bishop of Oxford 1737–58*, ed. A.P. Jenkins (Stroud, 1991), p. 248, William Freind to Secker, July 1755.

conversation be as becometh the gospel of Christ'.[40] Talbot's published writings owe as much to the sermon form as they do to conduct literature. The *Reflections* open with an unattributed quotation from Psalm 139, and unfold from the text in the manner of a sermon.[41] Her promotion of the psalms, her clarity of diction and the brevity of the daily discourses are in keeping with Secker's advice to his clergy.[42] Moreover, when Talbot wrote in her *Reflections* that 'In all my common Conversation, I shall have my Eye continually up to Him, who can alone direct my Paths to Happiness and Improvement, and crown all my Endeavours with the best Success', or urged her readers that 'Every Body can set a good Example', 'Every Body can in some Degree encourage Virtue and Religion', or set out 'the Path of Duty' as lying clearly between two extremes of gloom and superstition, she was engaging with fundamental questions of Anglican praxis which Secker tackled throughout his career in his exhortations to his clergy.[43] Both the form and content of Talbot's writings are usefully read in the context of Secker's publications and her wider reading of sermons: the topic of conversation in particular illuminates ways in which exemplary Christian behaviour might blur the distinctions between clergy and laity.

'Nothing will contribute more to make our public Instructions effectual, than private Conversation, directed with Prudence to the same end', urged Thomas Secker in his first visitation charge as bishop of Oxford in 1738.[44] His belief in the centrality of conversation to effective ministry remained strong all his life, and throughout his career he encouraged his fellow clergy to use conversation to convert, reform and educate. Secker, like Talbot, offered a good example in this respect, and according to Porteus would receive 'his Company with Politeness and good Humour, and entertained them, when he was in Health and Spirits, with lively and improving Conversation'.[45] Secker took a particular interest in training clergy, and in advising them on practical aspects of their ministry. As Jeremy Gregory notes, his instructions to clergy provided a valuable resource for a Church which did not provide formal pastoral training until the 1830s, and his charges proved lastingly popular.[46] Secker advised his pastorate to 'Speak to your People, as you would in Conversation … and vary both your Stile and your Elocution, as in Conversation you always do, suitably to your Matter'.[47] Secker urged his clergy

---

[40] Thomas Secker, 'Sermon CII', in Thomas Secker, *The Works of Thomas Secker* (new edn, 4 vols, Edinburgh, 1792), vol. 3, p. 108. Italics in original. Secker is quoting Phil. 1:27.

[41] Talbot, *Reflections*, p. 1; Psalm 139:1–3. On other eighteenth-century women writers and the sermon form, see Major, *Madam Britannia*, pp. 264–316.

[42] Secker, *Eight Charges*, pp. 316–19.

[43] Talbot, *Reflections*, pp. 10, 29.

[44] Secker, *Eight Charges*, p. 27.

[45] Porteus, *Life*, p. xcii.

[46] Gregory, 'Secker, Thomas', *Oxford Dictionary of National Biography*.

[47] Secker, *Eight Charges*, p. 310. His notes advising newly ordained ministers are painstaking: 'Talk with each as you can alone. Men are ashamed of letting not only their

to learn from Roman Catholic and Dissenting practices by increasing contact with the laity and conversing with them more often. Having recommended conversing with young people in the parish, he suggests: 'Other Means may be found with grown Persons: on the first settling of a Family in your Parish; on Occasion of any great Sickness, or Affliction, or Mercy; on many others, if you seek for them, and engage worthy Friends to assist you'.[48]

As I show below, Talbot was one of the 'worthy Friends' who often assisted Secker through talking with his parish, his clergy and his household. Conversation was central to Christian praxis for both Secker and Talbot: as the 'fruits' of faith, it was a key means of displaying virtue and an important way of detecting it in others.[49] Clergy and virtuous women alike were urged to pay heed to their duty to exemplify Christian virtues and promote them in others through their lives and conversation. It is not perhaps surprising in this context that Evelyn, struggling to articulate Godolphin's goodness, used words such as 'Apostless' and 'Fisheress' in an attempt to convey a virtue which through its power might have been understood as transcending an earthly gendered division of labour and entering the realm of Christian ministry.[50] Evelyn and Godolphin's friendship is perhaps one of the most famous examples of spiritual friendship between an Anglican man and woman.[51] Talbot and Secker's relationship had little of the intense language of High Church spiritual friendship, so troublingly often overlapping with that of romantic love. Yet the tradition of spiritual friendship is relevant here. Talbot and Secker had a profound respect and love for one another, and their interest in one another's spiritual welfare is an extremely important context for their joint efforts to put faith into practice. In this case, as we shall see, their friendship resulted in a blurring of normative gender roles, with Talbot writing not only for but as the bishop, and performing clerical duties. Here, friendship and affective kinship meant that Talbot and Secker both performed ecclesiastical duties notionally belonging only to the male bishop; but this was understood by both not as subversive, but as the natural result of their shared desire to live a truly Christian life.

---

sins, but their Ignorance be known. Ask no hard questions. Help them to answer by asking it this or thus. Be content with a bare yes or no. if they are long silent, answer the question yr self & do it thoroughly. Pray be not content with the words of the Catechism from yr Catechumens': Lambeth Palace Library, Archbishop Secker MS 1,350. I am grateful to the Trustees of Lambeth Palace Library for permission to quote from its holdings.

[48] Secker, *Eight Charges*, p. 269.

[49] Secker often uses biblical texts which reference fruit, and especially in reference to conversation and behaviour, echoing Matthew 7:16. See, for example, Secker, *Works*, vol. 1, p. 313.

[50] Evelyn, *Life*, pp. 10, 210.

[51] On this complex relationship, see Harris, *Transformations of Love*, esp. pp. 149–86. On earlier prominent Platonic friendships, such as those of Katherine Philips, 'the matchless Orinda', see Harris, *Transformations of Love*, pp. 154–5.

III. Talbot and Secker: Household and Institution

In a brief advertisement heading the contents page of the 1773 combined edition of Talbot's *Essays* and *Reflections*, readers were notified that more details about the author's life could be found in the biography of Secker included in his *Works*. Had the reference been pursued, the interested reader would have discovered that according to Beilby Porteus (later bishop of London and friend of Hannah More), Talbot 'added the gentlest Manners, and a Disposition thoroughly benevolent and devout to the finest Imagination and the most elegant Accomplishments of her Sex'.[52] However, the most detailed account of Talbot to appear in print before Montagu Pennington's publication of her letters was to be found not in Secker's biography, but in that of Mark Hildesley, where 10 pages of praise were bestowed upon her by his fellow cleric, Weeden Butler.[53] Talbot, indeed, is a concealed but significant presence in the lives of several clergymen: apart from Secker, most importantly in that of George Berkeley, whom she had refused in marriage due to family opposition to the match.[54] But beyond this, Talbot exercised indirect power and influence in the lives of many clergy because of her work for Secker – and as we shall see, the men who saw her in this role were happier to acknowledge it than Secker's twentieth-century historians have been.

Although it is clear that Talbot was the recipient of much affectionate admiration and respect from the clergy she encountered through Secker, her work in the Secker household tends to be omitted in recent accounts of his life.[55] However, the fact that she was named as his executrix in his will, alongside Daniel Burton, and that both were charged to make final decisions about the charitable bequests Secker made in his will, is evidence that hers was an active and responsible role. Secker enjoyed the company of active, intelligent, well-read women. His own wife, though not a brilliant student, was reputedly a woman of 'Courage, Activity, and good Sense'.[56] Secker not only recognized Talbot's abilities, but showed an interest in the work of contemporary male and female scholars. He did not

---

[52]   Porteus, 'Life of Archbishop Secker', vol. 1, p. xcv.

[53]   Butler, *Memoirs of Mark Hildesley*, pp. 582–92.

[54]   The reasons for this remain obscure; the families were friends before and after the two fell in love. (Secker refers to 'my good Friend Bishop Berkeley' in his *Autobiography*, p. 33.) George Berkeley later married, and his wife became Talbot's close friend. A scribbled note to posterity by Elizabeth Berkeley on a bundle of letters in the British Library recounts that she had not known of their love before her marriage; her husband would not allow 'My Dear Dear Friend the Divine Cath:ne Talbot to visit me before I married [.] That truly Angelic Friend asked me who told me of it? I replied Myself the first time I ever saw you together – I asked her how she liked me, she replied I thought I should have fainted at your feet when saluting you as his bride': BL, Add. MS 19,684, fol. 42.

[55]   She is entirely omitted from Leslie W. Barnard's *Thomas Secker: An Eighteenth-Century Primate* (Lewes, 1998) and only mentioned in the new *Oxford Dictionary of National Biography* entry.

[56]   Porteus, *Life*, p. ix.

publish any scholarly research of his own, but he advised Benjamin Kennicott and Thomas Sharp as well as Carter on their classical and theological publications. In his *Autobiography* he claimed that he not only 'corrected, with great Labour, every Page' of Carter's translation of Epictetus, but 'suggested many Notes, & wrote a considerable part of the Preface, & supervised the Whole'; afterwards, he recalled, he 'begged, without Shame, Subscriptions for her from every body every where'.[57] This account omits Carter's differences of opinion with him (which were, as Susan Staves points out, serious), but he did undoubtedly contribute to the publication, and provided financial support to her as well as to the impecunious Sarah Fielding and Mary Collier, whom he knew through Talbot and Samuel Richardson.[58]

Secker maintained that it 'is the peculiar glory of Christianity, to have extended religious instruction, of which but few partook before, and scarce any in purity, thro' all ages and ranks of men and even women'.[59] Though women have long assisted the male clergy, Secker seems here to be speaking of Christianity in relation to the increasingly popular narratives of progress and civilization generated by Enlightenment historians. His inclusion of Talbot in his work and his appreciation of educated women perhaps signal his engagement with a polite culture which placed a particular value on the positive treatment of women as a sign of civilization. Talbot became an integral part of Secker's ministry, acting as secretary and teacher as well as housekeeper: indeed, with obvious sacramental exceptions, she performed many of the duties of a curate. Secker was praised for promoting catechetical instruction. His lectures on the Catechism became the standard work, and they show a typically conscientious attitude: for instance, in a 1741 charge in which Secker insisted on the fundamental importance of teaching children the Catechism, he urged his Oxford clergy to ensure that the meaning of the words was explained, 'else Children will too often learn nothing but the Sound'.[60] In Secker's household and parish, the catechetical duties were often performed by Talbot, who was also frequently in charge of his generous charitable donations. She wrote letters for him, sometimes dictated by Secker, sometimes pursuing enquiries or offering advice for him.

Talbot's letters to the Berkeleys, especially George, blend Church business, comments on theological and literary texts, and clerical gossip. In one letter she jokes that the tales of cannibalism in Canada suggest that the priests there are at least spared the usual trouble of burying parishioners in church – the dark humour

---

[57] Secker, *Autobiography*, p. 36. See Susan Staves, *A Literary History of Women's Writing in Britain, 1660–1789* (Cambridge, 2006), pp. 314–15.

[58] 'This year [1763] I lent Mrs Carter, to whom I believe I had given about [£]50 before, [£]150 more upon her Note, without Interest. And I do not intend, that she shall repay it me': Secker, *Autobiography*, p. 46 (see also p. 49); Staves, *Literary History of Women's Writing*, pp. 314–15.

[59] Thomas Secker, *Lectures on the Catechism of the Church of England* (2 vols, London, [1769]), vol. 1, p. 10.

[60] Secker, *Eight Charges*, p. 50.

a useful reminder that Talbot had a personality beyond the hagiography.[61] (She memorably expressed a preference for the more spirited 'lions' over the 'lambs' amongst the eccentric and bullying antiquarian Browne Willis's daughters.)[62] Her sense of humour is as quick to appear as her sympathy, and though she clearly had a great respect for the clergy with whom she worked, she also preserved a sense of the ridiculous, noting to Berkeley in 1765 that the archbishop praised Mr Jones, but that she had heard from another quarter 'that he preaches to his Country Congregation about the Cherubim & matters that make them stare'.[63] Talbot's amiability was spiced with humour, and was a key element of all her close epistolary relationships. Although her humour was sometimes subversive, it may also have been an element of the exemplary amiability for which she was praised. Dullness and female virtue are not inseparable.

In one letter, she comforts Berkeley on what he felt to be an unglamorous lot:

> Some time or other I trust you will have a better House – how miserable would you be in it if, like I fear too many, you consider only the temporal advantages and comforts of such a paltry preferment: But while you have so ample a parish to range & do good in, how much nobler is your habitation than that of the plumpest Non-Resident, tho' he had Westminster Hall for his Dining Room![64]

Her letter combines friendship with encouragement, and although she was particularly fond of Berkeley, her ability to unite tactful advice and friendship was a gift she often drew upon in mediating between Secker and his clergy. A letter from Talbot to the newly ordained aristocratic Charles Poyntz shows her patiently responding to his anxieties regarding clerical dress: 'I am grieved from your perplexity my good Mr Poyntz, tho' I honour the Principles that cause it. I consulted the Bp as you desired me, & show'd him your letter. He thinks you need not be uneasy as to your motive in changing the short Cassock for a black Coat'.[65] Talbot may have envied Berkeley and Poyntz their professional occupations, for whilst capably advising and assisting the clergy, her own role was far less clearly defined. In her 'Essay on Employment', after considering the extremes of 'sublime Speculation' and 'soft Pleasure', she concludes with Anglican firmness that 'The right medium is a life busied in the exercise of duty'.[66] In her *Reflections* for Tuesday, Talbot enquired, 'What then is my proper Business and Employment, that I may diligently set to it?' and answered, 'In most Stations of Life, this is too

---

[61]   BL, Add. MS 39,311, fol. 155, Talbot to Berkeley, 13 February 1764, Canterbury.

[62]   Talbot to 'a lady of first-rate quality', 6 January 1738/9, in John Nichols, *Biographical and Literary Anecdotes of William Bowyer* (London, 1782), pp. 248–50.

[63]   BL, Add. MS 39,311, fol. 171, Talbot to Berkeley, 30 April 1765.

[64]   Ibid., fol. 143, Talbot to Berkeley, 8 October 1763.

[65]   Lambeth Palace Library, Archbishop Secker MS 1,349, fol. 181, Talbot to Charles Poytnz, 22 December 1757, St Paul's Deanery.

[66]   Talbot, 'Essay I', *Essays*, p. 2.

Evident to be asked'.[67] But the duties of an unmarried gentlewoman were vague, and Talbot constantly felt that she was failing in her duty to practice Christian virtues in the society in which she was placed: 'Alas, my great, my continual Failure is in social Duties!'[68] Talbot did not only look forward to an afterlife in which one could enjoy the 'conversation of Angels'; she also anticipated with eagerness a realm in which, as a member of the 'society of the Blessed', she might join the 'ministering Angels' who fill heaven with 'Life and Activity' beyond class and gender.[69]

IV. 'As a Christian'

'As a Christian, if indeed I behave like one, I am the equal of the greatest Monarch upon the Earth', wrote Talbot in her *Reflections*; 'as a Christian, I can look forward beyond Death to an Eternity of Happiness'.[70] Talbot is more confident in speaking about Christian than gendered duties, and it is significant that exemplary Churchwomen such as Talbot are often referred to in gender neutral terms by those who praise them. Talbot is 'the most pure, holy, & righteous' of 'all Persons' Montagu knew; for Carter, she is simply the 'perfect pattern of evangelical goodness'.[71] The question of at what point these women become defined by their faith more than their gender perplexed contemporaries and remains a controversial matter in the Church of England today.

Talbot's life and works exemplify the complex ways in which her identities as woman and Anglican might render private devotion of public significance. Yet that individual gendered identity itself might have been understood by women such as Talbot as less important than membership of the Church of England. Talbot's extensive work with Secker fitted better with the character of the unnamed Christian rather than the exemplary woman, and it is perhaps helpful to think in terms of religious communities as well as individuals when considering their joint labour. One letter to Berkeley, begun by Talbot and completed by Secker – who excuses her for not writing herself to the Berkeley ladies because she has been too busy with his correspondence – illustrates the merging of voices which could occur as one spoke or wrote for the other.[72] The institutional, devotional and personal strands identified by Nicky Hallett in her discussion of the life-writing of early modern nuns are useful for thinking about Talbot and Secker's personal

---

[67]   Talbot, *Reflections*, p. 16.

[68]   Talbot, 'Essay XXIV', *Essays*, p. 108.

[69]   Talbot, 'Essay XVIII', *Essays*, p. 84; Talbot, *Reflections*, p. 14.

[70]   Talbot, *Reflections*, p. 9.

[71]   Huntington Library, MO 3,361, Montagu to Carter, 31 October 1769; Pennington (ed.), *Series of Letters*, p. xxxi.

[72]   BL, Add. MS 39,311, fol. 249, Talbot and Secker to Berkeley, 10 October 176[?], Richmond.

and published papers.[73] Denominational differences apart – and both Talbot and Secker were notably ecumenical in their omnivorous reading – comparisons with religious communities are helpful here. Setting the Secker household alongside monastic houses places them in an unfamiliar but illuminating context, one which shows them as part of a religious house in which individual identity and gender mattered less than their shared endeavour towards true Christian praxis. Their moments of shared ministry in catechetical education, advice to the clergy, Christian conversation, dispensing charity and promoting Christian practice subvert normative gender roles and undermine a gendered division of labour, despite Talbot's posthumous fame as an exemplary woman. The blending of individual voices in letters and domestic practice might have been seen by Talbot and Secker as part of the Christian struggle against self. For Talbot, perhaps, the loss of the individual in the performance of religious and institutional duty could represent an epiphany of anonymous faith, a moment when she could find fulfillment in her ministrations as part of the Christian Church. It is in this largest of publics that she herself found consolation and purpose, in that realm in which, according to Galatians 3:28 (AV), 'There is neither Jew nor Greek, there is neither bond nor free, there is neither male nor female: for ye are all one in Christ Jesus'.

---

[73] Nicky Hallett, 'General Introduction', in Nicky Hallett (ed.), *Lives of Spirit: English Carmelite Self-Writing of the Early Modern Period* (Aldershot, 2007), pp. 5–11.

Bibliography

Manuscript Sources

Archives of the Archdiocese of Westminster, London
Augustinian Canonesses of Paris MS, 'A Relation of Some Remarkable Things that Happened to My Lady Abbesse in her Latter Dayes'.
Diurnall of the English Canonesses Regulars of St Augustin's Order Established in Paris.

Bodleian Library, Oxford
Rawlinson MSS, 983 C., D. 833, 1,125, 1,262.
Univ. Coll. D. 183.

British Library, London
Add MS 19,684.
Add MS 28,225, Letters of Royal and Other Persons to Mary, Queen of James II, 1685–88.
Add MSS 28,226, 28,229, Caryll Family Correspondence.
Add MS 38,146, Letter-Book of Sir Robert Southwell, 1690.
Add MS 39,311.
Add MSS 46,688, 46,690.
Sloane MS 2,569.

Dr Williams's Library, London
MS 59.V.170, 216–17, 234.

Huntington Library, San Marino, California
MO 3,361.

Lambeth Palace Library, London
Archbishop Secker MSS 1,349–50.
Miscellaneous Papers MS 2,165.

London Metropolitan Archives, London
P69/JS1/A/002/MS07894/002, Marriage Register of St James, Duke's Place.

The National Archives, Kew
SP 29/395, 398.
SP 84/216.

National Library of Scotland, Edinburgh
MS 1,668, Memoirs of John Brand, minister of Bo'ness.
Wod. Fol. LI, 'Reasons Against Forming Societies for the Reformation of Manners'.

National Records of Scotland, Edinburgh
CH3/27/1, Associate Presbytery Minutes, 1733–40.
CH3/269/1, Conclusions of the United Societies' General Meeting, 1681–1724.
CH3/319/3, Leslie Secession Congregation Minutes, 1739–58.
CH3/469/1, Glasgow Greyfriars (Shuttle Street) Kirk Session Minutes, 1739–55.
GD406/1/2,737, 3,165, 7,601.
PC1/50, Privy Council Acta, 1694–96.

Norfolk Record Office, Norwich
NRS 26,356.

Oulton Abbey, Stone
MS G.39, The English Benedictine Monastery at Ghent.

The Royal Archives, Windsor
Stuart Papers [accessed via microfilm].

Society of Antiquaries of London, London
MS 138.

Universiteitsbibliotheek Amsterdam, Amsterdam
Remonstrants MSS J. 57a.
UBA, MS D. III.16, 53.
UBA, MS.31.c.

Printed Primary Sources

Addison, Joseph, *The Spectator*, ed. Donald F. Bond (5 vols, Oxford: Clarendon Press, 1965).
———, *The Freeholder*, ed. James Leheny (Oxford: Clarendon Press, 1979).
Addison, Joseph and Richard Steele, *The Spectator*, 447, 2 August 1712 (London, 1712).
Addison, Lancelot, *West Barbary, Or, A Short Narrative of the Revolutions of the Kingdoms of Fez and Morocco* (Oxford, 1671).
Advice from Parnassus ([London, 1722]).
Aelred of Rievaulx, *Spiritual Friendship*, trans. L.C. Braceland, ed. and introd. M.L. Dutton (Collegeville: Liturgical Press, 2010).
Airy, Osmund (ed.), *The Lauderdale Papers*, n.s. 34, 36, 38 (3 vols, London: Camden Society, 1884–85).

Allestree, Richard, *The Ladies Calling* (Oxford, 1673).

Alsop, Vincent, *Duty and Interest United in Prayer and Praise for Kings and All that are in Authority from 1 Tim. II. 1, 2: Being a Sermon Preach'd at Westminster upon the Late Day of Thanksgiving, Sept. 8, 1695* (London, 1695).

Amhurst, Nicholas, 'To Mrs. Centlivre. Upon her Desiring him to Read and Correct a Poem', in *A New Miscellany of Original Poems, Translations and Imitations* (London, 1720).

Annals of the English Benedictines at Ghent, Now at St Mary's Abbey, Oulton in Staffordshire (Oulton: Privately Published, 1894).

'Appendix. Extract from a Manuscript Account of Dr. Hooper', in Arthur Trevor, *The Life and Times of William the Third, King of England, and Stadtholder of Holland* (2 vols, London, 1835–36).

Astell, Mary, *A Serious Proposal to the Ladies*, Parts I and II (London, 1694, 1697).

————, *Some Reflections upon Marriage* (London, 1700).

————, *An Impartial Enquiry into the Causes of Rebellion and Civil War in this Kingdom: In an Examination of Dr Kennett's Sermon, Jan. 31. 1703/4 and Vindication of the Royal Martyr* (London, 1704).

————, *Moderation Truly Stated: Or, A Review of a Late Pamphlet, Entitul'd, Moderation a Vertue* (London, 1704).

————, *The Christian Religion as Profess'd by a Daughter of the Church of England* (London, 1705).

————, *Reflections upon Marriage*, 3rd edn (London, 1706).

————, *A Serious Proposal to the Ladies Parts I & II*, ed. Patricia Springborg (Toronto: Broadview Press, 2002).

Astell, Mary and John Norris, *Letters Concerning the Love of God*, ed. E. Derek Taylor and Melvyn New (Aldershot: Ashgate, 2005).

The Athenian Gazette Or Casuistical Mercury (London, 1695).

Atterbury, Francis, *An Answer to Some Considerations on the Spirit of Martin Luther and the Original of the Reformation Lately Printed at Oxford* (Oxford, 1687).

Barker, Jane, *Poetical Recreations Consisting of Original Poems, Songs, Odes, &c. with Several New Translations: In Two Parts* (London, 1688).

Barlow, Thomas, *A Few Plain Reasons Why a Protestant of the Church of England Should Not Turn Roman Catholick* (London, 1688).

Baxter, Richard, 'The Introduction', in *The Life and Death of that Excellent Minister of Christ Mr. Joseph Alleine, Late Teacher of the Church of Taunton in Somerset-Shire, Assistant to Mr. Newton* (1671).

————, *A Breviate of the Life of Margaret, the Daughter of Francis Charlton of Apply in Shropshire, Esq. Wife of Richard Baxter* (London, 1681).

————, 'To the Reader', in Samuel Clark, *The Lives of Sundry Eminent Persons in this Later Age* (London, 1683).

————, *A Breviate of the Life of Margaret, the Daughter of Francis Charlton ... and Wife of Richard Baxter, Etc* (London, 1826).

———, *Richard Baxter and Margaret Charlton ... Being the Breviate of the Life of Margaret Baxter ... With Introductory Essay, Notes and Appendices by John T. Wilkinson, Etc.* (London: George Allen & Unwin, 1928).

———, *A Grief Sanctified: Passing Through Grief to Peace and Joy; J.I. Packer Presents Richard Baxter's Memoir of his Wife's Life and Death* (Leicester: Crossway, 1998).

Bayle, Pierre, *The Dictionary Historical and Critical of Mr. Pierre Bayle* (5 vols, New York: Garland, 1984).

Beer, E.S. De (ed.), *The Correspondence of John Locke* (8 vols, Oxford: Clarendon Press, 1976–89).

Birch, Thomas, *The Life of the Most Reverend Dr. John Tillotson, Lord Archbishop of Canterbury* (London, 1753).

Bland, James, *An Essay in Praise of Women: Or, A Looking-Glass for Ladies to See Their Perfections In* (London, 1733).

Blencowe, R.W. (ed.), *Diary of the Times of Charles the Second by Honourable Henry Sidney* (2 vols, London, 1843).

Boehme, Jacob, *Jacob Behmen's Theosophick Philosophy Unfolded,* trans. Edward Taylor (London, 1691).

Bond, Donald F. (ed.), *The Tatler* (3 vols, Oxford: Clarendon Press, 1987).

Boston, Thomas, *Memoirs of the Life, Time, and Writings of the Reverend and Learned Thomas Boston,* ed. George H. Morrison (Edinburgh: Oliphant, Anderson & Ferrier, 1899).

Bowber, Thomas, *A Sermon Preached in the Parish-Church of St. Swithin, London, March 10th, 1694/5, Upon the Much Lamented Death of Our Most Gracious Queen* (London, 1695).

Brereton, William, *Travels in Holland, the United Provinces, England, Scotland, and Ireland MDCXXXIV–MDCXXXV,* ed. Edward Hawkins (London: Chetham Society, 1844).

Bromley, Thomas, *The Way to the Sabbath of Rest* (London, 1678).

Brown, P. Hume, Henry Paton and E. Balfour-Melville (eds), *The Register of the Privy Council of Scotland,* 3rd series (16 vols, Edinburgh: H.M. General Register House, 1908–70).

Brown, Thomas, *A Legacy for the Ladies: Or, Characters of the Women of the Age* (London, 1705).

Burnet, Gilbert, *A Modest and Free Conference Betwixt a Conformist and a Non-Conformist, about the Present Distempers of Scotland,* 2nd edn ([Edinburgh?], 1669).

———, *A Discourse of the Pastoral Care* (London, 1692).

———, *An Essay on the Memory of the Late Queen* (London, 1695).

———, *Reflections upon a Pamphlet, Entituled [Some Discourses upon Dr. Burnet and Dr. Tillotson, Occasioned by the Late Funeral-Sermon of the Former upon the Latter]* (London, 1696).

———, *Bishop Burnet's History of His Own Time* (6 vols, Oxford, 1833).

———, *A Supplement to Burnet's History of My Own Time*, ed. H.C. Foxcroft (Oxford: Clarendon Press, 1902).

Butler, Weeden, *Memoirs of Mark Hildesley, D.D. Lord Bishop of Sodor and Mann, and Master of Sherburn Hospital* (London, 1799).

Cairns, Elizabeth, *Memoirs of the Life of Elizabeth Cairns* (Glasgow, [1762?]).

Calendar of the Stuart Papers Belonging to His Majesty the King, Preserved at Windsor Castle (7 vols, London: H.M.S.O., 1902–23).

Camden, Vera (ed.), *The Narrative of the Persecutions of Agnes Beaumont* (East Lansing: Colleagues Press, 1992).

Cartwright, James J. (ed.), *The Wentworth Papers, 1705–1739* (London, 1883).

Centlivre, Susanna, *The Beau's Duel: Or A Soldier for the Ladies* (London, 1702).

———, *The Basset-Table* (London, 1706).

———, *The Platonick Lady* (London, 1707).

———, *The Man's Bewitch'd* (London, 1709).

———, *The Perplex'd Lovers* (London, 1712).

———, *The Wonder: A Woman Keeps a Secret* (London, 1714).

———, *An Epistle to Mrs Wallup Now in the Train of Her Royal Highness the Princess of Wales* (London, 1715).

———, *The Gotham Election: A Farce* (London, 1715).

———, *A Poem. Humbly Presented to His Most Sacred Majesty George. King of Great Britain, France, and Ireland* (London, 1715).

———, 'An Invocation to Juno Lucina for the Safe Delivery of her Royal Highness the Princess of Wales', *The Protestant Packet*, 21 January 1716.

———, *An Epistle to the King of Sweden from a Lady of Great-Britain* (London, 1717).

———, *A Bold Stroke for a Wife* (London, 1718).

———, *A Woman's Case: In an Epistle to Charles Joye, Esq; Deputy-Governor of the South-Sea* (London, 1720).

———, *The Artifice* (London, 1723).

———, *The Works of the Celebrated Mrs. Centlivre* (3 vols, London, 1760–61).

Chudleigh, Mary, *Poems on Several Occasions* (London, 1703).

Churchill, Sarah and Nathaniel Hooke, *An Account of the Conduct of the Dowager Duchess of Marlborough* (London, 1742).

Cockburn, Catharine Trotter, *Philosophical Writings*, ed. Patricia Sheridan (Peterborough, ON: Broadview Press, 2006).

A Collection of State Songs, Poems, &c. That Have Been Publish'd since the Rebellion: and Sung in the Several Mug-Houses in the Cities of London and Westminster, Etc. (London, 1716).

A Compleat History of the Whole Proceedings of the Parliament of Great Britain Against Dr. Henry Sacheverell (London, 1710).

Considine, John and Sylvia Brown (eds), *N.H., The Ladies Dictionary (1694)* (Farnham: Ashgate, 2010).

Cooper, W.D. (ed.), *Savile Correspondence: Letters to and from Henry Savile Esq.* (London: Camden Society, 1858).

Crichton, Andrew (ed.), *Memoirs of the Rev. John Blackader*, 2nd edn (Edinburgh, 1826).

The Curate's Queries, and, the Malig[n]ant or Courtier's Answer Thereto (n.p., [1679?]).

The Daily Journal.

Defoe, Daniel, *An Essay upon Projects* (London, 1697).

———, *The Poor Man's Plea in Relation to All the Proclamations, Declarations, Acts of Parliament, &c., Which Have Been, or Shall be Made, or Publish'd, for a Reformation of Manners, and Suppressing Immorality in the Nation* (London, 1698).

———, *A New Test of the Church of England's Loyalty* (London, 1703).

De la Bédoyère, Guy (ed.), *The Diary of John Evelyn* (Boydell: Woodbridge, 2004).

Doebner, R. (ed.), *Memoirs of Mary, Queen of England, (1689–1693)* (Leipzig: Veit, 1886).

Dominicana: Cardinal Howard's Letters, English Dominican Friars, Nuns, Students, Papers and Mission Registers, Catholic Record Society, 25 (London: Catholic Record Society, 1925).

Elisabeth of Bohemia, Princess, *The Correspondence between Princess Elisabeth of Bohemia and René Descartes*, ed. and trans. Lisa Shapiro (Chicago: University of Chicago Press, 2007).

Evelyn, John, *The Life of Mrs Godolphin* (London, 1848).

Eyre-Todd, George (ed.), *The Book of Glasgow Cathedral* (Glasgow: Morison Brothers, 1898).

Finglas, John, *A Sermon Preached at the Chappel Royal in the Tower, upon Sunday the Sixth Day of January, 1694/5, being the Feast of the Epiphany as also the Day Whereon the Greatest Part of that Audience Appeared in Deep Mourning, upon the Death of Her Sacred Majesty, our Late Gracious Queen Mary* (London, 1695).

The Flying Post.

Fowler, Edward, *A Discourse of the Great Disingenuity & Unreasonableness of Repining at Afflicting Providences and of the Influence which they Ought to Have upon Us, on Job 2, 10, Publish'd upon Occasion of the Death of our Gracious Sovereign Queen Mary of Most Blessed Memory* (London, 1695).

A Funeral Oration on the Most High, Most Excellent, and Most Potent Princess, Marie Stuart (London, 1695).

A Funeral Oration, Pronounc'd upon the Death of the Most Serene and Potent Princess, Mary Stuart (London, 1695).

Furlong, Monica (ed.), *The Trial of John Bunyan and the Persecution of the Puritans: Selections from the Writings of John Bunyan and Agnes Beaumont* (London: Folio Society, 1978).

The Gentleman's Magazine.

Gillow, Joseph and Richard Trappes-Lomax (eds), *The Diary of the 'Blue Nuns': Or Order of the Immaculate Conception of Our Lady, at Paris, 1658–1810*, Catholic Record Society, 8 (London: Catholic Record Society, 1910).

Grevius, J.G., *A Funeral Oration of J.G. Grevius, Upon the Death of Mary II* (London, 1695).

H., N., *The Ladies Dictionary, Being a General Entertainment for the Fair-Sex: A Work Never Attempted Before in English* (London, 1694).

H., R. [Woodhead, Abraham], *A Discourse Concerning the Celibacy of the Clergy* (Oxford, 1687).

Hale, Matthew, *A Collection of Modern Relations of Matter of Fact, Concerning Witches & Witchcraft Upon the Persons of People*. Part I (London, 1693).

Hallett, Nicky (ed.), *Lives of Spirit: English Carmelite Self-Writing of the Early Modern Period* (Aldershot: Ashgate, 2007).

Hamilton, Adam (ed.), *The Chronicle of the English Augustinian Canonesses Regular of the Lateran, at St Monica's in Louvain* (2 vols, London: Sands and Co., 1904–6).

Hansom, Joseph (ed.), 'The English Benedictine Nuns of the Convent of Our Blessed Lady of Good Hope in Paris, now at St Benedict's Priory, Colwich, Staffordshire. Notes and Obituaries', *Miscellanea VII*, Catholic Record Society, 9 (London: Catholic Record Society, 1911).

Harrison, G.B. (ed.), *The Church Book of Bunyan Meeting, 1650–1821* (London: J.M. Dent, 1928).

HMC 15th Report, Calendar of Stuart Papers Belonging to His Majesty the King, Preserved at Windsor Castle (London: HMSO, 1902).

Hoeven, A. des Amorie van der, *De Joanne Clerico et Philippo a Limborch: Dissertationes Duae* (Amsterdam, 1843).

Hubberthorne, Richard, *A True Separation Between the Power of the Spirit, and the Imitation of Antichrist* (London, 1654).

Jacob, Giles, *The Poetical Register: Or, the Lives and Characters of the English Dramatick Poets* (2 vols, London, 1719–20).

Jerdan, William (ed.), *Letters from James Earl of Perth Lord Chancellor of Scotland to his Sister, the Countess of Erroll and Other Members of his Family* (London: Camden Society, 1845).

Johnson, Samuel, 'The Rambler', No. 80, in W.J. Bate and Albrecht B. Strauss (eds), *The Yale Edition of the Works of Samuel Johnson* (New Haven: Yale University Press, 1958–).

Jurieu, Pierre, *L'accomplissement des prophéties ou la deliverance* (Rotterdam, 1686).

———, *A Pastoral Letter Written on the Occasion of the Death of the Late Queen of England, of Blessed Memory with Reflections on the Greatness of that Loss to Europe* (London, 1695).

Keeble, N.H. and Geoffrey Nuttall, *Calendar of the Correspondence of Richard Baxter* (2 vols, Oxford: Clarendon Press, 1991).

Kelly, Gary (ed.), *Bluestocking Feminism: Writings of the Bluestocking Circle, 1738–1785* (6 vols, London: Pickering & Chatto, 1999).

Kennett, White, *Compleat History of England* (3 vols, London, 1706).

————, *The Excellent Daughter. A Sermon for the Relief of the Poor Girls Taught and Cloathed by Charity within the Parish of St. Botolph Aldgate, February 15. 1707/8* (London, 1708).

Kettlewell, John, *Of Christian Communion to be Kept on in the Unity of Christs Church and Among the Professors of Truth and Holiness* ([London], 1693).

Kidder, Richard, *The Life of the Reverend Anthony Horneck, D.D., Late Preacher at the Savoy* (London, 1698).

Kirkton, James, *A History of the Church of Scotland, 1660–1679*, ed. Ralph Stewart (Lewiston, NY: Edwin Mellen, 1992).

Knox, John, *John Knox on Rebellion*, ed. Roger A. Mason (Cambridge: Cambridge University Press, 1994).

Lake, Edward, 'Diary of Dr. Edward Lake, Archdeacon and Prebendary of Exeter', ed. G.P. Elliott, *Camden Miscellany*, vol. 1 (London: Camden Society, 1846).

Law, Robert, *Memorialls; Or, the Memorable Things that Fell Out within this Island of Brittain from 1638 to 1684*, ed. Charles Kirkpatrick Sharpe (Edinburgh, 1818).

Lead, Jane, *A Fountain of Gardens* (3 vols, London, 1697).

————, *A Living Funeral Testimony: Or, Death Overcome, and Drown'd in the Life of Christ* (London, 1702).

Lee, Francis and Richard Roach (eds), *Theosophical Transactions* (London, 1697).

Leibniz, G.W., *Die Philosophischen Schriften von Gottfried Wilhelm Leibniz*, ed. C.I. Gerhardt (7 vols, Berlin, 1875–90).

Letters of Lady Rachel Russell: From the Manuscript in the Library at Wooburn Abbey (London, 1801).

Lloyd, William, *Seasonable Advice to Protestants Shewing the Necessity of Maintaining the Established Religion in Opposition to Popery* (London, 1688).

Locke, John, *The Reasonableness of Christianity as Delivered in the Scriptures* (London, 1695).

————, 'An Essay for the Understanding of St. Paul's Epistles, by Consulting St. Paul Himself', in Victor Nuovo (ed.), *John Locke: Writings on Religion* (Oxford: Clarendon Press, 2002).

Long, Thomas, *Dr. Walker's True, Modest and Faithful Account of the Author of Eikon Basilike Strictly Examined and Demonstrated to be False, Impudent, and Deceitful* (London, 1693).

A Looking-Glasse for the Ranters (London, 1653).

Lucas, Richard, *The Influence of Conversation, with the Regulation Thereof; Being a Sermon Preach'd at St Clement Dane to a Religious Society* (1708; London, 1723).

Mackenzie, George, *A Vindication of the Government in Scotland during the Reign of King Charles II* (London, 1691).

Masham, Damaris, *A Discourse Concerning the Love of God* (London, 1696).

————, *Occasional Thoughts in Reference to a Vertuous or Christian Life* (London, 1705).

Mather, Cotton, *Observanda. The Life and Death of the Late Q. Mary* (Boston, MA, 1695).

Memoirs of the Life and Times of the Most Reverend Father in God, Dr. Thomas Tennison (London, 1716).

Mitchell, Gavin, *Humble Pleadings, for the Good Old-Way, or a Plain Representation* ([Edinburgh?], 1713).

Montagu, Matthew (ed.), *The Letters of Mrs Elizabeth Montagu, With Some of the Letters of Her Correspondents* (4 vols, London, 1809).

More, Henry, *A Modest Enquiry into the Mystery of Iniquity* (London, 1664).

A Most Excellent Ballad of S. George for England and the Kings Daughter of Aegypt (London, 1658).

Mullan, David G. (ed.), *Women's Life Writing in Early Modern Scotland: Writing the Evangelical Self,* c. *1670–c. 1730* (Aldershot: Ashgate, 2003).

——— (ed.), *Protestant Piety in Early-Modern Scotland: Letters, Lives and Covenants, 1650–1712* (Edinburgh: Scottish History Society, 2008).

Nichols, John, *Biographical and Literary Anecdotes of William Bowyer* (London, 1782).

Nicolson, Marjorie (ed.), *The Conway Letters: The Correspondence of Anne, Viscountess Conway, Henry More and their Friends, 1642–1684,* rev. Sarah Hutton (Oxford: Clarendon Press, 1992).

Norris, John, *Practical Discourses upon Several Divine Subjects* (4 vols, London, 1707).

The Officers Address to the Ladies (London, [1710]).

The Patriot.

Payne, William, *A Sermon Upon the Death of the Queen, Preached in the Parish-Church of St. Mary White-Chappel* (London, 1695).

Pennington, Matthew, 'Some Account of the Life of Mrs Catharine Talbot', *The Works of the Late Miss Catharine Talbot* (London, 1819).

Pennington, Montagu (ed.), *A Series of Letters Between Mrs Elizabeth Carter and Miss Catherine Talbot, From the Year 1741 to 1770. To Which are Added, Letters from Mrs Elizabeth Carter to Mrs Vesey, Between the Years 1763 and 1787,* 3rd edn (3 vols, London, 1819).

Perizonius, Jacob, *A Funeral Encomium upon the Queen. Most Serene and Potent Princess, Mary II* (London, 1695).

Pett, Peter, *The Happy Future State of England* (London, 1688).

Phillips, John, *The Secret History of the Reigns of K. Charles II and K. James II* ([London], 1690).

Pordage, John, *Innocencie Appearing Through the Dark Mists of Pretended Guilt* (London, 1655).

Porteus, Beilby, 'Life of Archbishop Secker', in Thomas Secker, *Sermons on Several Subjects* (4 vols, London, 1770).

The Protestant Packet.

Rabus, Pieter, *Uitvaart, Van Haar Grootmagtigte, Majesteit Maria, Koninginne van Groot Britanje, Vrankrijk en Yerland* (Rotterdam, 1695).

Raithby, John (ed.), *Statutes of the Realm* (11 vols, London, 1810–22).

The Ravished Maid in the Wilderness, Or, A True Account of the Raise, Causes and Continuunce of the Deference between a Suffering Party of Presbyterians, Commonly called Cotmure Folk, ond these that follows Mr John Mackmillan, Commonly called Mountain Men (n.p., 1708).

'Registers of the English Benedictine Nuns of Pontoise, Now at Teignmouth, Devonshire, 1680–1713', *Miscellanea X*, Catholic Record Society, 17 (London: Catholic Record Society, 1915).

Renwick, James, Alexander Shields, et al, *An Informatory Vindication of a Poor, Wasted, Misrepresented Remnant of the Suffering* ([Edinburgh?] 1707).

A Review of the State of the British Nation.

Roach, Richard, *The Great Crisis: Or the Mystery of the Times and Seasons Unfolded* (London, 1725).

———, *The Imperial Standard of Messiah Triumphant; Coming Now in the Power and Kingdom of his Father to Reign with his Saints on Earth* (London, [1727]).

Rose, Alexander, *A Sermon Preached Before the Right Honourable the Lords Commissioners of His Majesties Most Honourable Privy Council* (Glasgow, 1684).

Rumsey, M.J. (ed.), 'Abbess Neville's Annals of Five Communities of English Benedictine Nuns in Flanders, 1598–1687', *Miscellanea V*, Catholic Record Society, 6 (London: Catholic Record Society, 1909).

A Satyr upon Old Maids (London, 1713).

Secker, Thomas, *Eight Charges Delivered to the Clergy of the Dioceses of Oxford and Canterbury* (London, [1769]).

———, *Lectures on the Catechism of the Church of England* (2 vols, London, [1769]).

———, *The Works of Thomas Secker*, new edn (4 vols, Edinburgh, 1792).

———, *The Autobiography of Thomas Secker Archbishop of Canterbury*, ed. John S. Macauley and R.W. Greaves (Lawrence: University of Kansas Libraries, 1988).

———, *The Correspondence of Thomas Secker, Bishop of Oxford 1737–58*, ed. A.P. Jenkins (Stroud: Alan Sutton for the Oxfordshire Record Society, 1991).

A Series of Letters between Mrs. Elizabeth Carter and Miss Catherine Talbot, from the Year 1741 to 1770 (London, 1809).

Sharp, Thomas, *The Life of John Sharp D.D.* (2 vols, London, 1825).

Shields, Michael, *Faithful Contendings Displayed: Being an Historical Relation of the State and Actings of the Suffering Remnant of the Church of Scotland*, ed. John Howie (Glasgow, 1780).

Skippon, Philip, 'An Account of a Journey Made Thro' Part of the Low-Countries, Germany, Italy and France', in A. and J. Churchill (eds), *A Collection of Voyages and Travels*, 3rd edn (6 vols, London, 1746).

Smythe, George, *Letters of John Grahame of Claverhouse, Viscount of Dundee* (Edinburgh: Bannatyne Club, 1826).

Sodom Fair (London, 1688).

Some Choice Sentences and Practices of Emilia Geddie, Daughter to John Geddie of Hilton in Falkland, in the Sheriffdom of Fife, from her Infancy, to her Death on the 2d of Feb. 1681. in the Sixteenth Year of her Age (Edinburgh, 1717).

Stedman, Thomas (ed.), *Letters to and from the Rev. Philip Doddridge* (London, 1790).

Stephens, Edward, *A Letter to a Lady* (London, 1695).

———, *The More Excellent Way: Or, A Proposal of a Compleat Work of Charity* (London, 1695).

Stillingfleet, Edward, *Irenicum. A Weapon-Salve for the Churches Wounds, Or The Divine Right of Particular Forms of Church-Government* (London, 1661).

———, *The Unreasonableness of Separation: Or, An Impartial Account of the History, Nature, and Pleas of the Present Separation from the Communion of the Church of England* (London, 1681).

———, *A Discourse in Vindication of the Doctrine of the Trinity* (London, 1696).

St. James's Journal.

Swift, Jonathan, *The Tatler, Or, The Lucubrations of Isaac Bickerstaff Esq.* (London, 1709).

Talbot, Catherine, *Reflections on the Seven Days of the Week* (London, 1770).

———, *Essays on Various Subjects* (2 vols, London, 1772).

A Testimony to the Doctrine, Worship, Government and Discipline of the Church of Scotland (Edinburgh, 1734).

Tillotson, John, *The Rule of Faith: Or, An Answer to the Treatise of Mr. I.S. Entituled, Sure-Footing, &c.* (London, 1666).

Toland, John, *Christianity not Mysterious* (London, 1696 [1695]).

Trill, Suzanne (ed.), *Lady Anne Halkett: Selected Self-Writings* (Aldershot: Ashgate, 2007).

Tully, George, *An Answer to a Discourse Concerning the Celibacy of the Clergy* (Oxford, 1688).

Tyerman, Luke, *The Life and Times of Rev. Samuel Wesley, M.A.* (London: Simpkin, Marshall & Co., 1866).

Walker, Patrick, *Biographia Presbyteriana* (2 vols, Edinburgh, 1827).

Walpole, Horace, *Memoirs of King George II*, ed. John Brooke (3 vols, New Haven: Yale University Press, 1985).

The Weekly Journal, Or British Gazeteer.

Weekly Journal, Or Saturday's Post.

Wentworth, Anne, *A True Account of Anne Wentworths Being Cruelly, Unjustly, and Unchristianly Dealt with by Some of those People Called Anabaptists* (London, 1676).

———, *A Vindication of Anne Wentworth Tending to the Better Preparing of all People for Her Larger Testimony, which is Making Ready for Publick View* (London, 1677).

———, *Englands Spiritual Pill* (London, 1679).

———, *The Revelation of Jesus Christ Just as He Spake it in Verses at Several Times, and Sometimes in Prose, unto his Faithful Servant Anne Wentworth, who Suffereth for his Name* ([London], 1679).

West, Elizabeth, *Memoirs, Or, Spiritual Exercises of Elizabeth Wast* (Edinburgh, 1724).

Wharton, Henry, *A Treatise of the Celibacy of the Clergy Wherein its Rise and Progress are Historically Considered* (London, 1688).

Winstanley, Gerrard, *Fire in the Bush* (London, 1650).

Wodrow, Robert, *The History of the Sufferings of the Church of Scotland from the Restoration to the Revolution*, ed. Robert Burns (4 vols, Glasgow, 1828–32).

———, *Analecta: Or, Materials for a History of Remarkable Providences* (4 vols, Edinburgh: Maitland Club, 1842–43).

Wotton, William, *A Letter to Eusebia: Occasioned by Mr Toland's Letters to Serena* (London, 1704).

Printed Secondary Sources

Achinstein, Sharon, 'Women on Top in the Pamphlet Literature of the English Revolution', *Women's Studies*, 24/1–2 (1994): 131–63.

———, 'Romance of the Spirit: Female Sexuality and Religious Desire in Early Modern England', *English Literary History*, 69/2 (2002): 413–38.

———, 'Mary Astell, Religion and Feminism: Texts in Motion', in William Kolbrener and Michal Michelson (eds), *Mary Astell: Reason, Gender, Faith* (Ashgate: Aldershot, 2007).

Acworth, Richard, 'Cursory Reflections upon an Article Entitled "What is it with Damaris, Lady Masham?"', *Locke Studies*, 6 (2006): 189–97.

Allison, A.F, 'The English Augustinian Convent of Our Lady of Syon at Paris: Its Foundation and Struggle for Survival during the First Eighty Years, 1634–1713', *Recusant History*, 21/4 (1993): 451–96.

Anderson, James, *The Ladies of the Covenant. Memoirs of Distinguished Scottish Female Characters, Embracing the Period of the Covenant and the Persecution* (Glasgow: Blackie and Son, 1851).

Anderson, Misty G., *Female Playwrights and Eighteenth-Century Comedy: Negotiating Marriage on the London Stage* (Basingstoke: Palgrave, 2002).

Anderson, Paul Bunyan, 'Innocence and Artifice: Or, Mrs. Centlivre and "The Female Tatler"', *Philological Quarterly*, 16 (1937): 358–75.

Anderson, Penelope, *Friendship's Shadows: Women's Friendship and the Politics of Betrayal in England, 1640–1705* (Edinburgh: Edinburgh University Press, 2012).

Apetrei, Sarah, '"Call No Man Master Upon Earth": Mary Astell's Tory Feminism and an Unknown Correspondence', *Eighteenth-Century Studies*, 41/4 (2008): 507–23.

———, *Women, Feminism and Religion in Early Enlightenment England* (Cambridge: Cambridge University Press, 2010).

Atherton, Margaret, 'Women Philosophers in Early Modern England', in Steven M. Nadler (ed.), *A Companion to Early Modern Philosophy* (Oxford: Wiley-Blackwell, 2005).

Aveling, J.C.H., *The Handle and the Axe: The Catholic Recusants in England from Reformation to Emancipation* (London: Blond and Briggs, 1976).

Bailey, Joanne, *Unquiet Lives: Marriage and Marriage Breakdown in England, 1660–1800* (Cambridge: Cambridge University Press, 2003).

Barash, Carol, *English Women's Poetry, 1649–1714: Politics, Community, and Linguistic Authority* (Oxford: Clarendon Press, 1996).

Barker, Hannah and Elaine Chalus, Introduction to Hannah Barker and Elaine Chalus (eds), *Gender in Eighteenth-Century England: Roles, Representations, and Responsibilities* (Harlow: Longman, 1997).

Barker-Benfield, G.J., *The Culture of Sensibility: Sex and Society in Eighteenth-Century Britain* (Chicago: University of Chicago Press, 1992).

Barnard, Leslie W., *Thomas Secker: An Eighteenth-Century Primate* (Lewes: Book Guild, 1998).

Beaton, D., *Scottish Heroines of the Faith: Being Brief Sketches of Noble Women of the Reformation and Covenant Times* (London: D. Catt, 1909).

Bell, Ian A., *Literature and Crime in Augustan England* (London: Routledge, 1991).

Bennett, G.V., 'King William III and the Episcopate', in G.V. Bennett and J.D. Walsh (eds), *Essays in Modern English Church History* (London: Black, 1966).
——— , *To the Church of England* (Worthing: Churchmen Publishing Ltd., 1988).

Berger, Ronit, *Legalizing Love: Desire, Divorce, and the Law in Early Modern English Literature and Culture* (Saarbrücken: VDM Verlag, 2007).

Berry, Helen, *Gender, Society and Print Culture in Late-Stuart England: The Cultural World of the Athenian Mercury* (Aldershot: Ashgate, 2003).

Best, Geoffrey, *Temporal Pillars: Queen Anne's Bounty, the Ecclesiastical Commissioners and the Church of England* (Cambridge: Cambridge University Press, 1964).

Bodek, Evelyn Gordon, 'Salonières and Bluestockings: Educated Obsolescence and Germinating Feminism', *Feminist Studies*, 3/3–4 (1976): 185–99.

Borsay, Peter, *The English Urban Renaissance: Culture and Society in the Provincial Town, 1660–1770* (Oxford: Clarendon Press, 1991).

Bossy, John, *The English Catholic Community 1570–1850* (London: Darton, Longman & Todd, 1975).
——— , 'English Catholics after 1688', in Ole Peter Grell, Jonathan I. Israel and Nicholas Tyacke (eds), *From Persecution to Toleration: The Glorious Revolution and Religion in England* (Oxford: Clarendon Press, 1991).

Bots, Hans, 'William III and His Fellow Calvinists in the Low Countries', in J. Van Den Berg and P.G. Hoftijzer (eds), *Church, Change and Revolution* (Leiden: Brill, 1991).

Bowerbank, Sylvia, *Speaking for Nature: Women and Ecologies of Early Modern England* (Baltimore: Johns Hopkins, 2004).

Bowyer, John Wilson, *The Celebrated Mrs Centlivre* (Durham, NC: Duke University Press, 1952).

Broad, Jacqueline, *Women Philosophers of the Seventeenth Century* (Cambridge: Cambridge University Press, 2003).

Brown, Peter, *Body and Society: Men, Women, and Sexual Renunciation in Early Christianity* (New York: Columbia University Press, 1988).

Bugge, John, *Virginitas: An Essay in the History of a Medieval Ideal* (The Hague: Martinus Nijhoff, 1975).

Buickerood, James G., 'What is it with Damaris, Lady Masham?: The Historiography of One Early Modern Woman Philosopher', *Locke Studies*, 5 (2005): 179–214.

Bush-Bailey, Gilli, *Treading the Bawds: Actresses and Playwrights on the Late-Stuart Stage* (Manchester: Manchester University Press, 2006).

Bustin, Dennis C., *Paradox and Perseverance: Hanserd Knollys, Particular Baptist Pioneer in Seventeenth-Century England* (Milton Keynes: Paternoster, 2006).

Butler, Douglas R., 'Plot and Politics in Susanna Centlivre's *A Bold Stroke for a Wife*', in Mary Anne Schofield and Cecilia Macheski (eds), *Curtain Calls: British and American Women and the Theater, 1660–1820* (Athens, OH: Ohio University Press, 1991).

Calhoun, Craig (ed.), *Habermas and the Public Sphere* (Cambridge, MA: MIT Press, 1992).

Campbell, Jill, *Natural Masques: Gender and Identity in Fielding's Plays and Novels* (Stanford: Stanford University Press, 1995).

Carpenter, Edward, *Thomas Tenison, Archbishop of Canterbury: His Life and Times* (London: S.P.C.K, 1948).

Carter, Philip, *Men and the Emergence of Polite Society, Britain, 1660–1800* (Harlow: Pearson Education, 2001).

Castelli, Elizabeth, 'Virginity and its Meaning for Women's Sexuality in Early Christianity', *Journal of Feminist Studies in Religion*, 2/1 (1986): 61–88.

Cédoz, F., *Un couvent de religieuses Anglaises à Paris de 1634 à 1884* (London and Paris: Burns and Oates, 1891).

Chalus, Elaine, 'Women, Electoral Privilege and Practice in the Eighteenth Century', in Kathryn Gleadle and Sarah Richardson (eds), *Women in British Politics, 1760–1860: The Power of the Petticoat* (Basingstoke: Macmillan, 2000).

———, *Elite Women in English Political Life, c. 1754–1790* (Oxford: Oxford University Press, 2005).

———, 'Ladies Are Often Very Good Scaffoldings': Women and Politics in the Age of Anne', *Parliamentary History*, 28/1 (2009): 150–65.

Chamberlain, Jeffrey S., *Accommodating High Churchmen: The Clergy of Sussex, 1700–1745* (Urbana: University of Illinois Press, 1997).

Champion, Justin, '"Anglia Libera": Commonwealth Politics in the Early Years of George I', in David Womersley, Paddy Bullard and Abigail Williams (eds), *Cultures of Whiggism: New Essays on English Literature and Culture in the Long Eighteenth Century* (Newark: University of Delaware Press, 2005).

Chittister, Joan, *The Friendship of Women: The Hidden Tradition of the Bible* (New York: BlueBridge, 2006).

Claeys, Gregory (ed.), *Restoration and Augustan British Utopias* (New York: Syracuse University Press, 2000).

Clark, Elizabeth A., 'The Celibate Bridegroom and His Virginal Brides: Metaphor and the Marriage of Jesus in Early Christian Ascetic Exegesis', *Church History*, 77/1 (2008): 1–25.

Clark, J.C.D., *English Society, 1688–1832: Ideology, Social Structure and Political Practice during the Ancien Regime* (Cambridge: Cambridge University Press, 1985).

———, *English Society 1660–1832: Religion, Ideology and Politics during the Ancien Regime*, 2nd edn (Cambridge: Cambridge University Press, 2000).

Clarke, Basil F.L., *The Building of the Eighteenth-Century Church* (London: S.P.C.K., 1963).

Clarke, Elizabeth, *Politics, Religion and the Song of Songs in Seventeenth-Century England* (Basingstoke: Palgrave Macmillan, 2011).

Clarke, Norma, 'Bluestocking Fictions: Devotional Writings, Didactic Literature and the Imperative of Female Improvement', in Sarah Knott and Barbara Taylor (eds), *Women, Gender and Enlightenment* (2005; Basingstoke: Palgrave Macmillan, 2007).

Clarke, T.E.S., H.C. Foxcroft and C.H. Firth, *A Life of Gilbert Burnet, Bishop of Salisbury* (Cambridge: Cambridge University Press, 1907).

Clay, Christopher, *Public Finance and Private Wealth: The Career of Sir Stephen Fox, 1627–1716* (Oxford: Clarendon Press, 1978).

Claydon, Tony, *William III and the Godly Revolution* (Cambridge: Cambridge University Press, 1996).

———, 'The Sermon, the "Public Sphere" and the Political Culture of Late Seventeenth-Century England', in Lori Anne Ferrell and Peter McCullough (eds), *The English Sermon Revised: Religion, Literature and History, 1600–1750* (Manchester: Manchester University Press, 2000).

———, *Europe and the Making of England, 1660–1760* (Cambridge: Cambridge University Press, 2007).

Claydon, Tony and Ian McBride (eds), *Protestantism and National Identity: Britain and Ireland, c. 1650–c. 1850* (Cambridge: Cambridge University Press, 1998).

Coffey, John, *Politics, Religion and the British Revolutions: The Mind of Samuel Rutherford* (Cambridge: Cambridge University Press, 1997).

Cohen, Michèle, *Fashioning Masculinity: National Identity and Language in the Eighteenth Century* (London: Routledge, 1996).

Colie, Rosalie, *Light and Enlightenment: A Study of the Cambridge Platonists and the Dutch Arminians* (Cambridge: Cambridge University Press, 1957).

Collinson, Patrick, 'John Knox, the Church of England and the Women of England', in Roger A. Mason (ed.), *John Knox and the British Reformations* (Aldershot: Ashgate, 1998).

Colvin, Howard, 'The Church of St Mary Aldermary and its Rebuilding after the Great Fire of London', *Architectural History*, 24 (1981): 24–31.

Connolly, S.J., *Religion, Law and Power: The Making of Protestant Ireland 1660–1760* (Oxford: Clarendon Press, 1992).

Cornwall, Robert D. and William Gibson (eds), *Religion, Politics and Dissent, 1660–1832: Essays in Honour of James E. Bradley* (Farnham: Ashgate, 2010).

Cowan, Brian, 'What Was Masculine about the Public Sphere? Gender and the Coffeehouse Milieu in Post-Restoration England', *History Workshop Journal*, 51 (2001): 127–57.

———, *The Social Life of Coffee: The Emergence of the British Coffeehouse* (New Haven: Yale University Press, 2005).

Cowan, Ian B., *The Scottish Covenanters, 1660–1688* (London: Victor Gollancz, 1976).

Cranfield, G.A., 'The *London Evening-Post* and the Jew Bill of 1753', *The Historical Journal*, 8/1 (1965): 16–30.

Crawford, Patricia, *Women and Religion in England, 1500–1720* (London: Routledge, 1993).

Dabhoiwala, Faramerz, 'Sex and Societies for Moral Reform, 1688–1800', *Journal of British Studies*, 46/2 (2007): 290–319.

———, 'Lust and Liberty', *Past and Present*, 207 (2010): 89–179.

Davis, Richard Beale, *A Colonial Southern Bookshelf: Reading in the Eighteenth Century* (Athens, GA.: University of Georgia Press, 1979).

Dentz, Fredrik Oudschans, *History of the English Church at The Hague, 1586–1929* (Delft: Meinema, 1929).

DesBrisay, Gordon, 'Twisted by Definition: Women under Godly Discipline in Seventeenth-Century Scottish Towns', in Yvonne Galloway Brown and Rona Ferguson (eds), *Twisted Sisters: Women, Crime and Deviance in Scotland since 1400* (East Linton: Tuckwell, 2002).

———, 'Lilias Skene: A Quaker Poet and her "Cursed Self"', in Sarah M. Dunnigan, C. Marie Harker and Evelyn S. Newlyn (eds), *Woman and the Feminine in Medieval and Early Modern Scottish Writing* (Basingstoke: Palgrave Macmillan, 2004).

Ditchfield, G.M., 'Religion, "Enlightenment" and Progress in Eighteenth-Century England', *The Historical Journal*, 35/3 (1992): 681–7.

Dixon, Rosemary, 'The Publishing of John Tillotson's Collected Works, 1695–1757', *The Library*, 8/2 (2007): 154–81.

Dockrill, David and J.M. Lee, 'Reflections on an Episode in Cambridge Latitudinarianism: Henry More's Epistle Dedicatory to Gilbert Sheldon of his *Enchiridion Metaphysicum*', *Prudentia, Supplement* (1994): 207–23.

Dolan, Frances E., *Marriage and Violence: The Early Modern Legacy* (Philadelphia: University of Pennsylvania Press, 2008).

Donawerth, Jane, 'Conversation and the Boundaries of Public Discourse in Rhetorical Theory by Renaissance Women', *Rhetorica: A Journal of the History of Rhetoric*, 16/2 (1998): 181–99.

Donoghue, Emma, *Passions Between Women: British Lesbian Culture, 1668–1801* (London: Scarlet Press, 1993).

Duffy, Eamon, 'Primitive Christianity Revived: Religious Renewal in Augustan England', in Derek Baker (ed.), *Renaissance and Renewal in Christian History*, Studies in Church History, 14 (Oxford: Blackwell, 1977): 287–300.

———, '"Englishmen in Vaine": Roman Catholic Allegiance to George I', in Stuart Mews (ed.), *Religion and National Identity*, Studies in Church History, 18 (Oxford: Blackwell, 1982): 345–65.

Dunan-Page, Anne, *Grace Overwhelming: John Bunyan, The Pilgrim's Progress and the Extremes of the Baptist Mind* (Bern: Peter Lang, 2006).

Durrant, C.S., *A Link Between Flemish Mystics and English Martyrs* (London: Burns, Oates and Washbourne, 1925).

Eger, Elizabeth, *Bluestockings: Women of Reason from Enlightenment to Romanticism* (Basingstoke: Palgrave Macmillan, 2011).

Esdaile, K.A., 'Cousin to Pepys and Dryden: A Note on the Works of Mrs Elizabeth Creed of Tichmarsh', *The Burlington Magazine*, 77/448 (July 1940): 24–7.

Felch, Susan M., 'The Exemplary Anne Vaughan Lock', in Johanna Harris and Elizabeth Scott-Baumann (eds), *The Intellectual Culture of Puritan Women, 1558–1680* (Basingstoke: Palgrave Macmillan, 2011).

Fiering, Norman, 'The First American Enlightenment: Tillotson, Leverett, and Philosophical Anglicanism', *The New England Quarterly*, 54/3 (1981): 307–44.

Fincham, Kenneth and Nicholas Tyacke, *Altars Restored: The Changing Face of English Religious Worship, 1547–c. 1700* (Oxford: Oxford University Press, 2007).

Finlay, Richard J., 'Keeping the Covenant: Scottish National Identity', in T.M. Devine and J.R. Young (eds), *Eighteenth Century Scotland: New Perspectives* (East Linton: Tuckwell, 1999).

Forster, Ann M.C., 'The Chronicles of the English Poor Clares of Rouen – I', *Recusant History*, 18/1 (1986): 59–102.

———, 'The Chronicles of the English Poor Clares of Rouen – II', *Recusant History*, 18/2 (1986): 149–91.

Freeman, Lisa A., *Character's Theater: Genre and Identity on the Eighteenth-Century English Stage* (Philadelphia: University of Pennsylvania Press, 2002).

Friedman, Terry, *The Eighteenth-Century Church in Britain* (New Haven: Yale University Press, 2011).

Froide, Amy M., *Never Married: Singlewomen in Early Modern England* (Oxford: Oxford University Press, 2005).

Garnett, Jane and Colin Matthew (eds), *Revival and Religion since 1700: Essays for John Walsh* (London: Hambledon Press, 1993).

Garrett, Clarke, *Respectable Folly: Millenarians and the French Revolution in France and England* (Baltimore: Johns Hopkins University Press, 1975).

Gibbons, B.J., *Gender in Mystical and Occult Thought: Behmenism and its Development in England* (Cambridge: Cambridge University Press, 1996).

Gibson, William (ed.), *Religion and Society in England and Wales, 1689–1800* (London: Leicester University Press, 1998).

Gill, Catie, *Women in the Seventeenth-Century Quaker Community: A Literary Study of Political Identities, 1650–1700* (Aldershot: Ashgate, 2005).

Gillespie, Katharine, *Domesticity and Dissent in the Seventeenth Century: English Women's Writing and the Public Sphere* (Cambridge: Cambridge University Press, 2004).

Glickman, Gabriel, *The English Catholic Community, 1688–1745: Politics, Culture and Ideology* (Woodbridge: Boydell Press, 2009).

Goldie, Mark, 'John Locke, Jonas Proast and Religious Toleration, 1688–1692', in John Walsh, Colin Haydon and Stephen Taylor (eds), *The Church of England, c. 1689–c. 1833, From Toleration to Tractarianism* (1993; Cambridge: Cambridge University Press, 2002).

———, *John Locke and the Mashams at Oates* (Cambridge: Churchill College, 2004).

———, 'Mary Astell and John Locke', in William Kolbrener and Michal Michelson (eds), *Mary Astell: Reason, Gender, Faith* (Aldershot: Ashgate, 2007).

Goodare, Julian, 'Women and the Witch-Hunt in Scotland', *Social History*, 23/3 (1998): 288–308.

Goodman, Dena, *The Republic of Letters: A Cultural History of the French Enlightenment* (1994; Ithaca: Cornell University Press, 1996).

Graham, Michael F., 'Women and the Church Courts in Reformation-Era Scotland', in Elizabeth Ewan and Maureen M. Meikle (eds), *Women in Scotland, c. 1100–c. 1750* (East Linton: Tuckwell, 1999).

Gregg, Stephen H., '"A Truly Christian Hero": Religion, Effeminacy, and Nation in the Writings of the Societies for Reformation of Manners', *Eighteenth-Century Life*, 25/1 (2001): 17–28.

Gregory, Jeremy, *Restoration, Reformation and Reform, 1660–1828: Archbishops of Canterbury and their Diocese* (Oxford: Clarendon Press, 2000).

Guest, Harriet, *Small Change: Women, Learning, Patriotism, 1750–1810* (Chicago: University of Chicago Press, 2000).

Guilday, Peter, *The English Catholic Refugees on the Continent 1558–1795* (London: Longmans, Green and Co., 1914).

Guthrie, Neil, *The Material Culture of the Jacobites* (Cambridge: Cambridge University Press, 2013).

Habermas, Jürgen, *The Structural Transformation of the Public Sphere: An Inquiry into a Category of Bourgeois Society*, trans. and ed. Thomas Burger and Frederick Lawrence (Cambridge, MA: MIT Press, 1989).

———, *The Structural Transformation of the Public Sphere: An Inquiry into a Category of Bourgeois Society*, trans. and ed. Thomas Burger and Frederick Lawrence (Cambridge: Polity 1992).

———, *Religion and Rationality: Essays on Reason, God, and Modernity*, ed. and introd. Eduardo Mendieta (Cambridge: Polity, 2002).

Habermas, Jürgen and Joseph Ratzinger (Pope Benedict XVI), *Dialectics of Secularization: On Reason and Religion* (San Francisco: Ignatius Press, 2006).

Haggerty, George E., *Men in Love: Masculinity and Sexuality in the Eighteenth Century* (New York: Columbia University Press, 1999).

Hamel, Christopher De, *Syon Abbey: The Library of the Bridgettine Nuns and their Peregrinations after the Reformation* (Otley: Roxburghe Club, 1991).

Hamington, Maurice, *Hail Mary?: The Struggle for Ultimate Womanhood in Catholicism* (London: Routledge, 1995).

Hammond, Brean S., 'Is There a Whig Canon? The Case of Susanna Centlivre', *Women's Writing*, 7/3 (2000): 373–90.

Harding, Alan, *The Countess of Huntingdon's Connexion: A Sect in Action in Eighteenth-Century England* (Oxford: Oxford University Press, 2003).

Hardman, Anne, *Mother Margaret Mostyn: Discalced Carmelite 1625–1679* (London: Burns Oates and Washbourne, 1937).

Harris, Frances, *A Passion for Government: The Life of Sarah, Duchess of Marlborough* (Oxford: Clarendon Press, 1991).

——, *Transformations of Love: The Friendship of John Evelyn and Margaret Godolphin* (2002; Oxford: Oxford University Press, 2003).

Harris, Tim, *Revolution: The Great Crisis of the British Monarchy, 1685–1720* (London: Penguin, 2007).

Harris, Tim, Paul Seaward and Mark Goldie (eds), *The Politics of Religion in Restoration England* (Oxford: Basil Blackwell, 1990).

Harrison, Peter, *'Religion' and the Religions in the English Enlightenment* (Cambridge: Cambridge University Press, 1990).

Hart, A. Tindal, *William Lloyd, 1627–1717: Bishop, Politician, Author and Prophet* (London: S.P.C.K, 1952).

Hart, Vaughan, *Nicholas Hawksmoor: Rebuilding Ancient Wonders* (2002; New Haven: Yale University Press, 2007).

Harvey, Karen, 'The Century of Sex? Gender, Bodies, and Sexuality in the Long Eighteenth Century', *The Historical Journal*, 45/4 (2002): 899–916.

Haydon, Colin, *Anti-Catholicism in Eighteenth-Century England, c. 1714–80: A Political and Social Study* (Manchester: Manchester University Press, 1993).

Hayes, Kevin J., *A Colonial Woman's Bookshelf* (Knoxville: University of Tennessee Press, 1996).

Haynes, Clare, *Pictures and Popery: Art and Religion in England, 1660–1760* (Aldershot: Ashgate, 2006).

Haywood, Ian and John Seed (eds), *The Gordon Riots: Politics, Culture and Insurrection in Late Eighteenth-Century Britain* (Cambridge: Cambridge University Press, 2012).

A History of the Benedictine Nuns of Dunkirk (London: Burns and Oates, 1958).

Hitchcock, Tim, *English Sexualities, 1700–1800* (Basingstoke: Macmillan, 1997).

Hitchcock, Tim and Michèle Cohen, (eds), *English Masculinities 1660–1800* (London: Longman, 1999).

Hobby, Elaine, *Virtue of Necessity: English Women's Writing, 1649–1688* (London: Virago, 1988).

Hodgetts, Michael, 'The Yates of Harvington 1631–1696', *Recusant History*, 22/2 (1994): 152–81.

Hoffmann, Barbara, *Radikalpietismus um 1700. Der Streit um das Recht auf eine neue Gesellschaft* (Frankfurt: Campus Verlag, 1996).

Holmes, Geoffrey, *The Trial of Doctor Sacheverell* (London: Eyre Meuthen, 1973).

———, 'The Sacheverell Riots: The Crowd and the Church in Early Eighteenth-Century London', *Past and Present*, 72 (1976): 55–85.

Holmes, Geoffrey and W.A. Speck (eds), *The Divided Society: Parties and Politics in England 1694–1716* (London: Edward Arnold Ltd, 1967).

Houlbrooke, Ralph, *Death, Religion and the Family in England 1480–1750* (Oxford: Clarendon Press, 1998).

Hughes, Ann, 'Puritanism and Gender', in John Coffey and Paul C.H. Lim (eds), *The Cambridge Companion to Puritanism* (Cambridge: Cambridge University Press, 2008).

Hutton, Sarah, 'Damaris Cudworth, Lady Masham: Between Platonism and Enlightenment', *British Journal for the History of Philosophy*, 1/1 (1993): 29–54.

———, 'A Radical Review of the Cambridge Platonists', in Ariel Hessayon and David Finnegan (eds), *Varieties of Seventeenth- and Early Eighteenth-Century English Radicalism in Context* (Farnham: Ashgate, 2011).

———, 'Debating the Faith: Damaris Masham (1658–1708) and Religious Controversy', in Anne Dunan-Page and Clotilde Prunier (eds), *Debating the Faith: Religion and Letter Writing in Great Britain, 1550–1800* (Dordrecht: Springer, 2013).

Hyman, Elizabeth Hannan, 'A Church Militant: Scotland, 1661–1690', *The Sixteenth Century Journal*, 26/1 (1995): 49–74.

Ingle, H. Larry, *First Among Friends: George Fox and the Creation of Quakerism* (Oxford: Oxford University Press, 1994).

Ingram, Robert G., '"The Trembling Earth is God's Herald": Earthquakes, Religion and Public Life in Britain during the 1750s', in Theodore E.D. Braun and John B. Radner (eds), *The Lisbon Earthquake of 1755: Representations and Reactions* (Oxford: Voltaire Foundation, 2005).

Innes, Joanna, 'Review Article: Jonathan Clark, Social History and England's "Ancien Regime"', *Past and Present*, 115 (1987): 165–200.

Israel, Jonathan, 'Enlightenment! Which Enlightenment?', *Journal of the History of Ideas*, 67/3 (2006): 523–45.

Jacob, W.M., *Lay People and Religion in the Early Eighteenth Century* (Cambridge: Cambridge University Press, 1996).

Jantzen, Grace, *Power, Gender and Christian Mysticism* (Cambridge: Cambridge University Press, 1995).

Jeffery, Paul, *The City Churches of Sir Christopher Wren* (1996; London: Hambledon Continum, 2007).

Johnston, Warren, 'Prophecy, Patriarchy, and Violence in the Early Modern Household: The Revelations of Anne Wentworth', *Journal of Family History*, 34/4 (2009): 344–68.

———, *Revelation Restored: The Apocalypse in Later Seventeenth-Century England* (Woodbridge: Boydell, 2011).

Jones, M.G., *The Charity School Movement: A Study of Eighteenth-Century Puritanism in Action* (Cambridge: Cambridge University Press, 1938).

Katz, David S., *The Jews in the History of England, 1485–1850* (Oxford: Clarendon Press, 1994).

Keeble, Neil, '"Here is Her Glory, Even to be Under Him": The Feminine in the Thought and Work of John Bunyan', in Anne Laurence, W.R. Owens and Stuart Sim (eds), *John Bunyan and His England, 1628–88* (London: Hambledon, 1990).

Keeble, N.H. and Geoffrey Nuttall, *Calendar of the Correspondence of Richard Baxter* (2 vols, Oxford: Clarendon Press, 1991).

Kelley, Anne, *Catharine Trotter: An Early Modern Writer in the Vanguard of Feminism* (Aldershot: Ashgate, 2002).

Ketton-Cremer, R.W., *A Norfolk Gallery* (London: Faber & Faber, 1948).

Kilday, Anne-Marie, *Women and Violent Crime in Enlightenment Scotland* (Woodbridge: Boydell Press, 2007).

King, Kathryn R., *Jane Barker, Exile: A Literary Career 1675–1725* (Oxford: Clarendon Press, 2000).

———, 'Political Verse and Satire: Monarchy, Party and Female Political Agency', in Sarah Prescott and David E. Shuttleton (eds), *Women and Poetry, 1660–1750* (Basingstoke: Palgrave Macmillan, 2003).

Kishlansky, Mark, *A Monarchy Transformed: Britain, 1603–1714* (London: Allen Lane, 1996).

Kitch, Sally, *Chaste Liberation: Celibacy and Female Cultural Status* (Urbana: University of Illinois Press, 1989).

Klein, Lawrence E., 'Gender, Conversation and the Public Sphere in Early Eighteenth-Century England', in Judith Still and Michael Worton (eds), *Textuality and Sexuality: Reading Theories and Practices* (Manchester: Manchester University Press, 1993).

Knetsch, F.R.J., *Pierre Jurieu: Theoloog en Politikus der Refuge* (Kampen: J.H. Kok, 1967).

Knott, Sarah and Barbara Taylor (eds), *Women, Gender and Enlightenment* (2005; Basingstoke: Palgrave Macmillan, 2007).

Kolbrener, William, *Milton's Warring Angels: A Study of Critical Engagements* (Cambridge: Cambridge University Press, 1996).

———, '"Commonwealth Fictions" and "Inspiration Fraud": Milton and the *Eikon Basilike* after 1689', *Milton Studies*, 37 (1999): 166–97.

———, '*The Charge of Socianism*: Charles Leslie's High Church Defense of "True Religion"', *Journal of the Historical Society*, 3/1 (2003): 1–23.

————, 'Gendering the Modern: Mary Astell's Feminist Historiography', *The Eighteenth Century: Theory and Interpretation*, 44/1 (2003): 1–24.

————, 'The Jacobite Milton: Strategies of Literary Appropriation and Historiography', *Clio: A Journal of Literature, History and the Philosophy of History*, 32/2 (2003): 153–76.

————, '"Forc'd into an Interest": High Church Politics and Feminine Agency in the Works of Mary Astell', *1650–1850: Ideas, Aesthetics, and Inquiries in the Early Modern Era*, 10 (2004): 3–31.

Kolbrener, William and Michal Michelson (eds), *Mary Astell: Reason, Gender, Faith* (Aldershot: Ashgate, 2007).

Lachman, David C., *The Marrow Controversy, 1718–1723: An Historical and Theological Analysis* (Edinburgh: Rutherford House, 1988).

Langford, Paul, *Public Life and the Propertied Englishman, 1689–1798* (1991; Oxford: Clarendon Press, 1994).

Laqueur, Thomas, *Making Sex: Body and Gender from the Greeks to Freud* (Cambridge, MA: Harvard University Press, 1992).

Laslett, Peter, 'Masham of Otes', *History Today*, 3/8 (1953): 535–43.

Laurence, Anne, 'Women Using Building in Seventeenth-Century England: A Question of Sources?', *Transactions of the Royal Historical Society*, 6th ser., 13 (2003): 293–303.

————, 'Lady Betty Hastings (1682–1739): Godly Patron', *Women's History Review*, 19/2 (2010): 201–13.

Leckie, J.H., *Secession Memories: The United Presbyterian Contribution to the Scottish Church* (Edinburgh: T. & T. Clark, 1926).

Levack, Brian P., 'The Prosecution of Sexual Crimes in Early Eighteenth-Century Scotland', *Scottish Historical Review*, 89/2 (2010): 172–93.

Levine, Joseph M., *Dr. Woodward's Shield: History, Science, and Satire in Augustan England* (Berkeley: University of California Press, 1977).

Lloyd, Genevieve, *The Man of Reason: Male and Female in Western Philosophy* (London: Methuen & Co., 1984).

Lock, F.P., *Susanna Centlivre* (Boston: Twayne Publishers, 1979).

Logue, Kenneth J., *Popular Disturbances in Scotland, 1780–1815* (Edinburgh: John Donald, 1979).

Longfellow, Erica, *Women and Religious Writing in Early Modern England* (Cambridge: Cambridge University Press, 2004).

Luxon, Thomas H., 'One Soul Versus One Flesh: Friendship, Marriage, and the Puritan Self', in Vera J. Camden (ed.), *Trauma and Transformation: The Political Progress of John Bunyan* (Stanford: Stanford University Press, 2008).

Macdonald, Angus, *The Place-Names of West Lothian* (Edinburgh: Oliver and Boyd, 1941).

MacEwen, A.R., *The Erskines* (Edinburgh: Oliphant, Anderson & Ferrier, 1900).

Mack, Phyllis, *Heart Religion in the British Enlightenment: Gender and Emotion in Early Methodism* (Cambridge: Cambridge University Press, 2008).

Major, Emma, *Madam Britannia: Women, Church, and Nation, 1712–1812* (Oxford: Oxford University Press, 2011).

McCallum, John, *Reforming the Scottish Parish: The Reformation in Fife, 1560–1640* (Farnham: Ashgate, 2010).

McClain, Molly, 'Love, Friendship, and Power: Queen Mary II's Letters to Frances Apsley', *Journal of British Studies*, 47/3 (2008): 505–27.

McDowell, Paula, *The Women of Grub Street: Press, Politics, and Gender in the London Literary Marketplace, 1678–1730* (Oxford: Clarendon Press, 1998).

McElligott, Jason (ed.), *Fear, Exclusion and Revolution: Roger Morrice and Britain in the 1680s* (Aldershot: Ashgate, 2006).

McInnes, Angus, *The English Town, 1660–1760* (London: Historical Association, 1980).

McKeon, Michael, 'Historicizing Patriarchy: The Emergence of Gender Difference in England, 1660–1760', *Eighteenth-Century Studies*, 28/3 (1995): 295–322.

———, 'Parsing Habermas's "Bourgeois Public Sphere"', *Criticism*, 46/2 (2004): 273–7.

———, *The Secret History of Domesticity: Public, Private and the Division of Knowledge* (Baltimore: Johns Hopkins University Press, 2005).

McMahon, Marie P., *The Radical Whigs, John Trenchard and Thomas Gordon: Libertarian Loyalists to the New House of Hanover* (Lanham: University Press of America, 1990).

Mendieta, Eduardo and Jonathan VanAntwerpen (ed. and introd.), *The Power of Religion in the Public Sphere: Judith Butler, Jürgen Habermas, Charles Taylor, Cornel West* (New York: Columbia University Press, 2011).

Miller, John, *The Stuarts* (London: Hambledon and London, 2004).

Milling, Jane, '"A Gotham Election": Women and Performance Politics', *Restoration and Eighteenth-Century Theatre Research*, 21/2 (2006): 74–89.

M'Kerrow, John, *History of the Secession Church*, rev. edn (Glasgow, 1841).

Moltmann-Wendel, Elisabeth, *Rediscovering Friendship*, trans. John Bowden (London: SCM, 2000).

Morgan, Sue (ed.), *Women, Religion and Feminism in Britain, 1750–1900* (Basingstoke: Palgrave Macmillan, 2002).

Morrill, John, 'The Religious Context of the English Civil War', *Transactions of the Royal Historical Society*, 5th ser., 34 (1984): 155–78.

Muirhead, Andrew T.N., 'A Secession Congregation in its Community: The Stirling Congregation of the Rev. Ebenezer Erskine, 1731–1754', *Records of the Scottish Church History Society*, 22 (1986): 211–33.

Mullan, David G., *Scottish Puritanism, 1590–1638* (Oxford: Oxford University Press, 2000).

———, *Narratives of the Religious Self in Early Modern Scotland* (Farnham: Ashgate, 2010).

Mullett, Michael, *Catholics in Britain and Ireland, 1558–1829* (Basingstoke: Macmillan, 1998).

Myers, Sylvia Harcstark, *The Bluestocking Circle: Women, Friendship and the Life of the Mind in Eighteenth-Century England* (Oxford: Clarendon Press, 1990).

Ng, Su Fang, 'Marriage and Discipline: The Place of Women in Early Quaker Controversies', *The Seventeenth Century*, 18/1 (2003): 113–40.

Nicholson, Eirwen E.C., 'Sacheverell's Harlots: Non-Resistance on Paper and in Practice', *Parliamentary History*, 31/1 (2012): 69–79.

Nicolson, Marjorie, 'Christ's College and the Latitude Men', *Modern Philology*, 27/1 (1929): 35–53.

Nolan, Patrick, *The Irish Dames of Ypres: Being a History of the Royal Irish Abbey of Ypres Founded A.D. 1665 and Still Flourishing* (Dublin: Browne and Nolan, 1908).

Norbrook, David, 'Women, the Republic of Letters, and the Public Sphere in the Mid-Seventeenth Century', *Criticism*, 46/2 (2004): 223–40.

O'Brien, Karen, *Women and Enlightenment in Eighteenth-Century Britain* (Cambridge: Cambridge University Press, 2009).

O'Harae, Alison, 'Theology, Genre and Romance in Richard Baxter and Harriet Beecher Stowe', *Religion and Literature*, 37/1 (2005): 69–91.

Orr, Clarissa Campbell, 'The Late Hanoverian Court and the Christian Enlightenment', in Michael Schaich (ed.), *Monarchy and Religion: The Transformation of Royal Culture in Eighteenth Century Europe* (Oxford: Oxford University Press, 2007).

Oxford Dictionary of National Biography: From the Earliest Times to the Year 2000, ed. H.C.G. Matthew and Brian Harrison (Oxford: Oxford University Press, 2004).

Pask, Kevin, 'The Bourgeois Public Sphere and the Concept of Literature', *Criticism*, 46/2 (2004): 241–56.

Pearson, Jacqueline, *The Prostituted Muse: Images of Women and Women Dramatists 1642–1737* (Hemel Hempstead: Harvester Wheatsheaf, 1988).

Perry, Ruth, 'The Veil of Chastity: Mary Astell's Feminism', in Paul-Gabriel Boucé (ed.), *Sexuality in Eighteenth-Century Britain* (Manchester: Manchester University Press, 1982).

———, *The Celebrated Mary Astell: An Early English Feminist* (Chicago: University of Chicago Press, 1986).

Perry, T.W., *Public Opinion, Propaganda, and Politics in Eighteenth-Century England: A Study of the Jew Bill of 1753* (Cambridge, MA: Harvard University Press, 1962).

Peters, Christine, *Patterns of Piety: Women, Gender and Religion in Late Medieval and Reformation England* (Cambridge: Cambridge University Press, 2003).

Phemister, Pauline, '"All the Time and Everywhere Everything's the Same as Here": The Principle of Uniformity in the Correspondence between Leibniz and Lady Masham', in Paul Lodge (ed.), *Leibniz and his Correspondents* (Cambridge: Cambridge University Press, 2004).

Phemister, Pauline and Justin Smith, 'Leibniz and the Cambridge Platonists: The Debate over Plastic Natures', in Pauline Phemister and Stuart Brown (eds), *Leibniz and the English-Speaking World* (Dordrecht: Springer, 2007).

Pincus, Steve, *1688: The First Modern Revolution* (New Haven: Yale University Press, 2009).

Plumptre, E.H., *The Life of Thomas Ken, D.D.* (2 vols, London: W. Isbister, 1890).

Pocock, J.G.A., 'Clergy and Commerce: The Conservative Enlightenment in England', in R. Ajello et al. (eds), *L'età dei Lumi: studi storici sul settecento europeo in onore di Franco Venturi* (2 vols, Naples: Jovene, 1985).

———, *Barbarism and Religion: The Enlightenments of Edward Gibbon, 1737–1764* (Cambridge: Cambridge University Press, 1999).

Popkin, Richard H., 'The Spiritualistic Cosmologies of Henry More and Anne Conway', in Sarah Hutton and Robert Crocker (eds), *Henry More (1614–1687): Tercentenary Studies* (Dordrecht: Kluwer Academic, 1989).

Porter, Roy, 'The Enlightenment in England', in Roy Porter and Mikuláš Teich (eds), *The Enlightenment in National Context* (Cambridge: Cambridge University Press, 1981).

Potts, Richard, *Dame Sarah's Legacy: A History of the Lady Hewley Trust* (York: Lady Hewley Trust, 2005).

Powicke, F.M., *Handbook of British Chronology* (London: Offices of the Royal Historical Society, 1939).

Prescott, Sarah, 'The Cambrian Muse: Welsh Identity and Hanoverian Loyalty in the Poems of Jane Brereton (1685–1740)', *Eighteenth-Century Studies*, 38/4 (2005): 587–603.

———, 'Elizabeth Singer Rowe: Gender, Dissent, and Whig Poetics', in David Womersley, Paddy Bullard and Abigail Williams (eds), *Cultures of Whiggism: New Essays on English Literature and Culture in the Long Eighteenth Century* (Newark: University of Delaware Press, 2005).

Prescott, Sarah and David E. Shuttleton (eds), *Women and Poetry, 1660–1750* (Basingstoke: Palgrave Macmillan, 2003).

Pugh, Martin, *The March of the Women: A Revisionist Analysis of the Campaign for Women's Suffrage, 1866–1914* (Oxford: Oxford University Press, 2000).

Quantin, Jean-Louis, *The Church of England and Christian Antiquity: The Construction of a Confessional Identity in the 17th Century* (Oxford: Oxford University Press, 2009).

Rabin, Dana, 'The Jew Bill of 1753: Masculinity, Virility, and the Nation', *Eighteenth-Century Studies*, 39/2 (2006): 157–71.

Raffe, Alasdair, 'Presbyterianism, Secularization, and Scottish Politics after the Revolution of 1688–1690', *The Historical Journal*, 53/2 (2010): 317–37.

———, 'Presbyterians and Episcopalians: The Formation of Confessional Cultures in Scotland, 1660–1715', *English Historical Review*, 125/3 (2010): 570–98.

————, *The Culture of Controversy: Religious Arguments in Scotland, 1660–1714* (Woodbridge: Boydell, 2012).

Rivers, Isabel, *Reason, Grace, and Sentiment: A Study of the Language of Religion and Ethics in England, 1660–1780* (2 vols, Cambridge: Cambridge University Press, 1991–2000).

Roberts, Alasdair F.B., 'The Role of Women in Scottish Catholic Survival', *The Scottish Historical Review*, 70/2 (1991): 129–50.

Robertson, John, *The Case for the Enlightenment: Scotland and Naples 1680–1760* (Cambridge: Cambridge University Press, 2005).

Rogers, John, 'The Enclosure of Virginity: The Poetics of Sexual Abstinence in the English Revolution', in Richard Burt and John Michael Archer (eds), *Enclosure Acts: Sexuality, Property and Culture in Early Modern England* (Ithaca: Cornell University Press, 1994).

Rosa, Susan, 'Religion in the English Enlightenment: A Review Essay', *Eighteenth-Century Studies*, 28/1 (1994): 145–9.

Rose, Craig, 'Providence, Protestant Union and Godly Reformation in the 1690s', *Transactions of the Royal Historical Society*, 6th ser., 3 (1993): 151–69.

————, *England in the 1690s: Revolution, Religion and War* (Oxford: Blackwell, 1999).

Rosenthal, Laura J., *Playwrights and Plagiarists in Early Modern England: Gender, Authorship, Literary Property* (Ithaca: Cornell University Press, 1996).

Roseveare, Henry, *The Financial Revolution, 1660–1760* (London: Longman, 1991).

Rubik, Margarete, *Early Women Dramatists, 1550–1800* (Basingstoke: Macmillan, 1998).

Rupp, Gordon, *Religion in England, 1688–1791* (Oxford: Clarendon Press, 1986).

Schmidt, Leigh Eric, *Holy Fairs: Scotland and the Making of American Revivalism*, 2nd edn (Grand Rapids, MI: W.B. Eerdmans, 2001).

Schwoerer, Lois G., 'Propaganda in the Revolution of 1688–89', *The American Historical Review*, 82/4 (1977): 843–74.

————, 'Images of Queen Mary II, 1689–95', *Renaissance Quarterly*, 42/4 (1989): 717–48.

————, 'The Queen as Regent and Patron', in Robert P. Maccubbin and Martha Hamilton-Phillips (eds), *The Age of William III & Mary II: Power, Politics, and Patronage, 1688–1702* (Williamsburg, VA.: College of William and Mary in Virginia, 1989).

————, (ed.), *The Revolution of 1688–1689: Changing Perspectives* (Cambridge: Cambridge University Press, 1992).

Scott, Geoffrey, *'Sacredness of Majesty': The English Benedictines and the Cult of King James II*, Royal Stuart Papers, 23 (Huntingdon: Royal Stuart Society, 1984).

Shapiro, Barbara J., *A Culture of Fact: England, 1550–1720* (Ithaca: Cornell University Press, 2000).

Shaw, Jane, 'Fasting Women: The Significance of Gender and Bodies in Radical Religion and Politics, 1650–1813', in Timothy Morton and Nigel Smith (eds), *Radicalism in British Literary Culture, 1650–1830 from Revolution to Revolution* (Cambridge: Cambridge University Press, 2002).

———, *Miracles in Enlightenment England* (New Haven: Yale University Press, 2006).

Sheehan, Jonathan, 'Enlightenment, Religion and the Enigma of Secularization: A Review Essay', *The American Historical Review*, 108/4 (2003): 1061–80.

Sher, Richard and Alexander Murdoch, 'Patronage and Party in the Church of Scotland, 1750–1800', in Norman Macdougall (ed.), *Church, Politics and Society: Scotland, 1408–1929* (Edinburgh: John Donald, 1983).

Sheridan, Patricia, 'Reflection, Nature, and Moral Law: The Extent of Catharine Trotter Cockburn's Lockeanism in her "Defence of Mr. Locke's Essay"', *Hypatia*, 22/3 (2007): 133–51.

Simonutti, Luisa, 'Circles of *Virtuosi* and "Charity under Different Opinions": The Crucible of Locke's Last Writings', in Sarah Hutton and Paul Schuurman (eds), *Studies on Locke: Sources, Contemporaries and Legacy* (Dordrecht: Springer, 2008).

Skinner, Quentin, 'Motives, Intentions and the Interpretation of Texts', in James Tully (ed.), *Meaning and Context: Quentin Skinner and His Critics* (Princeton: Princeton University Press, 1988).

Skoczylas, Anne, *Mr Simson's Knotty Case: Divinity, Politics, and Due Process in Early Eighteenth-Century Scotland* (Montreal: McGill-Queen's University Press, 2001).

Sleigh, Robert C., 'Reflections on the Masham-Leibniz Correspondence', in Christia Mercer and Eileen O'Neill (eds), *Early Modern Philosophy: Mind, Matter, and Metaphysics* (Oxford: Oxford University Press, 2005).

Smith, Hannah, 'English "Feminist" Writings and Judith Drake's *An Essay in Defence of the Female Sex* (1696)', *The Historical Journal*, 44/3 (2001): 727–47.

———, 'The Idea of a Protestant Monarchy in Britain, 1714–1760', *Past and Present*, 185 (2004): 91–118.

———, 'Mary Astell, *A Serious Proposal to the Ladies* (1694) and the Anglican Reformation of Manners in Late-Seventeenth-Century England', in William Kolbrener and Michal Michelson (eds), *Mary Astell: Reason, Gender, Faith* (Ashgate: Aldershot, 2007).

———, 'Politics, Patriotism, and Gender: The Standing Army Debate on the English Stage, circa 1689–1720', *Journal of British Studies*, 50/1 (2011): 48–75.

Smith, Hilda L., *Reason's Disciples: Seventeenth-Century English Feminists* (Urbana: University of Illinois Press, 1982).

Smith, Hilda L., Mihoko Suzuki and Susan Wiseman (eds), *Women's Political Writings, 1610–1725* (4 vols, London: Pickering & Chatto, 2007).

Smith, Lacy Baldwin, *This Realm of England, 1399–1688*, 8th edn (New York: Houghton Mifflin, 2000).

Smyth, Adam, *Autobiography in Early Modern England* (Cambridge: Cambridge University Press, 2010).

Smyth, Charles H.E., *The Art of Preaching: A Practical Survey of Preaching in the Church of England, 747–1939* (London: S.P.C.K, 1940).

Snell, K.D.M., *Parish and Belonging: Community, Identity and Welfare in England and Wales 1700–1950* (Cambridge: Cambridge University Press, 2006).

Sobo, Elisa Janine and Sandra Bell (eds), *Celibacy, Culture and Society: The Anthropology of Sexual Abstinence* (Madison: University of Wisconsin, 2001).

Sokol, B.J. and Mary Sokol, *Shakespeare, Law, and Marriage* (Cambridge: Cambridge University Press, 2003).

Sommerville, C. John, *The Secularization of Early Modern England: From Religious Culture to Religious Faith* (Oxford: Oxford University Press, 1992).

Sorkin, David, *The Religious Enlightenment: Protestants, Jews and Catholics from London to Vienna* (Princeton: Princeton University Press, 2008).

Speck, W.A., *Reluctant Revolutionaries: Englishmen and the Revolution of 1688* (Oxford: Oxford University Press, 1988).

———, 'William – and Mary?', in Lois G. Schwoerer (ed.), *The Revolution of the 1688–1689: Changing Perspectives* (Cambridge: Cambridge University Press, 1992).

Spellman, W.M., *The Latitudinarians and the Church of England, 1660–1700* (Athens, GA.: University of Georgia Press, 1993).

Springborg, Patricia, 'Mary Astell (1666–1731); Critic of Locke', *American Political Science Review*, 89/3 (1995): 621–33.

———, *Mary Astell: Theorist of Freedom from Domination* (Cambridge: Cambridge University Press, 2005).

Spurr, John, '"Latitudinarianism" and the Restoration Church', *The Historical Journal*, 31/1 (1988): 61–82.

———, 'Schism and the Restoration Church', *The Journal of Ecclesiastical History*, 41/3 (1990): 408–24.

———, *The Restoration Church of England, 1646–1689* (New Haven: Yale University Press, 1991).

———, *England in the 1670s: 'This Masquerading Age'* (Oxford: Blackwell, 2000).

Starkie, Andrew, *The Church of England and the Bangorian Controversy, 1716–1721* (Woodbridge: Boydell and Brewer, 2007).

Staves, Susan, 'Investments, Votes, and "Bribes": Women as Shareholders in the Chartered National Companies', in Hilda L. Smith (ed.), *Women Writers and the Early Modern British Political Tradition* (Cambridge: Cambridge University Press, 1998).

———, 'Church of England Clergy and Women Writers', *Huntington Library Quarterly*, 65/1–2 (2002): 81–103.

———, *A Literary History of Women's Writing in Britain, 1660–1789* (Cambridge: Cambridge University Press, 2006).

Stell, Christopher, *An Inventory of Nonconformist Chapels and Meeting-Houses in South-West England* (London: HMSO, 1991).

————, *An Inventory of Nonconformist Chapels and Meeting-Houses in the North of England* (London: HMSO, 1994).

————, *An Inventory of Nonconformist Chapels and Meeting-Houses in Eastern England* (Swindon: English Heritage, 2002).

Stewart, Laura A.M., 'Jenny Geddes', in Elizabeth Ewan, Sue Innes, Rose Pipes and Siân Reynolds (eds), *The Biographical Dictionary of Scottish Women: From the Earliest Times to 2004* (Edinburgh: Edinburgh University Press, 2006).

Stitziel, Judd, 'God, the Devil, Medicine, and the Word: A Controversy Over Ecstatic Women in Protestant Middle Germany 1691–1693', *Central European History,* 29/3 (1996): 309–37.

Stott, Anne, *Hannah More: The First Victorian* (Oxford: Oxford University Press, 2003).

Stretton, Tim, 'Marriage, Separation and the Common Law in England, 1540–1660', in Helen Berry and Elizabeth Foyster (eds), *The Family in Early Modern England* (Cambridge: Cambridge University Press, 2007).

Strickland, Agnes, *Lives of the Queens of Scotland and England and English Princesses Connected with the Regal Succession of Great Britain* (New York: 1851–59).

Sykes, Norman, *Church and State in England in the XVIIIth Century* (Cambridge: Cambridge University Press, 1934).

————, 'The Sermons of Archbishop Tillotson', *Theology,* 58/422 (1955): 297–302.

Tadmor, Naomi, *The Social Universe of the English Bible: Scripture, Society and Culture in Early Modern England* (Cambridge: Cambridge University Press, 2010).

Tayler, Edward, *Milton's Poetry: Its Development in Time* (Pittsburgh: Duquesne University Press, 1979).

Taylor, Barbara, 'The Religious Foundations of Mary Wollstonecraft's Feminism', in Claudia L. Johnson (ed.), *The Cambridge Companion to Mary Wollstonecraft* (Cambridge: Cambridge University Press, 2002).

————, *Mary Wollstonecraft and the Feminist Imagination* (Cambridge: Cambridge University Press, 2003).

Taylor, Charles, *A Secular Age* (Cambridge, MA: Belknap Press of Harvard University Press, 2007).

Taylor, Stephen, 'Sir Robert Walpole, the Church of England, and the Quakers Tithe Bill of 1736', *The Historical Journal,* 28/1 (1985): 51–77.

————, 'Church and Society after the Glorious Revolution', *The Historical Journal,* 31/4 (1988): 973–87.

————, '"The Fac Totum in Ecclesiastic Affairs"? The Duke of Newcastle and the Crown's Ecclesiastical Patronage', *Albion,* 24/3 (1992): 409–33.

————, 'Queen Caroline and the Church of England', in Stephen Taylor, Richard Connors and Clyve Jones (eds), *Hanoverian Britain and Empire: Essays in Memory of Philip Lawson* (Woodbridge: Boydell Press, 1998).

Thomas, Keith, 'Women and the Civil War Sects', *Past and Present*, 13 (1958): 42–62.

Thompson, Andrew C., 'Popery, Politics, and Private Judgement in Early Hanoverian Britain', *The Historical Journal*, 45/2 (2002): 333–56.

———, *Britain, Hanover and the Protestant Interest, 1688–1756* (Woodbridge: Boydell Press, 2006).

Trumbach, Randolph, *Sex and the Gender Revolution, Volume 1: Heterosexuality and the Third Gender in Enlightenment London* (Chicago: University of Chicago Press, 1998).

Wakely, Alice, 'Mary Davys and the Politics of Epistolary Form', in David Womersley, Paddy Bullard and Abigail Williams (eds), *Cultures of Whiggism: New Essays on English Literature and Culture in the Long Eighteenth Century* (Newark: University of Delaware Press, 2005).

Walker, Claire, 'Prayer, Patronage, and Political Conspiracy: English Nuns and the Restoration', *The Historical Journal*, 43/1 (2000): 1–23.

———, *Gender and Politics in Early Modern Europe: English Convents in France and the Low Countries* (Basingstoke: Palgrave Macmillan, 2003).

———, 'Loyal and Dutiful Subjects: English Nuns and Stuart Politics', in James Daybell (ed.), *Women and Politics in Early Modern England, 1450–1700* (Aldershot: Ashgate, 2004).

———, 'Continuity and Isolation: The Bridgettines of Syon in the Sixteenth and Seventeenth Centuries', in E.A. Jones and Alexandra Walsham (eds), *Syon Abbey and its Books: Reading, Writing and Religion, c. 1400–1700* (Woodbridge: Boydell, 2010).

———, 'Crumbs of News: Early Modern English Nuns and Royalist Intelligence Networks', *Journal of Medieval and Early Modern Studies*, 42/3 (2012): 635–55.

Walsh, John, Colin Haydon and Stephen Taylor (eds), *The Church of England, c. 1689–c. 1833: From Toleration to Tractarianism* (Cambridge: Cambridge University Press, 1993).

Ward, W.R., *The Protestant Evangelical Awakening* (Cambridge: Cambridge University Press, 1992).

Weatherill, Lorna, *Consumer Behaviour and Material Culture in Britain, 1660–1760* (London: Routledge, 1988).

Wedgwood, C.V., 'Sir John Hewley, 1619–1697', *Transactions of the Unitarian Historical Society*, 6/1 (1935): 3–13.

Weil, Rachel, *Political Passions: Gender, the Family and Political Argument in England, 1680–1714* (Manchester: Manchester University Press, 1999).

———, 'The Female Politician in the Late Stuart Age', in Julia Marciari Alexander and Catharine MacLeod (eds), *Politics, Transgression, and Representation at the Court of Charles II* (New Haven: Yale Center for British Art, 2007).

Weir, David R., 'Rather Never than Late: Celibacy and Age at Marriage in English Cohort Fertility, 1541–1871', *Journal of Family History*, 9/4 (1984): 340–54.

Whatley, Christopher A., *Scottish Society, 1707–1830: Beyond Jacobitism, Towards Industrialisation* (Manchester: Manchester University Press, 2000).

Whitley, Laurence A.B., *A Great Grievance: Ecclesiastical Lay Patronage in Scotland until 1750* (Eugene: Wipf & Stock, 2013).

Wiesner-Hanks, Merry, *Christianity and Sexuality in the Early Modern World: Regulating Desire, Reforming Practice* (London: Routledge, 2000).

Williams, Abigail, *Poetry and the Creation of a Whig Literary Culture, 1681–1714* (Oxford: Oxford University Press, 2005).

Wilson, Kathleen, *The Sense of the People: Politics, Culture and Imperialism in England, 1715–1785* (Cambridge: Cambridge University Press, 1995).

———, *The Island Race: Englishness, Empire, and Gender in the Eighteenth Century* (London: Routledge, 2003).

Wormald, Jenny, 'Godly Reformer, Godless Monarch: John Knox and Mary Queen of Scots', in Roger A. Mason (ed.), *John Knox and the British Reformations* (Aldershot: Ashgate, 1998).

Yeoman, Louise, '"Away with the Fairies', in Lizanne Henderson (ed.), *Fantastical Imaginations: The Supernatural in Scottish History and Culture* (Edinburgh: John Donald, 2009).

Young, B.W., 'The Anglican Origins of Newman's Celibacy', *Church History*, 65/1 (1996): 15–27.

———, *Religion and Enlightenment in Eighteenth-Century England: Theological Debate from Locke to Burke* (Oxford: Clarendon Press, 1998).

———, 'Religious History and the Eighteenth-Century Historian', *The Historical Journal*, 43/3 (2000): 849–68.

Zaller, Robert, 'Breaking the Vessels: The Desacralization of Monarchy in Early Modern England', *The Sixteenth Century Journal*, 29 (1998): 757–78.

Zook, Melinda, '"History's Mary: The Propagation of Queen Mary II, 1689–1694', in L.O. Fradenburg (ed.), *Women and Sovereignty* (Edinburgh: Edinburgh University Press, 1992).

———, 'Nursing Sedition: Women, Dissent, and the Whig Struggle', in Jason McElligott (ed.), *Fear, Exclusion and Revolution: Roger Morrice and Britain in the 1680s* (Aldershot: Ashgate, 2006).

———, 'The Shocking Death of Mary II: Gender and Political Crisis in Late Stuart England', *British Scholar*, 1/1 (2008): 21–36.

———, *Protestantism, Politics, and Women in Britain, 1660–1714* (Basingstoke: Palgrave Macmillan, 2013).

Theses

Jardine, Mark, 'The United Societies: Militancy, Martyrdom and the Presbyterian Movement in Late-Restoration Scotland, 1679 to 1688', University of Edinburgh PhD thesis, 2009.

MacKenzie, Niall, 'Gender, Jacobitism and Dynastic Sanctity', University of Cambridge PhD thesis, 2003.
Yeoman, Louise A., 'Heart-Work: Emotion, Empowerment and Authority in Covenanting Times', University of St Andrews PhD thesis, 1991.

Databases

Brown, Keith M., et al. (eds), *The Records of the Parliaments of Scotland to 1707*, http://www.rps.ac.uk.
Goodare, Julian, Lauren Martin, Joyce Miller and Louise Yeoman, *The Survey of Scottish Witchcraft*, http://www.shca.ed.ac.uk/Research/witches.
Who Were the Nuns?, http://wwtn.history.qmul.ac.uk/search/csearch.php.

Index